FROM HOSEA TO ZEPHANIAH

FROM HOSEA TO ZEPHANIAH

THE MINOR PROPHETS·BEFORE THE EXILE

Fred Pearce

THE CHRISTADELPHIAN
404 SHAFTMOOR LANE
BIRMINGHAM B28 8SZ

1991

First published 1979
Reprinted 1991

ISBN 0 85189 099 7

Printed and bound in Great Britain by
Billing & Sons Ltd., Worcester

Contents

		Page
1	The Life and Times of the Prophets	1
2	The Role of the Prophets	10
3	Joel: "The Day of the Lord Cometh"	19
4	Obadiah: The Judgement of Edom	41
5	Amos: "Prepare to Meet thy God, O Israel"	49
6	Jonah: Mercy For Nineveh	79
7	Hosea: The Love of God for His People	93
8	Micah: "Thou Wilt Perform the Truth to Jacob"	128
9	The Overthrow of Assyria and Judah	157
10	Nahum: Judgement on Nineveh	161
11	Zephaniah: "Seek Ye the Lord, All Ye Meek of the Earth"	171
12	Habakkuk: "The Just Shall Live by His Faith"	183
13	Epilogue	197

List of Special Notes

		Page
1	The Day of the Lord	25
2	The Lord's Great Army	28
3	How can the Lord "repent"?	30
4	Who is "The Northerner"?	32
5	The Interpretation of Prophecy	36
6	"The Lord God": Adonai Yahweh	52
7	Divine Judgements on the Pagan Nations	55
8	The Poor and the Meek	57
9	The Purpose of God's Judgements	62
10	James and the "Tabernacle of David"	75
11	The Pride of Ephraim	106
12	Matthew's quotation from Micah 5:2	142
13	"What doth the Lord require of thee …?"	148
14	The "Vengeance of the Lord"	170

Preface

The substance of these studies in the Minor Prophets was first given in the London Bible Class of 1961 and has since appeared in a revised form in the Study Section of *The Christadelphian* of 1975–77. This has been further revised to form the material of this book.

The work has been designed for the individual reader or the member of the ecclesial Bible Class who wants a readable summary of the prophets' message. It has therefore been written not in the form of verse by verse study, but of a "running commentary" on groups of verses. This makes it possible to read straight through the comments on any one of these prophets and obtain a ready impression of his message. Each section commences with observations upon the historical circumstances of the time and concludes with reflections upon the general significance of the prophecy for us in our day. The chapters will be found to contain numerous allusions to the meaning of the original terms used by the inspired writers, as well as to parallel passages in other parts of Scripture, and to political developments in the Middle East which throw light on the prophets' meaning. Special notes are added upon subjects of difficulty or particular interest.

The order of the studies varies a little from that of the Minor Prophets in the Old Testament because there appeared to be in this some advantage of exposition.

That the reader may feel the same marvel at the spiritual and practical qualities of "the word of the Lord through the prophets", its substantial identity with that word through Jesus and the apostles, and the same utter conviction of its divine origin as has the author as the result of his study, is the main object in issuing this book.

FRED PEARCE

1

THE LIFE AND TIMES OF
THE PROPHETS

Why should we spend time studying the prophets of the Old Testament? Would we not do better in these perilous times to give our whole attention to the sayings of Jesus and of his apostles in the New Testament, the final revelation of God?

But to put the matter in this way is to misrepresent it, as though it were a case of "either ... or", which of course it is not. And then it is to ignore this very important fact: the New Testament writings are infused with the ideas and expressions and spirit of the Old Testament. How could it be otherwise? Jesus and the apostles were Israelites brought up in the knowledge of "the law, the psalms and the prophets" and they used those inspired writings in their teaching and in their preaching of the Gospel to men and women who had no other writings to refer to. Inevitably they quote from those writings and comment on them. To ignore the sources of their exposition is to run a grave risk of misunderstanding what they are saying. It is not just a question of recognising their allusions to Israel's history; we need even more to know the meaning of the terms and the ideas they are quoting, so that we may better understand the use they are making of them.

The Old Testament is furthermore a rich store of examples of the will and work of God. The principles of its instruction and exhortation apply to us today. To neglect it is folly. To study it is to gain a precious treasure: a deeper understanding of the Scriptures as a whole, the one Word of the one God, of which Jesus, the "Word made flesh", is the greatest manifestation.

In this short study we shall not spend much time considering the views of Biblical scholars who do not accept that the prophets' writings were "given by inspiration of God". They treat them as the work of men, not as the word of God, and naturally have little time for prophecy. While they may give a little help in making clear the meaning of a term or a local allusion here and there, their writings are largely based upon their own theories, often mutually contradictory, and are barren largely of spiritual power. It is true that some critics are more ready these days to acknowledge that the prophets' writings are far older than was previously maintained, yet the greater part of "theological teaching" in schools and colleges

2 *The Life and Times of the Prophets*

still follows the destructive theories so prevalent 50 years ago and more. There is no real help for the earnest servants of God to be found there. As he turns to the writings of the prophets themselves, he cannot fail to realise how wonderfully consistent they are with the circumstances of the times when they were written, how marvellously they agree with one another, and how full they are of spiritual truth. God spoke through His servants the prophets: that is why there is nothing else like them in the writings of pre-Christian times. Nothing else can possibly explain their words.

Nevertheless there are difficulties in their study. They lived and wrote several centuries before Christ, in Eastern conditions so different from ours. Further, the message of the prophets was meant *first* for their fellow Israelites, and dealt with *their* problems and in *their* language and ideas. As he spoke or wrote, the prophet did not know that his words would still be studied over 2500 years later; so he does not go out of his way to make clear *for us* allusions which were no difficulty at all to his fellow Israelites. Mercifully the Spirit of God has given to his words a fullness and a significance which he could not foresee; and for the understanding of this the New Testament is the most valuable commentary on the Old. Still, if we are fully to understand the prophets and especially to benefit by the riches their writings contain, we must be prepared to give their words some special study.

Israel and the Surrounding Nations

For this purpose the actual circumstances in which the prophets spoke and wrote are of first importance.

Israel became a nation, a political unity, at a moment chosen by God through the call and the leadership of Moses and the great signs of the Exodus. Why did God choose *this* particular moment in history for the independent existence of His people rather than any other? The moment turns out to be very significant. Since they were not a numerous people, Israel in Canaan could not be a great world power. Their country, acting as a "bridge" between the great land powers of Egypt and the valley of the Euphrates, was certain to become a battleground. It is interesting to discover however that at the time of the Exodus the threat from "the south", the power of Egypt, had declined politically; from the 18th to the 14th centuries B.C. she had dominated the land of Canaan, but from the time of the Exodus the Egyptian empire was rent by internal divisions; her military strength was greatly reduced. How remarkable to discover that the great powers from "the north", as they were later to prove themselves, Assyria and Babylon, were in a similar position. The significant result was that the land of Canaan was not regularly dominated by any *great* power for a period of 600 years. *It is into this period that the bulk of Israel's history fits.* These circumstances are a remarkable illustration of the mercy and foresight of God; mercy in that Israel were given a land of their own and opportunity to develop freely in it under God's guidance, relatively unoppressed, at least by any *great* power; and foresight in that God used for His purpose these great powers when they arose. When the corrupt nation of Israel was ripe for judgement, the invading powers of Assyria and Babylon were at hand to carry out, though they did not realise it, the will of God. (See Fig. 1)

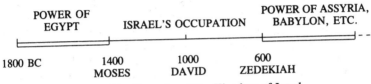

Fig. 1 The Centuries of the Kingdom of Israel

But if Israel were delivered from the pressure of the great powers of the Middle East during the early centuries of their occupation of the land, their contacts with the smaller powers were close indeed. Phoenicia, Philistia, Ammon, Moab, Edom, Syria, and the Arabians (the Arabs of the desert) were active peoples who were bound to exert an influence. Their trading activities were remarkably varied; they manufactured articles in wood, metal, fabric; they made jewelry and weapons. Great trade routes existed for the distribution of these goods; one ran from North to South on the East of the Jordan, from Syria through Bashan, Gilead, and the land of the Ammonites, Moabites and Edomites; another crossed Canaan from East to West near the Sea of Chinnereth (Galilee) and then branched, northwards for the great port of Tyre, or southwards down the coastal plain for Egypt. There seems little doubt that taxes were levied by the powers through whose territories the trading caravans passed and that some of the petty wars we read of in the Old Testament were fought to gain possession of these routes and so to acquire a source of wealth. (See Fig. 2)

Wars were not always fought for the purpose of holding the territory overrun, but rather to capture slaves who were then put to work in the industries of the conqueror or just sold for cash; or in order to levy a tribute, which then became a regular source of income as long as it could be extracted. Such domination could only be maintained by frightfulness, and, as we shall see later in the case of the Assyrians, the treatment of the vanquished in war was horrifying. The dynastic alliances made by certain of Israel's kings (Solomon married a daughter of the Egyptian Pharaoh and Ahab a Tyrian princess) were no doubt for commercial reasons largely; they offered the prospect of profitable trade.

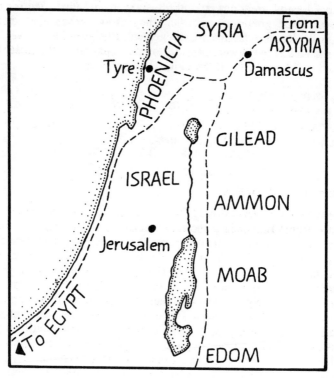

Fig. 2 Trade Routes

In their religious worship Israel did not achieve that separation from the idolatry of the pagan nations which God had commanded them to observe. The Canaanites were not cleared out of the land; inevitably their religious rites went on in the midst of Israel. They carried on certain fertility cults, seeking the favour of their gods ("the baals") for the increase not only of their fields but also of the human body, and accompanied them by corrupt practices such as debauchery (Canaan was particularly the "land of the grape") and sacred prostitution. So there grew up in Israel a mixed worship; the people did not wholly abandon Yahweh; they continued to observe

The Life and Times of the Prophets 5

the ceremonies of the Law, while at the same time joining in the religious rites of their Canaanite neighbours. Later the worship of foreign gods, like the Ammonite Milcom and the Tyrian Baal, was openly established by the leaders of the nation themselves. Now the language of Israel, Hebrew, resembled in some ways the languages of the peoples of Canaan, for they are all varieties of Semitic. Men and ideas could therefore pass easily from Canaan into Israel and be readily understood. The result in Israel of this ease of inter-penetration becomes clear in the writings of the prophets.

Further, during the centuries of their occupation of the land the character of Israel's life changed. From being nomads in the desert, and then chiefly farmers and shepherds in the early years of their life in Canaan, the Israelites became dwellers in walled towns with a materialistic civilisation. They became involved in the common life and ideas of their neighbours. The effect on their religion and the test for their faith become obvious in the writings we are to study.

The Rise of the Great Powers

From the 8th century B.C. Israel began to feel the power of Assyria. Egypt remained a second-rate power, whose influence was only occasionally felt, but Assyria exerted pressure on Palestine for nearly 200 years (compare this with the later domination by Babylon of only 70 years). At first Israel enjoyed a respite: Shalmaneser II was held off by a strong coalition of Syrian powers about 850 B.C.* Syria was weakened by this exhausting conflict with Assyria, and for Israel under Jeroboam II and Judah under Uzziah there followed a period of great prosperity from about 780 to 740 B.C. It is surprising to learn that the area of their two kingdoms combined actually exceeded that of Solomon's. This period of respite gave opportunity for the return of the people to God. Instead, material prosperity resulted in still greater corruption both social and religious. The writings of Amos and Hosea make that abundantly clear.

By 738 B.C. Tiglathpileser III (745–727) was exacting tribute from Menahem of Israel, and in 734 he delivered Ahaz of Judah from the hostile alliance of Pekah (Israel) and Rezin (Syria)—at a price. Israel was overrun; Ahaz went to Damascus to do homage to the Assyrian king. By 725 Shalmaneser IV (727–722) had found Hoshea of Israel guilty of conspiring with So, king of Egypt, and had overrun the Northern kingdom; Samaria was laid waste, 27,000

---

* All dates quoted are of course only approximations.

6   *The Life and Times of the Prophets*

people were deported to Mesopotamia and Media, being replaced
by captives from Babylonia and Syria. So the kingdom of Israel
came to an end; in their territory dwelt a mixed population among
whom, in the time of Christ, the Samaritans were found.

Under Sargon II (722–705) the pressure continued upon the
Southern kingdom of Judah. The reverse suffered by Sennacherib
(705–681) before Jerusalem when the angel of the Lord intervened
on behalf of faithful Hezekiah, a reverse of which the Assyrian
monuments naturally have nothing to say (defeats were never
recorded), gave a respite of 20 years; but by 678 B.C. Manasseh of
Judah was paying tribute to Esarhaddon (681–668) as were Tyre,
Edom, Moab, and the Philistine cities. In 670 Esarhaddon overran
Egypt and was the first of the Assyrian kings to be proclaimed
"king of the kings of Egypt". Little is known of the effect in Judah
of the long reign of the last great Assyrian king Ashurbanipal
(668–626), except that Manasseh was taken in chains to Babylon
(probably for being false to his allegiance), but was afterwards
restored to his throne.

After the death of Ashurbanipal the collapse of Assyria was
startling in its swiftness. Sheer military weakness brought about by
centuries of almost continuous war, the pressure of rising nations
like the Scythians and the Medes, and the revival of Babylonian
power under the father of Nebuchadnezzar, led, within 15 years of
the death of its last great ruler, to the sack of Nineveh. So the great
power which had so ruthlessly dominated the Middle East for two
centuries was shattered, to the accompaniment of a cry of
exultation from the oppressed peoples.

For Judah it was but the replacement of one oppressor by
another. Babylon swiftly occupied the vacancy left by the Assyrian,
overran Palestine, and swept even into Egypt. Judah, first subservient and content to pay tribute, was later convicted of treachery
under Zedekiah, and Jerusalem finally in 588 B.C. was sacked (as
Samaria had been 130 years before) and her people deported. It
was apparently the end of the kingdom of the Lord; the purpose of
God with His people seemed to have been frustrated.

Israel under Assyria

For the nation of Israel what did the "Assyrian experience"
mean?

The Assyrian rulers were utterly ruthless. For them mercy was
weakness. They judged human beings solely by their usefulness; so
the rebellious, the sick and the old were exterminated at once. The

The Life and Times of the Prophets

effect can be gauged from an inscription like the following, describing Ashurbanipal's treatment of the city of Tela:

"I drew near to the city of Tela. The city was very strong: three walls surrounded it ... With battle and slaughter I assaulted and took the city. Three thousand warriors I slew in the battle. Their booty and possessions, cattle and sheep, I carried away; many captives I burned with fire. Many of their soldiers I took alive; of some I cut off hands and limbs; of others the noses, ears, and arms; of many soldiers I put out the eyes. I reared a column of the living and a column of heads. I hung up on high their heads on trees in the vicinity of their city. Their boys and girls I burned up in the flame. I devastated the city, dug it up, in fire I burned it; I annihilated it." (Standard Inscription col. I, 113–118, quoted Goodspeed, *The Babylonians and Assyrians*, p. 197.)

The full horror of the situation is borne upon us when we realise that Ashurbanipal is proud of what he has done. It comes as a shock to observe that the same spirit is arising in our own lands in modern times.

Here is a list of typical spoil taken by the Assyrians from conquered nations in the 9th century B.C.:

Horses, cattle, sheep; metals like copper, gold, silver, lead; corn and wine; chariots, harness and weapons; manufactured goods in linen, wood, metal; furniture in ivory, gold; beads, pendants, silver baskets. Timber, like cedars from Syria; elephant tusks; female slaves.

The list reveals how active was the commerce of the time in the Middle East, and gives some idea of the burden imposed by these heartless conquerors.

From the 8th century the Assyrians began to deport captives from conquered areas. These were settled in other conquered areas, always many hundreds of miles distant, and their homes were occupied by other captives. The mixed community of the natives who remained and the deported captives who had arrived was then ruled by an Assyrian governor; and since the arrival of the deportees was usually resented by the natives, the governor was able to control the territory with a far smaller military force than he would otherwise have required. The extent of these deportations can be judged from the following list, which applies to the reign of Tiglathpileser III: 135,000 from Babylonia, 65,000 from the Eastern Highlands, 70,000 from the Northern Highlands, 30,000 from the Hamath region. The Syrians were sent North and East;

the Babylonians went to Syria; the 27,200 who were deported from Samaria and the thousands (exact number unknown) removed by Nebuchadnezzar from Judah formed part of the same policy (Fig. 3). The figures are impressive enough. What they cannot do, however, is to give any real idea of the sheer misery and heartbreak involved in this ruthless removal of human beings from their homes and the bitter separation of families, in most cases for ever.

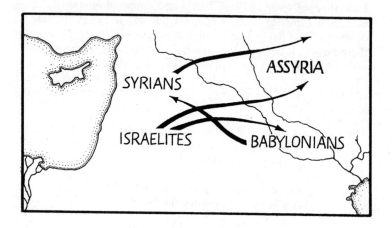

Fig. 3   Assyrian Deportations

For the Assyrians the supreme god was Ashur, whose sign was a winged disc. From popular superstitions it is clear that the basis of Ashur's worship was fear, not admiration for his moral character. The worshipper acknowledged his "sin", of which he became conscious when some misfortune overcame him, and he made expiation by purely ritual means. What was of more significance for the conquered peoples, however, was that Ashur was predominantly the god of the Assyrians, who demanded vengeance upon the enemies of his people (hence the slaughter of captives was regarded as a religious act) and the submission in worship of those who survived. When Ahaz built in Jerusalem a replica of the altar of Damascus, he was certainly carrying out an act of political submission.

Finally, the rise of the great empires of Assyria and Babylon raised new questions for the faithful in Israel: How could these powers prosper? Why did God allow them to oppress His people? Had God then a purpose with the nations of the world as well as

The Life and Times of the Prophets

with Israel? From the ruthless nature of these foreign oppressions we may form some idea of Israel's strong temptation to resort to purely political expedients (such as foreign alliances), and of the real faith demanded by the words of the prophets. Herein lies the great value of the prophetic word for ourselves; for the same temptation to rely on material things and the same call to faith are inevitably part of our experience too.

2
THE ROLE OF THE PROPHETS

Who *were* the prophets? What was their message?

Modern critical theory really denies that the prophets ever received direct messages from God. The critics believe neither in the divine inspiration of the prophets, nor in their power to predict what was still future; the prophets must therefore be "men of outstanding insight", artists, poets, and even patriots. Their words must be the product of "the religious genius of Israel" and stem largely from natural causes. This religious genius is regarded as reaching its perfection in the "ethical monotheism" of the "eighth century prophets". The religion of Israel is thus a "development" from the "primitive" and "barbarous" ideas of the wilderness wanderings to the spiritual understanding of the prophets. In other words, this is a theory of evolution applied to the development of religion.

The theory having been accepted, everything which does not agree with it must be explained away or just ruthlessly removed; so whole sections are denied to the prophet whose name they bear and are ascribed to some "later hand" (usually unknown!), very often upon no stronger evidence whatever than that their contents do not agree with the critical theory.

In recent years there have been encouraging signs of a reaction against these views, for it is now more widely recognised that the critical theories totally fail to explain the facts. "Ethical monotheism", that is the worship of one God of a highly moral nature, did not first arise in the writings of the prophets; it is found consistently much earlier. Nothing in the circumstances of Israel or of the world of the Middle East can explain the lofty character of the prophetic message. Certainly it could not be the "religious genius" of a nation whose main desire was to reject it and to prefer the ideas of their pagan neighbours. Still less can "natural causes" explain how such a rare and spiritual message was consistently preserved over several centuries in the Old Testament writings. After reading the barren speculations of the critics, noting how divided they are among themselves, realising upon what little evidence they base their confident assertions (and tasting a little of the humour of the situation when one critic is found to be accusing

The Role of the Prophets

another of "excisions" which are "violent and arbitrary"!) one turns anew to the words of the prophets themselves, appreciating their sanity and spiritual truth, conscious that there is no explanation possible but that they were holy men of God who spoke because they were moved by the Holy Spirit.

What was their origin? For the answer to this question Deuteronomy 18 is very valuable. The two earlier sections of the chapter treat of the duties and privileges of priests and Levites (vv. 1–8). Then follows a passage warning Israel against the practices of the heathen, who, for their spiritual guidance, had turned to diviners, enchanters, and necromancers: "For these nations which thou shalt possess hearkened unto observers of times and unto diviners"; but as for Israel, "*not so* hath the Lord thy God given unto thee" (v. 14), as the Hebrew literally means. Then follows the great declaration: "The Lord thy God will raise up unto thee a prophet from the midst of thee, of thy brethen, like unto me (Moses)"; and the authority of the prophet is underlined by the declaration from God Himself: "I will put my words in his mouth; and he shall speak unto them all that I shall command him. And it shall come to pass, that whosoever will not hearken unto my words which he shall speak in my name, I will require it of him."

Of course the passage has special reference to the Lord Jesus Christ, as the New Testament distinctly shows. But as is the case with other Old Testament prophecies, this one must have had a more immediate application.

(1) In a section of Deuteronomy dealing with institutions this one is dealing with the institution of the prophets.

(2) If this passage has not that sense, then it seems there is no other passage of the Old Testament which gives authority to the prophets as such.

(3) Amos 2: 10–11 speaks of the prophets as a distinct *gift* of God following His redemption of His people from the land of Egypt.

(4) The comment of Jesus in Luke 11: 49–50: "Therefore also said the wisdom of God: I will send them prophets and apostles, and some of them they shall slay and persecute; that the blood of all the prophets, which was shed from the foundation of the world may be *required* of this generation ...", in which the same expression as that of Deuteronomy 18 is used.

(5) The concluding section of Deuteronomy 18 itself requires a succession of prophets, for it declares that the prophet who presumed to speak a word God had not given him should die; and that Israel would be able to distinguish the true prophet from the false because the words of the true would come to pass. We may

The Role of the Prophets

therefore conclude that God had instituted in Israel an order of prophets, who would provide the spiritual leadership of the people.

About the precise meaning of the word *nabhi*, prophet, much ink has been spilt with little result. The declaration of Deuteronomy 18: "the words which (the prophet) shall speak in my name", seem exactly to express the function. So Aaron was the appointed spokesman for Moses, and Jeremiah was told: "Behold, I have put my words in thy mouth ... Arise and speak unto (Israel) all that I command thee ..." (1: 9, 17). *Roeh* (seer) is used chiefly of Samuel, and I Samuel 9: 9 suggests that it was an older word for prophet: "For he that is now called a prophet was beforetime called a seer." Isaiah 30: 9–10, "This is a rebellious people ... that will not hear the word of the Lord; which say to the seers (*hozeh*, beholder), See not; and to the prophets, Prophesy not. Speak unto us smooth things ...", suggests that a beholder was no different from a *roeh*, seer. Indeed Amos is called a *hozeh* at a time when he had not been seeing visions but declaring the word of the Lord.

Spokesmen for God

The prophets, then, were the spokesmen of God, never inventing what they had to say, always conscious that their message came by the Spirit of the Lord. They were always individuals, called of God, never inheriting their position from their fathers or acquiring it by becoming members of a guild or "school"; and because of their unique call, no one in Israel seemed to be in any doubt as to who was a genuine prophet.

After Moses the next great prophet was Samuel, who left no "heir". We may therefore be inclined to think that the prophets were a rather rare phenomenon, appearing at great intervals and crises. A careful reading of Kings and Chronicles reveals, however, that genuine prophets of the Lord were known to exist very frequently. The following list is instructive:

> The "old prophet" of Bethel, 1 Kings 13: 11; Ahijah, sent to Jeroboam, 1 Kings 14: 2–16 (about *930 B.C.*); Shemaiah the prophet and Iddo the seer, 2 Chron. 12: 15; Azariah, the son of Obed, 2 Chron. 15: 1; Hanani the seer, 2 Chron. 16: 7 (about *910*); Jehu, son of Hanani, 1 Kings 16: 1 *(900)*; Elijah *(870–750)*; one of the "sons of the prophets", 1 Kings 20: 35–42 *(860)*; Micaiah, son of Imlah, 1 Kings 22: 8-28 *(850)*; Elisha *(840)*; Zechariah, son of Jehoida, 2 Chron. 24: 20 *(830)*; a "man of God", 2 Chron. 25: 7 *(790)*; "a prophet", 2 Chron. 25: 15; Jonah, son of Amittai, 2 Kings 14: 25 *(780)*; Oded, 2 Chron.

The Role of the Prophets

28: 9 *(735)*; prophets who spoke to Manasseh, 2 Kings 21: 10 *(680–650)*; Hulda the prophetess, 2 Kings 22: 14–20 *(635)*; prophets, classed separately from priests under Josiah, 2 Kings 23: 2 *(630)*.

This list spans more than 300 years, and *includes none of the great "writing" prophets*. It shows that God spoke to His people through His inspired messengers far more frequently than may have been thought. The list makes a little more understandable the statement in 2 Chronicles 36: 15 that God "sent to them by his messengers, rising up betimes (marg. *continually*) and sending ..."

There are occasional references to a company or group of prophets. The first allusion of this kind is the appointment by the Spirit of the 70 elders to assist Moses. It is noticeable nevertheless that these elders do not then make any independent pronouncements, but reinforce the already established authority: Moses himself. Saul, having been given "another heart" by God, is joined temporarily to "a company of prophets" and prophesies among them when the Spirit of God comes upon him. The incident seems to prove that there existed in Saul's day men who were known as prophets and of whom God evidently did not disapprove, since He granted a Spirit sign to Saul in their midst. There are however no further references to such groups until the days of Elijah and Elisha. From 1 Kings 20: 35 we learn that "a certain man of the sons of the prophets said unto his neighbour *in the word of the Lord*, Smite me I pray thee". The "neighbour" refused, and is told that because he had "not obeyed the voice of the Lord" judgement would come upon him. The king of Israel later discerned that the speaker was "of the prophets" and received from him a message from God, announcing his doom. The passage proves that there existed 170 years after Saul's day a group of men known as prophets and that God used one of them for His message.

The "sons of the prophets" evidently lived together in one place, for they told Elisha, "The place where we dwell with thee is too strait for us", and suggested making a new dwelling. Bethel and Gilgal were certainly two such centres. Their comparative prominence in the days of Elijah and Elisha was probably due to the fact that the Levitical system had largely broken down; the prophets became custodians of the written word of God, and His historians too. Their relation to the temple itself is hard to settle, but one thing is certain:there was no opposition whatever between the *true* prophet and the *true* priest.

The False Prophets

But the Old Testament record leaves us in no doubt that there existed in Israel false prophets as well as true. Though nothing explicit is said as to their origin, with what we have already learned about the existence of companies of prophets and our knowledge of human nature, it is not difficult to imagine what must have happened. Organised bodies tend to become established; so these groups of prophets would be joined in time by some who had received no Divine calling, following perhaps in the footsteps of a father or just choosing an agreeable way of earning a living. Such men were undoubtedly "professional" prophets, receiving payment for their services and therefore having a natural tendency to utter things pleasing to those who "footed the bill".

The episode of Micaiah in 1 Kings 22 is a most interesting example. Ahab, supported by Jehoshaphat of Judah, was about to attack the Syrians, and when Jehoshaphat wished to "enquire at the word of the Lord", Ahab called his prophets. There were 400 of them, and they unanimously prophesied success for Ahab in his enterprise. Jehoshaphat evidently had no high opinion of these "prophets", for he pointedly enquired whether there was not a "prophet of the Lord" besides. The messenger, who went to fetch Micaiah in response to this request, urged the prophet to give the same message as the others, who incidentally were continuing their prophesying before Ahab, one of them making horns of iron to symbolise the coming victory. Micaiah replied uncompromisingly: "What the Lord saith unto me, that will I speak." Standing before Ahab, Micaiah, having first ironically counselled the king to do as his prophets bade him, revealed the coming defeat of Israel and ascribed the fair words of the prophets to a "lying spirit", or spirit of deception which God had put into their mouth. It is a spirit which finds its best explanation in the words of Jeremiah: "Hearken not unto the words of the prophets ... they speak of a vision *of their own heart* ... they prophesy lies ... they are prophets of the *deceit of their own heart*" (23:16, 26). The character of their "inspiration" is shown by the violence used by Zedekiah, the leader of the false prophets, who struck Micaiah in the face, while Ahab, displeased, ordered him to be put in prison.

The episode throws light on the situation of the prophets about 850 B.C., before the work of the great writing prophets had begun: the large number, 400; their unanimity—"the words of the prophets, declare good unto the king with one mouth", as if they had agreed beforehand; their determination to please the king; the fact that Micaiah was known to stand apart from them; the

The Role of the Prophets

remarkable quality of his words contrasted with their platitudes. These features combine to prove that false, or purely human, prophecy existed in Israel alongside of the true and throw a deal of light upon the denunciations by the inspired prophets we are about to study. The "human" message of the false prophets naturally concentrated on features pleasing to the people (in Jeremiah 23 God condemned them because they did not turn the people from their evil way). Such features were a trust in foreign alliances in place of faith in God, and an emphasis upon the purely ritual aspects of their religion to the neglect of the spiritual. For the sake of completeness it should be pointed out here that there existed also another type of false prophet, one devoted to the service of a particular idol, such as the prophets of Baal, who were probably not Israelites at all.

The Inspiration of the Prophets

What was the character of the inspiration of the true prophets? Modern criticism, failing to distinguish between false prophecy and true, has sought to trace their descent through the Canaanite prophets of the idolatrous cults, an attempt which has clearly failed, as some of the critics themselves concede. These pagan prophets were characterised by physical excitement (the frenzied antics of the devotees of Baal in their contest with Elijah come to mind), whereas the prophets of Yahweh remained calm and rational (upon this point more later); they were associated with certain sanctuaries, whereas Israel's ranged freely through the land; they had no moral message and have perished, leaving no lasting legacy; whereas the spiritual power of the words of Israel's prophets was echoed and developed in the inspired utterances of the New Testament. The contrast between the two could not be more striking.

Others have classed Israel's prophets as "ecstatics", visionaries capable of going into a trance and so entering into contact with the "unseen" or "spiritual". But the basic principle of the heathen ecstatics was that the soul was distinct from the body, was in fact "God within the breast". They claimed by "spiritual" means to enter into communion with God, seeking an escape from the turmoil of the present in a higher sphere. The Hebrew conception is totally opposed to this: man is an animated body, a "living soul", incapable of knowing God by any of his natural powers. The prophet does not acquire his inspiration by introspective brooding, but by an objective word *from without*, which comes to him with the force of a command, often obliging him to utter words which he

16   *The Role of the Prophets*

would rather have left unsaid. He does not seek to evade the difficulties of the present, but to give the counsel of God in the light of them in order that they may be faced and endured.

Concerning the question of ecstasy, the testimony of some of the critics themselves is highly significant:

> "The first prophet (Moses) and the last (Jesus) like unto him, seem both to have received and to have uttered truth *with a calm demeanour,* free from all perturbation of mind or excitement of manner."

> "(God) speaks to His prophets not in magical processes nor through the visions of poor phrenetics, but by a clear and intelligible word, *addressed to the intellect and the heart.* The characteristic of the true prophet is that he retains his *consciousness* and *self control* under revelation."

> "The content (of the prophetic utterance) is a rational, intelligible, communicable word, directed to certain peculiar circumstances in the national life ... It is impossible to deny the eminent rationality of the prophetic discourse. The prophets show themselves to be sane, logical, lucid, and to be equipped with dialectical powers (the ability to present a reasoned argument) which render them expert in controversy. They exhibit the intellectual grasp which permits them to comprehend and elicit the far-reaching implications of the positions they take up."[*]

How did God speak to His prophets? In Numbers 12: 6–8 He said He would do it by vision and dream, though He spoke face to face with Moses. From 2 Kings 20 it is clear that sometimes He must have spoken to them very clearly indeed. Isaiah delivered to Hezekiah the message from God that he was to die. After the prophet's departure, the king prayed to God, and "afore Isaiah was gone out into the middle court" he received from God the command to go back and deliver an important modification of the original message: God would add to the life of Hezekiah 15 years. Here the change of message must have been both very rapidly and very clearly received, since it involved various points of important detail in a short space of time. The complication and detail of other prophetic utterances on behalf of God show that they must have been received by equally clear means. As to how exactly this was done, we simply do not know, but are just told: "The word of the Lord came ...", or, "Thus saith the Lord ..."

Inspiration, however, could not have made the prophet a mere

---

[*] Davidson, *Old Testament Prophecy,* p. 88; Robertson Smith, *The Old Testament in the Jewish Church,* p. 289; Knight, *Hebrew Prophetic Consciousness,* p. 101.

The Role of the Prophets

recording machine, reproducing words which made no sense to him. Of course his words very frequently (as the comments of the New Testament show) had a wider application than he knew; but they were always directed to a particular situation arising in his own day, and *made sense* both to him and to his hearers. In our study we shall do well to try and ascertain first what that sense was as a vital preliminary to grasping the wider implications for us. To the prophet himself the divine inspiration must have seemed an intense compulsion (cf. Jeremiah's expression: "His word was in my heart as a burning fire shut up in my bones, and I was weary with forbearing and I could not stay", 20: 9). To this the prophet made his own complete surrender. It was his whole mind and heart that he gave, and so he preserved his individuality; Amos used the language natural to a countryman and Isaiah that of a cultivated townsman. Common to them all was their intense conviction that God had spoken: what else could they then do but prophesy?

The Prophets' Message

What was the message of the prophets?

Certainly they were not the innovators, the leaders in the "evolution of religious thought", which some moderns would make them out to be. Their whole message was a recall to old truths and an old faith, a faith first found in the books of Moses. In his book *The Law in the Prophets* (1891) Stanley Leathes traced all the allusions to the Pentateuch in the prophetical writings. The following list gives the number of verses in the Minor Prophets where such allusions are present: Hosea 79; Joel 22; Amos 45; Obadiah 4; Jonah 9; Micah 39; Nahum 10; Habakkuk 15; Zephaniah 20; Haggai 7; Zechariah 35; Malachi 14. Despite the fact that these allusions vary in directness, the list is impressive. Evidently the prophets were steeped in the writings of Moses and were well aware that their hearers or readers knew them too. This undoubted fact is a tremendous testimony to the antiquity of the Pentateuch and an equally tremendous obstacle to the theories of the critics.

To the prophets Yahweh was supreme, the God of the whole earth, controlling life upon it. He had intervened on behalf of His people in the deliverance from Egypt, and constantly made that the ground of His appeal to them. But this great God of the whole world, the Lord of the nations even, was at the same time a personal God, possessing a clear moral character of truth, mercy and righteousness; but a righteousness which was retributive, in that it judged men when they sinned, but always with a deep desire

18   *The Role of the Prophets*

for their correction, repentance, and redemption. Yahweh was first
in covenant relation with His people as a whole. But as His people
turned away from Him and would not be reformed, He showed
Himself through His prophets ever ready to dwell with the
individual worshipper, the poor and contrite who trembled at His
word. His kingdom of Israel, corrupted now by sin, would
ultimately triumph. So the prophets predict the coming climax (it
has been observed that there is no prophet of Israel whose words do
not contain predictions) and the intervention of God. But the day of
the Lord, at first regarded by Israel as the time when they would be
triumphantly delivered from their pagan oppressors, was now seen
to be a day of redemption for a *faithful remnant* only, and a dire
day of judgement for the ungodly, whether Israelite or Gentile. To
these coming events belonged the expectation of the Messiah, the
glorious son of David; even more, Immanuel and the Servant of the
Lord.

To the faithful Israelite, dismayed at the disasters coming upon
his people, grieved at the ways of the wicked, especially in his own
nation, the words of the prophets were a clarion call to faith and
trust in God in spite of all appearances to the contrary. This is
where their great value lies as exhortation and instruction for us
today, for we face just the same problem. We need the serene
authority of their message, their deep appreciation of the holy
righteousness and the mercy of God, their entire belief in Him as a
Person who will act in His own cause at the time He will choose.
The words of the prophets have only one explanation, the one which
the prophets themselves unitedly assert; that in speaking and
writing what they did, they were moved not by the will of man, but
by the Holy Spirit.

3
Joel
"THE DAY OF THE LORD COMETH"

Introduction

Of Joel's personal life nothing whatever is known. The name is not uncommon, but it is impossible to identify the prophet with any known historical character, and we are compelled therefore to turn to the internal evidence and to the evidence of tradition. Since the prophecy contains a number of references to Jerusalem and shows familiarity with the temple, the priests and the offerings, while on the other hand there is no allusion at all to the Northern Kingdom, we may safely conclude that Joel must have been a native of Judah and that his prophecy was uttered in their midst.

But what is his date? This is a subject upon which the commentators are most deeply divided, some placing Joel very early and others very late. What can we find to guide us?

There is first of all the place of his book in the canon of the Old Testament. It is now fashionable to discount this as evidence on the ground that the canon was fixed long after the prophet's days, which is true enough. Nevertheless the Israelites who fixed it were considerably nearer those days than we are and were likely, to put it as its lowest, to have known *something* of the origin of books which held a revered place among all their own people. Further, the arrangement of the prophetical books clearly follows some sort of order; the "great" prophets, Isaiah, Jeremiah, Ezekiel, and Daniel, are unquestionably in chronological order. Some such order can be discerned in the arrangement of the Minor Prophets, too, for no one disputes that Amos, Hosea and Micah belong to the period of Assyrian domination; Nahum, Habakkuk and Zephaniah to the period of Babylonian power; Haggai, Zechariah and Malachi to the period of restoration after the exile. Now this is generally the order of the groups of prophets in the canon, which surely suggests that the others, whose dates are less certain to us (for example, Obadiah, Joel), would be inserted in approximate chronological order. We should expect Joel then to belong to a relatively *early* period.

20   *Joel*

Internal Evidence

Does the other internal evidence confirm this? Very striking is
the absence of any mention whatever of Assyria or Babylon. In view
of the frequent mention of these powers by the majority of the
prophets, this fact suggests that they had not yet begun seriously to
affect Israel at the time of Joel. In his prophecy the enemies of
Israel are the Philistines, the Phoenicians, Moab and Egypt.

Equally striking is the absence of all allusion to the Northern
Kingdom. Now this could mean, as some think, that Samaria was
already destroyed and the people deported; but arguments from
silence, whether about the absence of allusion to Assyria-Babylon
or to Israel, are only indications, and we must seek for corro-
boration elsewhere. One fact seems certain: the temple was
standing and the priests were officiating. Now this means that the
prophecy must apply either to a long time *before* the Babylonian
destruction or to a period substantially *after* the restoration. The
"spiritual" atmosphere of the prophecy, however, seems more in
accord with the earlier date. Remarkably there is no condemnation
of any particular vices among the people (as is found so vigorously
expressed in Amos and Hosea); the priests are depicted as faithful
and zealous, and the people as likely to respond to a call to
repentance. The absence of all mention of the king *could* argue that
he did not exist, but could also mean that at the time he was not a
decisive national figure. The allusion to the valley of Jehoshaphat
argues a time when God's deliverance of His people there had not
faded from their memory. Further, the commencement of the
prophecy of Amos suggests that he may well have had the
conclusion of Joel's prophecy before him: "The Lord shall roar from
Zion and utter his voice from Jerusalem" (Amos 1:2) is almost
identical with Joel 3:16; and the continuation: "... and the
habitations of the shepherds shall mourn and the top of Carmel
shall wither" recalls Joel's detailed descriptions of the desolations of
the famine. It is very probable, therefore that Joel preceded Amos.

Language and Style

It is a mark of the unreliable nature of arguments from style and
language that directly contrary conclusions have been drawn from
those of Joel. Kirkpatrick remarks: "It is a strange misrepresen-
tation to say that 'the language of Joel plainly bears the character
of the latest period of Hebrew literature'. If any argument can be
drawn from it, it is in favour of the *earlier* date"; a comment which
shows that the alleged linguistic evidence for the late date of Joel

cannot be all that strong. The comment of G. A. Smith is interesting; he remarks upon "Joel's archaic style" and then assumes that the prophet must have been writing in imitation of *older* models! One would have thought that a style which was so evidently "archaic" required an equally "archaic" date! E. J. Young declares that the literary style of Joel is quite different from that of the post exilic prophets such as Haggai, Zechariah and Malachi.

Historical Setting

Does there exist a period in Judah's history when the indications we have noted: absence of Assyrian or Babylonian menace, absence of allusion to the Northern Kingdom, high standing of the temple and the priests, a strong element of faithfulness still existing among the people, relative unimportance of the king, could all apply? It is remarkable that there does. The long dominance of Jezebel in Israel had been a disaster; her devotion to Baal, and her thorough lack of justice and mercy, illustrated in the murder of Naboth, coupled with the weakness of her husband Ahab, were at length punished about the year 840 B.C. by the revolt of Jehu who destroyed her house. Her daughter Athaliah, embarking upon a similar career as queen mother in Judah, was overthrown by the resolute action of Jehoiada the priest, who raised to the throne of the Southern kingdom a seven year old prince of the house of David, Jehoash. There followed a period of reform:

> "And Jehoiada made a covenant between the Lord and the king and the people that they should be the Lord's people; ... and all the people of the land went to the house of Baal and brake it down ... And Jehoiada appointed the officers of the House of the Lord under the hand of the priests the Levites ... to offer the burnt offerings of the Lord, as it is written in the law of Moses ... So all the people of the land rejoiced and the city was quiet" (2 Kings 11: 17–20; 2 Chron. 23: 16–18).

During the lifetime of Jehoiada, the picture is that of a community whose leaders are devoted to the service of God.

Into this period the prophecy of Joel would obviously fit. The deliverance of Jehoshaphat was a recent memory, having occurred perhaps only 30 years before; the Northern Kingdom was in a strange state: delivered from an idolatrous queen and her ungodly house, yet ruled now by Jehu, a far from godly character. The prime concern of the prophet was evidently with Judah, among whom this vigorous revival had recently taken place. It is in this

22   *Joel*

context that we shall seek to find the immediate relevance of Joel's
words.

Joel's name means "The Lord is God"—a fitting summary of the
sovereignty of the Lord, both in judgement and in salvation, which
pervades the whole prophecy.

1.   Desolation (1: 1-20)

1: 1-4. It was the pride and duty of the faithful Israelite to
impress upon his son the great works God had done for His
people, "His praises and his strength", for it was a command to
their fathers "that they should make them known to their children",
in order that future generations might make them known in turn to
their children; the whole purpose being "that they might set their
hope in God" (Psa. 78: 1-7). Joel, however, solemnly calls upon the
old men, and *all* inhabitants of the land even, to consider whether
the dread events he is about to describe have ever taken place
before; events so dire that they will tell their children and their
children's children of them (vv. 1-3). A great scourge of locusts is
to lay waste the land. The four names given in the A.V. mean
literally the shearer, the swarmer, the lapper, and the devourer. In
the original verse 4 is very terse: "Shearer's remnant, swarmer eats,
swarmer's remnant, lapper eats, lapper's remnant, devourer eats" is
the attempt of the Century Bible to render the abruptness of the
Hebrew. The terms for locust probably signify not different kinds of
the insect, nor even different stages of its life development, but
rather the devastating effects of successive swarms, rising to a
climax with the "devourer".

vv. 5-7: After summoning the "drunkards" to weep because there
will be no more new wine, the prophet abruptly changes the figure
from locusts to a nation. The word he uses suggests a *foreign*
nation, numerically strong, with great destructive power, since its
"cheek teeth" are the grinding teeth of a lioness (the figure
reappears in Revelation 9: 8: "... their teeth were as the teeth of
lions"). In verse 7 however Joel reverts to the thought of locust
destruction, for stripping the bark of the fruit trees was one of their
characteristic activities. This union of the figurative (the locust
plague) and the literal (the foreign desolator) is found frequently in
the first two chapters. Most probably there had been in Judah a
literal locust plague; the reality of the scourge which the people had
just suffered would be a powerful demonstration of the reality of
the one to come. It is interesting to note that God refers to *my* vine

Joel 1   23

and *my* fig tree, both used as figures of Israel in the Scriptures;
another indication that it is foreign invasion which is really meant.

vv. 8–12: There follows a series of calls to lamentation. The first is
addressed to the land ("Lament", v. 8, is fem. sing.), mourning like
a young widow. The next to the priests (their description: "the
Lord's ministers" suggests that they are faithful) because the "meat
offering and the drink offering is cut off from the house of the
Lord"; as part of these offerings were to be given to the priests, they
therefore lose some of their livelihood. Then the call is to tillers of
the ground and the tenders of vines and fruit trees, because all is
"withered". The natural blessings of God for His people—the corn,
the new wine, the oil, the wheat, the barley, and all the pleasant
fruits of the trees, the traditional sources of "joy"—are "dried up"
(v. 10) and "withered" (twice in v. 12). In each case it is the same
word, really meaning "ashamed" (see R.V.m.), thus showing that
the mourning of the land is but a symbol for the mourning of the
people. The Hebrew of verse 10 has 5 couplets of words, "sounding
like a dirge" (Cent. Bible).

vv. 13–15: The priests are now called upon directly to clothe
themselves in sackcloth and lament before the altar. Joel's exact
phrasing is remarkable, for he addresses them as "ye ministers of
my God" and then refers to "the house of *your* God". Since the
priests are not distinctly criticised, this is probably a reminder that
the God who inspired His prophet was also *theirs*. The situation is
so serious that the elders and *all* the inhabitants of the land are
urged to "cry unto the Lord" and to "hallow" a solemn day of
mourning in His house; not just to "hold" one, but to "proclaim a
fast" as Jehoshaphat had done (2 Chron. 20: 3–4) at a crisis in
Israel's affairs. Joel now ascribes this destruction directly to a
divine source: "for the day of the Lord is at hand, and as a
destruction from the Almighty shall it come". (For "day of the
Lord" see note following.) It is significant in this context that the
word Almighty is used. The Hebrew is *Shaddai,* a plural word not
unlike *Elohim,* but one used early in the Scriptures, conveying the
sense of the supreme power of God and especially that power
expressed in judgement. It was the name (*Ail Shaddai*) by which
God spoke of Himself to the patriarchs, and it is found frequently
in the book of Job.

vv. 16–20: In Deuteronomy Israel had been told that when they
entered the land, they were to break down the idols of the heathen,
and to bring their offerings "to the place which the Lord your God
shall choose, ... and there ye shall eat before the Lord your God

24   *Joel 1*

and rejoice in all that ye put your hand unto" (12: 4–7). Joel
however foresees such desolation that there will be nothing left in
the land to offer, so "joy and gladness" would be "cut off from the
house of our God". This is the kind of indirect allusion to the
Pentateuch, and especially to Deuteronomy, of which there are
many examples in the prophetic writings, to say nothing of the
much more direct ones. The chapter concludes with a picture of the
beasts of the field suffering affliction. "The sheep are made
desolate", literally "are punished" (R.V.m.), in the sense of "suffer
for sin" (*Speaker's*), is another example of a "human" term being
applied to the natural creation (see "dried up ... withered", vv. 10,
12). The "beasts of the field pant up to thee", for the land is
parched and as though burned with fire. The prophet evidently
recognises that the visitation is from the hand of God: "O Lord, to
thee will I cry"; and wishes his people to realise it too.

Travellers in the East have left such graphic pictures of plagues
of locusts that Joel's scene of destruction is evidently not at all
exaggerated. Their numbers are incredible and their onward
progress was utterly irresistible in ancient times; their multitudinous gnawing sounds like roaring flames, and leaves the
ground behind black as though it had been actually burnt. They
devour literally every green thing. At a time when regions were far
more isolated than today and had to depend almost wholly upon
their *own* food supplies to last them through the coming winter,
such a devastation must have been catastrophic. The force of the
prophet's words could not pass unnoticed.

2. The Army of the Lord (2: 1–11)

2: 1–11: The second chapter opens with an alarm sounded on "the
trumpet", or *shophar,* the horn used to gather Israel to religious
assembly (still blown to this day in the synagogue on the Day of
Atonement), but also to summon the people to war or to warn of
the approach of an enemy (Ezek. 33: 3). It is sounded in no less a
place than in Zion, "my holy mountain", and on hearing it "*all* the
inhabitants of the land (of Judah)" were to tremble; and well they
might, for was not Zion, the holy mountain, the dwelling place of
God Himself among His people? Why then should an *alarm* be
sounded there? Joel explains "For the day of the Lord cometh ... it
is nigh at hand" (v. 1). Evidently Israel were to learn something
about the "day of the Lord" which they had not altogether expected
(v. 1).

Joel 2

Note 1: THE DAY OF THE LORD

In the writings of the prophets the idea that God would intervene in the affairs not only of His own people but of the nations generally, occurs frequently and grows in importance. Since it is probable, however, that this striking use of the term by Joel was the *first* in prophetic literature, it is interesting to enquire how Joel's contemporaries understood the term and what impression his prophecy must have made upon them.

From the earlier inspired writings the books of Moses, the first historical books, and many of the Psalms, the earnest Israelite would certainly have derived a fairly optimistic view of the future of his people. To Abraham had been promised blessing for a numerous seed, possession for ever of the land, and a means of extending the blessings to all the nations of the earth. Jacob's blessings of the tribes in Genesis 49 speaks of the coming of a ruler who would receive the obedience of the nations. In his song of triumph after the deliverance at the Red Sea Moses contemplates the planting of the people in their inheritance, where the Lord should rule over them for ever (Exod. 15). Balaam, finding no curse for Israel, says their kingdom shall be exalted; the Star and the Sceptre are to rule and "have dominion" over the surrounding nations (Num. 23 and 24). To David God promised that He would plant His people, deliver them from affliction, and establish the throne of His anointed; as David himself expresses it immediately after receiving this promise: "What one nation in the earth is like thy people ... For thou hast confirmed to thyself thy people Israel to be a people unto thee for ever ..." (2 Sam. 7: 9–24). The future of Israel seemed assured.

But surely, it may be said, the great prophecies of Deuteronomy 28 and Leviticus 26, with their long detailed list of all the afflictions which were to follow their disobedience, must have warned the Israelites that their path to glory and dominion would not be quite so smooth? The scattering among the nations, the persecutions, the contempt and the sufferings are so vividly described that surely the earnest Israelite would have allowed for them in his expectations?

No doubt there were a few who did; but the fact that *we* know the disastrous course which their history eventually followed must not blind us to the equally important fact that for the Israelites *these prophecies of affliction were conditional:* "But it shall come to pass, *if* thou wilt not hearken unto the voice of the Lord thy God, ... that all these curses shall come upon thee ..." (Deut. 28: 15); and Leviticus 26 even concludes with a section suggesting

26   *Joel 2*

that *if* Israel "confess their iniquity", God will remember His covenant with them and not cast them away. The majority of the Israelites must have believed that their people would never so far forsake God as to bring His severe judgements upon them; repentance would always come in time, and since God was clearly by His own proclamation a God of mercy, doubtless the rigours of Deuteronomy were meant as a warning rather than as a literal forecast of history. The future to Joel's contemporaries, despite local setbacks, was in the long run full of promise.

For them, too, at first the expression "*the day*" of the Lord had a *retrospective* rather than a prospective sense; for in Israel's history Yahweh's great day had been one of deliverance, that of His people from Egypt. That day, celebrated annually afterwards in the Feast of the Passover, was to be remembered "all the days of thy life" (Deut. 16: 3). The constant basis of the appeal of Yahweh to His frequently heedless people, as well as that of His prophets, was to remember that it was He who, by a mighty hand and a stretched-out arm, had delivered them from the house of bondage, that "furnace of iron", to be a holy people unto Himself. The assertion even stands at the head of the ten commandments: "I am the Lord thy God which brought thee forth from the land of Egypt." This had been emphatically "the day" when God had shown His wonders among the nations and redeemed Israel, His inheritance; "the day when (God) delivered us from the enemy" (Psa. 78: 42).

It was therefore to be expected that any future "day of the Lord" would in the same way demonstrate the power of God in the deliverance of His people. David, "in spirit", declares of his Lord: "Thy people shall be willing *in the day of thy power*", and adds: "The Lord at thy right hand shall strike through kings *in the day of his wrath*" (Psa. 110: 3, 5). No doubt the anticipation of *that* day of the Lord formed the consolation of the large majority in Israel.

We may judge therefore of their dismay when Joel proceeds to foretell a day of fearful judgement; so fearful that all the inhabitants of the land are bidden to "hear" and to consider whether they have ever heard the like before. The fruits of the field are to be utterly destroyed, the land is to be full of lamentation, for a ruthless enemy is to ravage it; it shall be covered with darkness, burnt by fire, and shaken by earthquake. *This* day of the Lord is to be one of destruction, a cause of trembling, so great and terrible that the question is raised whether anyone will be able to survive it.

It is true that the prophecy goes on to speak of repentance and eventual deliverance for Israel; it ends on a note of hope. But the description of the desolation is so thorough and so detailed that no

Joel 2   27

sincere and devoted Israelite could have hoped that this judgement
would be averted; he would see that the suffering had to come first.
Final glory, when it came, would be the end of a process in which
Israel were to be purged and only a remnant inherit the fulness of
the promise. We have here in Joel the elementary statement of
principles which receive much fuller treatment in the later prophets.

vv. 2–11: The next ten verses contain a remarkable description of
the remorseless advance of an immense swarm of locusts, like an
invading host of soldiers. There is darkness over the land, as the
locust swarm actually obscures the light of the sun. The word for
morning is unusual (from *shachar,* to be black) and suggests
twilight. The severity of the attack is shown by the use of the
traditional formula: "there hath not ever been the like, neither shall
be any more after it, even to the years of many generations" (v. 2;
cf. Exod. 10: 14.) Their fiery depredations make even the garden of
Eden into a desolate wilderness (see Ezek. 36: 33–35 for the
reversal of this) The remarkable resemblance between the heads of
the locust and the horse is commented upon in Relevation 9: 7.
Here Joel dwells upon the comparison, and upon the noise like that
of chariots, because he sees the locusts as typical of a "strong
people set in battle array" (v. 5). Before this invading host the
"peoples" (R.V.) are in anguish and their faces grow pale; the
allusion is doubtless primarily to all the nations of Canaan, "Tyre,
Sidon and all the coasts of Palestine" (3: 4).

And now the locust figure recedes into the background as the
prophet sees the invading host swarming over the walls into the city,
plunging through the missiles of the enemy ("they burst through
the weapons and are not halted" of the R.S.V. is the generally
agreed sense of A.V.'s "When they fall upon the sword they shall
not be wounded", a rendering which has caused some to interpret
this passage of the angelic army of God, an untenable exposition as
the sequel shows). The "city" is doubtless Jerusalem itself, whose
"windows" present no serious obstacle either to locusts or to men,
for they are the lattice type, without any glass. The great physical
signs of upheaval, the quaking of the earth, the darkening of the
heavenly bodies, become in later prophets the familiar language of
the judgements of God (cf. the well-known passage in Luke 21);
Joel is probably the first of the prophets to make use of the figure.
The section concludes with the assertion that the leader of this
army is no less than the Lord Himself; it is *His* army, numerous
and powerful, carrying out *His* will. The result is a "great and
terrible" day of the Lord. Who in Israel will be able to survive?

28   *Joel 2*

Note 2: THE LORD'S "GREAT ARMY"

What would Joel's contemporaries make of the great invading, locust-like force which was to be God's "great army" for the judgement of His people?

Whether they would be able to identify this force with any great political power must remain a question difficult to answer, since Joel does not name the aggressor; but if they did so identify it, surely it must have been with Assyria, although the period of Assyria's great supremacy in Palestine had not yet arrived. It seems inevitable however that they expected *one* great calamity, spread over a number of years notwithstanding; *one* invading enemy who would accomplish all the desolation; and *one* signal act of deliverance when the "northerner" (v. 20) would come to his end in their land; inevitable too that they should expect both the invasion and the deliverance to be not too far distant in time. To the contemporaries of Joel there was to be a great crisis, and then a great deliverance, and apparently a final one, for in the end Israel were to *know* that Yahweh was their God and no strangers were to pass through their land any more.

To us, over 2500 years later, the words of Joel take on a much fuller significance; for not only the Assyrians, but also the Babylonians and the Romans carried out a judgement of God upon His people and were in turn His "army" for the purpose; they all desolated the land, and eventually came to their end. Among various attempts to extract a meaning from the names of the locusts, the following is of considerable interest. Hebrew consonants are also numbers, so Hebrew words possess numerical values. The four words for locust in Joel 1: 4 work out like this:

Palmerworm: *gazam:* Gimel (3), Zain (7), Mem (40)—Total 50.
Locust: *arbeh:* Aleph (1), Resh (200), Beth (2), He (5)—208.
Cankerworm: *yelek:* Yod (10), Lamed (30), Koph (100)—140.
Caterpillar: *chesil:* Cheth (8), Samech (60), Yod (10), Lamed (30)—108.

In these calculations vowel points, which were not in the original texts, are ignored. These numerical values were confirmed for the writer by a Jewish rabbi, to whom the four words for locust were submitted.

Now it has been pointed out that Babylonian desolation of Jerusalem and its temple lasted from 588 B.C. to 538, the year that Cyrus took Babylon, that is for 50 years; that Persian domination lasted from 538 to 330 B.C., the year of the victory of Alexander the Great, or for 208 years; that the period of Seleucid domination

Joel 2 29

lasted from 330 to their defeat by the Romans at the battle of Magnesia in 190, or for 140 years; then followed the period of the Maccabees and liberty, to be followed in its turn by Roman domination from 38 B.C. to 70 A.D., a period of 108 years. The locust figure is therefore a composite designation for the "kingdoms of men" (of which Daniel's image is another) in their oppression of the "people of God".

Now there are difficulties in this exposition. For example, is B.C. 38 a really firm date for the commencement of *Roman* domination? But when all is said, it is astonishing that it is possible to offer it *at all;* for one would have said that the chances of being able to do so with even an appearance of truth were heavily against. The correspondence is so detailed that we are justified in regarding the locusts as a concealed prophecy of the coming upon the land of Israel of the great Gentile desolators who are yet "one army" because they are carrying out one Divine purpose.

3. The Call to Repentance (2: 12–17)

vv. 12–14: "Yet *even now* (R.V.), *saith* the Lord, turn *ye quite* unto me with all your heart ..." The words in italics show the special emphasis: the dire destruction prophesied could "even now" be averted, if only the people would "wholly turn" to the Lord; and this is a solemn appeal, the word "saith", no ordinary word, implying an authoritative utterance (cf. "The Lord *saith* to my Lord", Psa. 110). It is a call to repentance. Israel were to offer not merely the conventional signs of affliction—fasting, weeping, mourning and the rending of their garments, all of which have ever played a prominent part in the lamentations of the peoples of the East, but nothing less than the *rending of their hearts;* no mere ceremonial conformity, but *real* repentance was what God desired. This was evidently the purpose of the affliction; which explains how He could at one moment tell them that His great army was coming for their punishment, and at the next command them to repent.

Here doubtless the words of the prophet merge into those of God Himself; the Lord is *your* God, turn unto Him, because *He* (very emphatic) is "gracious and merciful, slow to anger and of great kindness and repenteth him of the evil". No doubt there were those in Israel who found it as difficult to reconcile the judgements and the mercy of God as any of our moderns do. The description of the character of Yahweh is taken straight from the revelation of Himself granted to Moses (Exod. 34: 5–6)—no new conception of the Lord, this, but a recall to an old one (see also Jonah 4: 2). The prophet joins in the call: Who knows that God might not still grant

30 *Joel 2*

a blessing instead of the curse of desolation, and it would again be possible to offer the meal and the drink offering in the temple? (vv. 12–14).

Note 3: HOW CAN THE LORD "REPENT"?

"Who knoweth if (God) will return and *repent* ...?", Joel urges his people. His words pose a problem to us, readers of Scripture in English, for they suggest limitations to the understanding and to the power of God which are quite inconsistent with the general Bible portrait of Him who is infinite in wisdom and knowledge. And the matter is not made easier by apparently contradictory assertions like that of Samuel to Saul: "The Strength of Israel will not lie *nor repent:* he is not a man that he should repent", compared with the calm statement of the inspired historian of the Flood, "It repented the Lord that he had made man on the earth" (Gen. 6: 6).

But the problem is in our English, not in the Bible's Hebrew. A Hebrew verb is composed of three consonants (repent is *n-ch-m*), representing first a broad, general idea; special forms and emphases are then given to it by adding the vowels, the points of the Jewish scholars of later centuries (the Masoretes). So, says Gesenius' Hebrew Lexicon, *nacham* can mean variously to lament or grieve, and so to repent; to pity or have compassion; to be comforted, and to comfort others; and to take vengeance, that is to exact a righteous retribution.

Now add to the two quotations above the following:

Jer. 4: 28—I have purposed (judgement on Judah) and *will not repent* ...
Jer. 18: 8—If that nation, against whom I have spoken, turn from their evil way, *I will repent* of the evil that I had thought to do unto them ...
Isa. 1: 24—I will *ease me* of my adversaries ...
Isa. 57: 6—Should I *receive comfort* (be appeased, R.V.) from these (offerings of Israel to idols)?
Isa. 40: 1—*Comfort ye,* comfort ye, my people

Nacham, then, when used of God, represents His reaction to a given situation. When men, whom He has created, turn to evil, He is grieved; and as long as they continue in their evil way He will not repent of the judgement that He has pronounced upon them. Persistent sin demands His righteous retribution (A.V., vengeance) and when it is carried out He is "comforted". But when sinners "turn" to Him, He is quick to alter His action and so to "repent of the evil", and bring comfort to the sufferers. (For a more detailed

Joel 2

treatment of the subject, see the author's "Knowledge of God" series, *The Christadelphian*, Aug. 1967, pp. 355–59).

vv. 15–17: The call to repentance is taken up by all sections of the people; a solemn trumpet (*shophar*, a call this time to assemble for worship) is blown; a fast is "hallowed" as a national act of humiliation. The call is to the whole nation, including children; even the bridegroom, normally exempt from service for one year, and the bride are called from their festivities. The priests act as the people's intercessors and lament "between the porch and the altar", a space enclosed in front of the Holy of holies where the altar for burnt offerings stood. Their plea is that God will spare His people and His heritage; otherwise the pagan nations will rule over them and say in contempt, "Where is this God of theirs? Either He does not exist, or He cannot save them"—both blasphemous assertions in the ears of every devout Israelite.

4. The Divine Blessings Restored (vv. 18–27)

The repentance has been real; God sets out to restore His people to favour. In interpretation, however, theological prejudice plays a great part in this section of the prophecy.

The difficulty is caused by the fact that the Hebrew verb has nothing approaching the definiteness of *time* which Western languages all possess. The interpretation therefore is made to depend almost entirely upon the context. Those modern critics who refuse to admit prophecy of the future, understand the verbs in this passage in the past tense: "The Lord *was* jealous for his land and pitied his people." More conservative scholars defend the *future* tense, as in the A.V. and R.V. When the full implications of the restoration promised to Israel in this section are explored, it becomes clear that a complete fulfilment has not yet occurred, even in our day. The prophecy, then, definitely has long term future applications.

vv. 18–20: The Lord, full of zeal ("jealous") for *His* land, and of pity for *His* repentant people, promises restoration of the blessings of the soil, the corn and the wine, reversing the devastation caused by His "great army"; the pagan nations too shall no longer refer to Israel contemptuously. The "northerner" ("army" is not in the original) is to be removed. The term is new in the prophecy; it evidently cannot be solely applied to an army of locusts, since they would hardly come into Palestine from the North, nor would they be destroyed between the Dead and the Mediterranean Seas (in Hebrew the east "faces" you; the western or "hinder" sea is

32   *Joel 2*

therefore behind you). Nor would locusts stay in a barren land; nor
would it be said of the locust power: "He hath magnified to do
great things." The stink of decaying locust bodies is well known,
but so would be that of any decaying flesh in quantity. In other
words we have here a prophecy of the destruction of a great latter
day invader from the North. (See note.)

vv. 21–27: And now the whole land is to rejoice, for it is the Lord
who hath done "great things" (as He did at the Exodus). The
beasts and the trees of the field shall alike recover strength. The
"former rain", "the rain", and "the latter rain" allude to the three
rainy seasons in Israel: October, December–February, and April.
"In the first month" is a mistaken translation for "as at the first".
The Hebrew word rendered "former rain" can also mean "instruc-
tor", and the one rendered "moderately" means literally "for
righteousness"; hence some have interpreted that God was
promising to His people "a teacher of righteousness", that is the
Messiah; the context of verse 23 however is definitely that of
material blessings, and so we may render, "the former rain for
righteousness"; that is, just as the previous desolation had come on
account of their forsaking of God (how otherwise would they need
to turn unto the Lord with their whole heart?), so their repentance
brings material blessings in its train. God will restore "the years
that the locust hath eaten" (the expression suggests that the
desolation had been spread over a considerable time, rendering void
the attempt to interpret the destruction of one great locust plague
as some wish to do). The four locust names of chapter 1: 4 are
repeated, and are described as "*my great army* which I sent among
you", thus identifying the locust desolators with the great power
described in chapter 2, and equally clearly, linking "the northerner"
with them. Because God had dealt "wondrously" as He had done in
the great deliverance from Egypt, His people shall "know" that
God is in their midst (this was the aim of the chastisement); they
will recognise His absolute supremacy, and the pagan nations will
never have occasion to reproach them any more. The great
judgement will have been reversed.

Note 4: WHO IS "THE NORTHERNER"?
   From our exposition so far it appears that the locust power is a
composite figure for all the invading forces of the nations, from the
Assyrians to the Romans (750 B.C.–A.D. 70), sent by God against
His people and His land on account of persistent rebellion and sin.
Since their deliverance from "the northerner" (2: 20) reverses at
last the desolations of the previous Gentile powers, that expression

Joel 2   33

must represent the last great invasion of the Land for the purpose of
plunder. In later prophecy that event is the invasion of the army of
Gog (Ezek. 38), who comes, like all invaders except Egypt, "out of
the north", and whose hosts, in the very language of the locust
plagues, "ascend like a storm, ... like a cloud to cover the land",
and whose carcases, devoured by "ravenous birds", yet corrupt the
land so that it needs to be "cleansed" (39: 4, 14). The Lord's
address to Gog: "Art thou he of whom I spake in old time by my
servants, the prophets of Israel, which prophesied in those days
(for) many years that I would bring thee against them?" (Ezek.
38: 17) is therefore a direct allusion to prophecies like Joel's. By
Gog's destruction God will cause his Name to be known among the
nations, and Israel to realise that He is their God (Ezek. 38: 23;
39: 21–22) just as Joel declares.

5. The Outpouring of the Spirit (2: 28–32)

vv. 28–29: There follows a remarkable section of the prophecy
which must have been greatly encouraging to those faithful in Israel
who were dismayed by the "day of darkness" to come. "Afterward"
(that is after the judgement and deliverance of verses 18–27), "I
will pour out of my spirit upon all flesh." The outpouring is to be
upon "your sons and your daughters ... your young men and your
old men ... servants and handmaids ..."; that is, upon all sections
of the nation. Joel and his contemporaries, remembering the gift
made in the wilderness to the 70 elders to enable them to assist
Moses, would expect a nationwide repetition. Since it was by dream
and by vision that God had promised to speak to His prophets
(Num. 12: 6), and the gift was to come even upon the servants, the
prophecy was really saying that the whole people of Israel were to
become prophets, or spokesmen of God. But verse 32 shows that the
prophecy really applied to "the remnant whom the Lord doth call".
  But more than the gift of miraculous powers is ultimately
implied, as other passages from the prophets show. Through
Jeremiah God was to promise that, as a result of the "new
covenant" He would make with Israel, "I will put my law in their
inward parts, and write it in their hearts" (31: 33); and through
Ezekiel that, once they were delivered from Gog, they would "know
that I am the Lord ... for I have poured out my spirit upon the
house of Israel" (39: 29); and through Zechariah that, upon their
repentance, "I will pour out upon the house of David ... the spirit
of grace and of supplication" (12: 10). No doubt Joel, and certainly
those who read the prophets in later times, would see in his

34   *Joel 2*

prophecy not merely the reappearance of miraculous gifts, but the promise of spiritual reconciliation with God.

When we come to consider Peter's application of this prophecy to the events of the Day of Pentecost (Acts 2), God's promise through Joel, "I will pour out my spirit upon *all* flesh" becomes very significant. While the terms used appear to restrict the promise to Israel, the use of "all flesh" in the Scripture is striking: "All flesh had corrupted God's way ... The end of all flesh ..." (Gen. 6); "O thou that hearest prayer, unto thee shall all flesh come" (Psa. 65: 2; cf. "All nations whom thou hast made shall come and worship before thee", 86: 9). Joel's prophecy looked forward, then, to the extension of God's Spirit blessing to "all nations". And so the process took a decisive step forward on the Day of Pentecost: the appeal was first to those in Israel who would repent, and was supported by the visible signs of God's power; it then went out in the preaching of the Gospel to "all nations", who were called to the "new covenant" and to be "an epistle of Christ, written ... with the Spirit of the living God ... in tables that are hearts of flesh" (2 Cor. 3: 3; see Heb. 8: 9–12).

vv. 30–32: Peter, himself speaking by the Spirit, made an application of Joel's prophecy to that first Pentecost, but a further application is required at the time of the end, as is shown by verses 30–32 here. God will shew "wonders", as in the deliverance from Egypt (Deut. 6: 22). The great signs in the heavens and in the earth, including "blood, fire and pillars of smoke", speak of judgements to come, not now upon Israel only, but upon all nations (cf. Jesus' words in Luke 21: 25), for the "day of the Lord" will be "great and terrible". The deliverance will be for "those that call upon the name of the Lord", that acknowledge Him as their Redeemer and seek to do His will. In Romans 10: 13 the Apostle Paul quotes this phrase as a prophecy of the call of the Gentiles.

Although verse 32 is the first occurrence of the doctrine of "the remnant" in Scripture, there had been earlier examples of the principle. The survivors from the judgements of the Flood and the wilderness wanderings, were only a remnant. Other prophetic allusions can be found in Isaiah 10: 20; 28: 5; Jeremiah 23: 3; 31: 7. In the New Testament the Apostle Paul declares that there will be "a remnant according to the election of grace" (Rom. 11: 5). In the latter day the remnant will prove to be of two kinds: the redeemed faithful, whether of Israel or of the Gentiles, who through Christ will inherit immortality at his coming; and the remnant of the natural seed of Israel, who will have survived the "purging" and are

Joel 3 35

not "rebels" and will enter the Kingdom of the Son of David as his mortal subjects (Ezek. 20: 33–38).

6. The Judgement of the Nations (3: 1–16)

3: 1–8: The opening words of the new section, "For, behold, in those days and at that time", link it with what has preceded: the time of Israel's redemption. God, however, makes the time still more precise: "When I shall bring again the captivity of Judah and Jerusalem." Modern critics, finding it incredible that there could be a reference to the Babylonian captivity over 200 years into the future, prefer the marginal reading: "restore the fortunes of ..." But of the 22 occurrences of the word translated "captivity" here (it is never translated in any other way), 12 are distinct allusions to a return of a people from exile, mostly of Israel, and many of the remainder could well be the same. We may take it therefore that the Spirit foretells here the final return of Israel to their land.

But the restoration of Israel is to be a time of reckoning for "all nations", who will be brought to judgement by God Himself; they will be charged with scattering the people of Israel and dividing up their land, crimes which occurred long after Joel's day. Why are the nations to be brought into the valley of Jehoshaphat? The allusion is unquestionably to the great deliverance from the invading armies of Ammon, Moab, and Edom, when Jehoshaphat led Judah in a cry for help to God and was heard because of his faith (2 Chron. 20). This striking event had occurred probably not more than 50 years before Joel's days. The precise place of this deliverance is difficult to determine; it seems to have been near Tekoa, 10 miles south of Jerusalem. In that case the traditional "valley of Jehoshaphat", the valley of the Kedron between Jerusalem and the mount of Olives, cannot be meant. The Century Bible asserts that the tradition linking the valley of Jehoshaphat with this valley close to Jerusalem cannot be traced back further than the historian Eusebius of the 4th century A.D. Since "Jehoshaphat" means "Yahweh will judge", it is likely that the name was chosen because of the act of judgement to be performed there in very similar circumstances of invasion and repentance at a much later date. The choice of the name "valley of decision" in verse 14 of the same chapter suggests that it is the act which is to be performed there which gives its name to the valley. There God will "plead with the nations"; that is, He will accuse them of crimes and will act as judge.

To Joel and his contemporaries "all nations" meant, as verse 4 shows, "Tyre, Sidon, and all the coasts (regions) of Palestine (Philistia)"; in other words, the surrounding nations with whom

36   *Joel 3*

Israel had been in conflict. In the reign of Jehoram, who succeeded Jehoshaphat, the Philistines and the Arabs of the desert invaded Judah and sacked Jerusalem (2 Chron. 21). Now they are bluntly warned that they have no claim upon God. For acts of pillage they would be judged, as for selling the Israelites as slaves to the Greeks, almost certainly through Tyre, a notorious port for the slave traffic (see Ezek. 27: 13). The mention of "the Grecians" is no proof of late date for this prophecy, as some allege. The word is *Javan,* found as early as Genesis 10: 2, and there is evidence that the Greeks had colonised parts of Asia Minor 200 years before Joel's day.

The time was to come when the tables would be turned; Israel would be restored from captivity, and the nationals of these invading Palestinian powers would themselves be sold as slaves, as far away as to the Sabeans, or "men of Sheba" (R.V.), a great trading race in farthest Arabia, perhaps chosen because it was in the opposite direction to the land of the "Grecians". There does not seem to be any record of Judah themselves indulging in this slave selling, as verse 8 asserts they would, but they may well have done so, when Uzziah and Hezekiah were dominating the Philistines for example (740–700 B.C.).

Note 5: THE INTERPRETATION OF PROPHECY

Before proceeding further, it is necessary to say something about the interpretation of prophecies like Joel's.

The prophet's message always treated first of some crisis which was close in time and therefore of *immediate* concern to those who heard it, creating in them a need for faith. So to Joel's contemporaries the immediate threat came from the nations of Canaan, and would next come from Assyria and Babylon. But then, by the Spirit, the prophet's message leaps forward to the final conclusion of God's controversy with His people and with the invading nations, without giving any hint that *a gap of several centuries is to intervene.* A simple example is found in the reassuring message given to Hezekiah at the invasion of Sennacherib (Isa. 37: 31–32); and a perfect New Testament example is the Olivet Prophecy of the Lord himself, who refers in it first to events soon to come to pass upon Jerusalem, and then to those of his Second Coming without giving any hint that 1900 years were to intervene between the two (Luke 21). This "prophetic gap", unnatural as it may seem to us who look backwards, is not a sign of forced interpretation but was a necessity of the phenomenon of prophecy. By it the faithful were encouraged to trust that God would eventually bring His words of

Joel 3   37

comfort and deliverance to pass; and at the same time He avoided discouraging them by revealing to them the long periods involved.

There is a further point: in seeking to make latter-day interpretations of prophecy, we must look for those powers which play a corresponding role in relation to Israel. For example, when the Spirit through Isaiah declares that "Israel shall be the third with Egypt and Assyria, a blessing in the midst of the earth, etc." (see 19: 24–25), we must first appreciate that Egypt and Assyria were chosen as typical Gentile powers, because *they* were the immediate enemies of Israel in the days of Isaiah. In the latter-day application, however, they stand for all the nations of the Gentiles, who will come to worship the Lord of Hosts in Jerusalem.

The second lesson is the unfolding character of Biblical prophecy, for the faithful in both Babylonian and in Roman times saw in their oppressors the scourging army of God and looked forward to deliverance. The idea therefore that a Biblical prophecy may have a double application is not far-fetched, but sometimes a necessity, and this may help us to understand more easily the mind of the New Testament writers who sometimes make applications of Old Testament prophecy which seem to us premature or local. The applications are there; the prophecy is constructed so that they shall be; the minds of the believers are constantly exercised to see how the words of God come perennially true; how otherwise could faith have been maintained through long centuries of waiting?

And how is it possible for the words of God to find their application through different crises extending over many centuries? Surely because the two main elements in the situation remain ever the same: God is the same today as He was in the days of Moses, His righteousness unchanging and his purpose firm to redeem *to* that righteousness those who will hear; and the wayward tendencies of human kind to prefer "the lust of the flesh, the lust of the eyes and the pride of life" to the Divine righteousness remain as unchanging as ever. Inevitably the reactions between these two forces will be very much alike in every age and a forecast of God about one situation will apply generally to the succeeding ones. But it is important to notice that only *true* estimates of the righteousness of God and of the tendencies of human flesh could have produced such a forecast at all.

vv. 9–16: In harmony with the foregoing, what now follows in Joel's prophecy is an early forecast of that great crisis in the land of Israel, described in more detail in Ezekiel's account of the invasion of the hosts of Gog (38–39). In its general effects it must also include the results of the overthrow of the nations of Europe, the

38   *Joel 3*

beast and the ten kings, who deliberately choose to go to make war
with the Lamb (Rev. 19). God now addresses "the Gentiles" (same
original as "all nations", v. 2), summoning them to assemble all
their mighty men, turn all their instruments of peace to weapons,
and to "hallow" or "sanctify" war. The expression occurs several
times in the Old Testament; the Medes were God's "sanctified
ones" for the destruction of Babylon (Isa. 13: 3); Judah's enemies
say: "Sanctify ye war against her" (Jer. 6: 4), that is, proclaim a
holy war. (Two comments of interest: Antichrist will do just this in
the final conflict—see Rev. 17: 12–14; and the nations, subdued
under Christ, will turn weapons to peaceful uses and *sanctify* war
no more, Isa. 2.) To this hostile gathering of the nations who are
assembled "round about", God will bring down His "mighty
ones"—the angels "mighty in strength" (Psa. 103: 20), the chariot
of Israel. The gathering is to "the valley of Jehoshaphat" because
there "the Lord will judge" (see comment on v. 2). There follow
two figures of the harvest: first the wheat harvest, cut with a sickle;
second the grape harvest, trodden under foot in the winepress,
always used for God's anger (Lam. 1: 15; Isa. 63: 3); its "over-
flowing" represents the judgement for wickedness which is "great".
Both these figures reappear in the book of Revelation. The order to
put in the sickle and to tread the winepress (see R.V.m. for: "get
you down") is evidently given to the mighty ones. The emphatic
repetition: "multitudes, multitudes" (the original means "hum")
suggests the noise of vast numbers (in Psa. 2: 1, "why do the
heathen rage" means literally "tumultuously assemble"). The
valley is one of "decision"—the word is used of sharp, threshing
instruments in Isaiah 28: 27; 41: 15; Amos 1: 3. There follow the
darkening of the heavens and the shaking of the earth, no doubt
literal as well as political: cf. 2: 10, 31; Isaiah 13: 10 and the Olivet
prophecy. The Lord roars like a lion from Zion (Amos 1: 2), but for
His people He becomes a place of refuge and a stronghold (R.V.).

7. Judah at Peace (3: 17–21)

vv. 17–21: The prophecy concludes with a few verses describing the
blessings of Judah and Jerusalem. The remnant of Israel will
"know" (acknowledge) that Yahweh is their God (as after the
destruction of Gog, Ezek. 39: 22) and that He really dwells among
them in Zion, after all the doubts raised by the locust-like scourge.
Jerusalem shall be "holiness" for ever, untrodden by strangers: "no
unclean ... no uncircumcised" (Isa. 35: 8; 52: 1); "no wicked"
(Nahum 1: 15); "no Canaanite" (Zech. 14: 21). The prosperity of
the vines and the flocks and abundant waters will return to Judah; a

Joel 3   39

special stream will issue from the house of the Lord, as from the
temple in Ezekiel 47, from Jerusalem in Zechariah 14: 8; like the
"river of water of life" from the throne of God and the Lamb in
Revelation 22: 1. It will water the valley of Shittim (acacias), a
valley on the East of Jordan known for its dryness; but more
significantly it was there that Israel had their last camp before
entering the land under Joshua; hence there that Balaam delivered
his blessing and that Israel committed the great sin of idolatry with
the gods of Moab. The memory of this is finally to be washed away.
Egypt, the great oppressing power, and Edom the hostile neighbour,
are both to remain desolate. The reason given is obscure: "for the
violence against the children of Judah, because they have shed
innocent blood in their land". The most probable sense is that these
two enemies of Israel had been guilty of murdering Jewish captives.
(See Amos 1: 11–12.)

For Judah and Jerusalem however, the restoration and the
pardon are permanent; they shall "abide for ever". The blood that
is to be cleansed is doubtless that of the sinners in Israel, who as a
community are at last reconciled to God, but the work will
emphatically be that of Yahweh Himself, known as the God who
dwells in Zion. The prophecy thus has moved from the dread tones
of warning of coming desolation to the full assurance of restoration
and eventual peace with God; but it is He alone who will be the
architect of the work.

Concluding Reflection

What does Joel's prophecy mean to us?

It is probably the first prophetic account of the events to be
expected at the "time of the end". There will be signs and wonders
when the day of the Lord comes: the armies of the assembled
nations are judged for wickedness; the remnant of Israel is delivered
and restored; Zion is the seat of deliverance, and from there the
Lord's reign of peace will go forth.

Joel's prophecy is predominantly one of judgement to come, first
upon Israel and then on the nations, and its first clear message is
this: in the purpose of God, when wickedness is "great", that is
when it is so deep rooted that repentence is no longer possible, then
God's ultimate action in dealing with it is drastic and complete. So
it was in the case of the Flood (Gen. 6) and the final overthrow of
the Kingdom, first of Israel and then Judah, when there was "no
remedy" (2 Chron. 36: 15–16). The conclusion is that God will not
be mocked and that He is jealous (zealous) for His Holy Name in
the earth and intends that it shall be honoured among the nations.

40   *Joel 3*

The lesson for us is clear: in these days of man's self-assertion (even in religion) and general neglect of divine authority, we must remember that the God we serve is "holy" and "righteous" (see Jesus' address to the Father in John 17: 11, 25), and while rejoicing to the full in His infinite mercy and grace, we should serve Him in "godly fear".

Its second message is that, though the "time is long", the purpose of God stands sure. The devastations of the locust powers were spread over centuries, unsuspected as this was by those who heard Joel's words. But in our own day the tide has shown unmistakable signs of its turn; the day of the final crisis cannot be far off.

The call therefore to the servants of God, whether in Israel in Joel's day or to us in this Gentile age, is to humble submission and to faith, to a trust in Him and His word, despite all appearances; for "the just shall live by his faith" (Hab. 2: 4). We are privileged indeed to live so near to the "time of the end", for our encouragement is great. "Fear not ... be glad and rejoice: for the Lord will do great things" (Joel 2: 21) is still the message for the faithful, just as it was over 2500 years ago.

4

OBADIAH

THE JUDGEMENT OF EDOM

The prophecy of Obadiah—the shortest book in the Old Testament—recounts how Edom is to be brought low by the very allies whom she has trusted, on account of her treachery against Jacob in the day of the latter's calamity; but the "day of the Lord" would reveal God's judgement upon *all* the nations. In that day there would be salvation in Zion for the remnant of Israel, who would regain their dominion, for "the kingdom shall be the Lord's".

But when, and in what circumstances, was the prophecy delivered? No details are given about the prophet himself; Obadiah is a common name and simply means "servant of Yahweh". At first sight the sack of Jerusalem referred to by the prophet would appear to be the final one by Nebuchadnezzar in 588 B.C., when the Edomites are known to have "helped on the affliction" (Zech. 1: 15). But there are objections to this view, for the tenses of the verbs are indefinite; they may refer to events which are either past or future. The result is that critics who cannot believe in prediction insist on taking them all in the past tense, give a late date to the prophecy and understand Obadiah's references as alluding to the final overthrow of Jerusalem by the Babylonians; others see them as prophetic of a calamity to come. If Obadiah did write after the destruction of Jerusalem by Nebuchadnezzar, then it is certainly remarkable that there is no allusion to the ruin of the city or temple, nor to Nebuchadnezzar or the Chaldeans, nor to the deportation of Judah to Babylon. If the prophecy is to be put after 588 B.C., then it must be put quite a lot later, to a date, in fact, which its tone and allusions do not fit.

In favour of an earlier date is the position of the book in the canon (see introduction to Joel, p. 19). The absence of allusion to Nebuchadnezzar and the Chaldeans as well as to the actual destruction of Jerusalem and its temple could argue a *much* earlier date, one consistent with its place in the canon, in fact. The linguistic evidence agrees with this, for "nowhere ... can one word or form be alleged of which it can even be said that it was used more frequently in later Hebrew" (Pusey, *Minor Prophets*, Vol. III, p. 306), and allusions in Obadiah are always to the *earlier* writings of the Old Testament (to one of Balaam's pronouncements in

Numbers, to a psalm of David, and perhaps to Amos and Joel, but never to any prophet of later date. The really important piece of evidence, however, is that without much doubt Jeremiah, in writing his prophecy of Edom (49: 7–22), must have been acquainted with the prophecy of Obadiah and echoed parts of it. The prophecy of Obadiah is a carefully constructed and compact whole; Jeremiah alludes to no less than eight of the verses, but does so in such a scattered manner, interspersing them with his own material, as to suggest that he was making his own use of an already existing prophecy. (Jeremiah also made use of 8 verses of Isaiah for his prophecy about Moab.) A further striking fact is that in the material common to himself and Obadiah in chapter 49 Jeremiah uses no expressions characteristic of himself, whereas in the rest of the passage such expressions are found. (See Pusey, Vol. III, p. 278 ff.; Kirkpatrick, *Doctrine of the Prophets*, pp. 35–6, for the detailed evidence.)

On balance then the evidence is strikingly in favour of the conclusion that Obadiah must have written before Jeremiah, and in that case probably a long time before.

Now it seems very likely that Obadiah wrote this "judgement" of Edom because there had been some historical event, involving Israel's affliction and Edom's triumph, to call it forth. Can such an event be found long before the overthrow of Jerusalem by Nebuchadnezzar? That the opportunities for such an event were great is obvious when we consider that Judah and Edom were neighbours and that an almost constant state of war existed between them. During the wilderness journey Israel were refused permission to pass through the land of Edom (Num. 20); David completely subdued the Edomites and put garrisons in their land (2 Sam. 8); about 860 B.C. occurred the striking deliverance of Judah under Jehoshaphat from the confederacy of Ammon, Moab and Edom; but about 10 years later Edom revolted against Jehoshaphat's son, Jehoram. Doubtless there were many wars and raids which have never found their way into the Divine records, because they were not specially significant. Of calamities involving Judah and Jerusalem, the most interesting for our purpose is the attack by the Philistines and the Arabians in the reign of Jehoram, shortly after Jehoshaphat's death, when the invaders broke into Jerusalem, carried away a great deal of spoil and also many people belonging to the king's family and household (2 Chron. 21: 16–17). Now the Edomites had just regained their independence from Judah and it seems incredible that they did not seize this opportunity to add to Judah's affliction, to take plunder and captives, and to cut off stragglers. Here was a situation which Obadiah's allusions would fit

Obadiah 43

very well. Since the Philistine–Arabian invasion took place about 840 B.C., and since a fairly early date seems required, we may regard Obadiah's prophecy as written not very long after that date, at a time when the memory of these events was still fresh.

1. The Judgement of Edom (vv. 1–9)

vv. 1-2: The prophecy opens with the assertion that the move to destroy Edom has come from Yahweh, who has sent "an ambassador" to this effect to the nations. This "messenger" or "herald" may have been an actual person or even an angel, but consistently with similar usages in the Old Testament it is more likely to be an allusion to God's method of using the political ambitions of the nations for His own purpose. For example Nebuchadnezzar, King of Babylon, was God's "servant" in His judgement upon Judah and Jerusalem (Jer. 25: 9). "The nations" to whom the messenger was sent were in the first instance "all the kingdoms of the earth of (Nebuchadnezzar's) dominion" (Jer. 34: 1). As a result there is a general move to "rise up" against Edom "to battle" (v. 1).

Edom is now addressed directly: "I have made thee small among the nations": the A.V. translates in the past tense, but all commentators are agreed that since Edom, in Obadiah's day was not yet destroyed, but was a formidable nation possessing considerable territory the tense must be taken as a *future* looked upon as already accomplished. The R.S.V. has: "I will make you small ... you shall be utterly despised ..." As already remarked in the study of Joel (see p. 31), the Hebrew verb lacks the definiteness of time which modern versions are compelled to give—an indication that its action will be more gradual and comprehensive than might at first appear.

vv. 3-4: The charge against Edom is one of pride of heart, encouraged by a fortress home, built at the head of deep defiles easily defended by a few men and blessed with abundant water supplies. The word "rock" is Hebrew *selah*, the name of the Edomite capital. The revelation in modern times of the astonishing city of Petra, with its dwellings cut out of the rock, has provided remarkable archaeological confirmation of the prophet's description, written centuries before Christ. As the eagle builds a nest in inaccessible places, so Edom has "set her nest among the stars". The expression "set thy nest" occurs in the words of Balaam's prophecy (Num. 24: 21) and *nowhere else*. Though the Edomites

44   *Obadiah*

felt confident—"Who shall bring me down to the ground?"—God
declares, "Thence will *I* bring thee down."

vv. 5–6: Even thieves and marauders leave some of "the spoil"
behind; but Edom's ruin, brought about by the judgement of God,
will be complete. So the prophet, like many others who have
contemplated the retribution of God upon the wicked, exclaims:
"How art thou cut off! How Esau has been pillaged and his
treasures (probably the spoil taken from others—Petra was a great
storehouse of the Syria-Arabia trade) sought out!" (R.S.V.). The
exclamation is not at all "vindictive" as some would contend; the
prophet is awe-struck at the judgement of God. The use of "Esau"
is striking, for rarely does it stand for the *nation* of Edom. Its use in
Jeremiah 49 is almost certainly an echo of this passage; in Malachi
1: 2–3 it is used for the *ancestor* of the people; but in Deuteronomy
2 "the children of Esau" five times represents the Edomites as a
people. Obadiah's use here is one more illustration of the knowledge
of the Pentateuch so often shown by the prophets.

vv. 7–9: Edom's allies, her intimate friends who ate her bread, were
traditionally Ammon and Moab, who, together with Tyre and
Sidon, united with her eventually to resist Nebuchadnezzar. Even
they have deceived her, laid a "snare" (R.V., for A.V. "wound",
obscure) under her, and driven her fugitives back to their own
border, presumably instead of giving them shelter. Edom, renowned
for "wisdom" and "understanding" of the worldly sort, is to be
destroyed "in that day"—clearly the judgement is still future. Her
warriors, too, are to be "cut off".

2. The Crime against Israel

vv. 10–14: According to the law Israel were not to abhor an
Edomite, "for he is thy brother" (cf. "your brethren ... the
children of Esau", Deut. 23: 7; 2: 4–5). They were to admit him
into the congregation of the Lord in the third generation. Edom,
however, had adopted a consistently hostile attitude towards Israel,
which would culminate in a cry of exultation at Nebuchadnezzar's
sack of Jerusalem. Obadiah charges Edom with "violence against
thy brother Jacob" (Jacob being used as a counterpart to Esau of
v. 8), and declares he shall be cut off "for ever", which came
historically to pass, but not all at once.

In the next 4 verses the rendering of the verbs makes a great
difference to the interpretation. The A.V. translation: "In the day
thou stoodest on the other side, in the day that strangers *carried
away captive his forces,etc. ... thou shouldest not have looked* on

Obadiah   45

the day of thy brother ... neither shouldest thou have rejoiced ..."
and so on for 7 more verbs to the end of verse 14, inevitably
suggests that the actions are past, that Obadiah is writing *after*
these events, and that therefore the interpretation must be of
Edom's malicious participation in the destruction accomplished by
Nebuchadnezzar. The grammatical facts however suggest an
entirely different view. The *time* of verse 11 is not stated: literally,
"In the day of thy standing over against (Israel, doubtless to gloat
over their misfortunes), in the day of the strangers' carrying
away, ... even thou as one of them ..." The action could refer to
the past, but equally to the future. Concerning the succession of
verbs: "Thou shouldest not have ...", Pusey contends with great
force that they are mistranslations; they should be rendered "Do
not ..." etc. "It is absolutely certain that *al* with the future forbids
or deprecates a thing future. In all the passages, in which *al* occurs
in the Hebrew Bible, it signifies 'Do not' " (Vol. III, p. 275). Upon
which the *Speaker's Commentary* adds: "... This is undoubtedly
so, for *al* with the future must express a dehortatory future. The
grammatical argument in favour of the A.V.m. is irrefragable and
sufficient". The *Century Bible,* wishing to see here a reference back
to an historical event, comments: "This sudden change to the
imperative, *implying that the event had not yet happened,* is very
perplexing"! The R.V. translates as imperatives throughout: "Look
not thou ... rejoice not ... neither speak proudly", etc. Obadiah,
then, is not speaking of a past calamity for Israel, but is foreseeing
one to come, a point which has considerable force in the argument
about the date of the prophecy.

The fact that the Edomites were to "stand on the other side"
while "strangers" spoiled Israel suggests clearly that Edom was not
to be the main aggressor, but a mere ally. (We will return to this
point later when we come to consider the scope of the prophecy.)
Ultimately the subjection of Israel is complete, for the foreigners
enter the gates of Jerusalem and divide up the city by lot. In this
day of calamity Edom would not only rejoice in his pride, but would
actually enter the city himself, loot it, and cut off the fugitives
fleeing for their lives, and hand over some of them, probably to be
sold as slaves. For these crimes against his "brother Jacob", Edom
is to be "cut off for ever". (For other passages accusing Edom of
the same attitude, see Psa. 137: 7; Joel 3: 19; Amos 1: 11; Ezek.
35.)

46   Obadiah

3. The Day of the Lord: Deliverance in Zion (vv. 15–21)
vv. 15–18: The ultimate judgement of Edom now merges into a
wider one involving "all the nations". As Edom would revel in
exultant drunkenness, so would all the nations upon the holy
mountain itself, but the cup God would give them and of which
they would drink "continually" there (that is, in a series of Gentile
triumphs) would be that of His wrath: and the power of the nations
would disappear.

Zion, the place of their triumph, would now become the
dwelling-place of an "escaped remnant" (see R.V., and Isa.
37: 31–32; Joel 2: 32 for same word). Its holiness will not be marred
by the presence of the unclean of the nations: and Israel would
regain their "possessions" which they had lost. "The possessions"
could, however, be those of the Gentile nations, an interpretation
which agrees well with the rest of this part of the prophecy. Israel,
now described as "the house of Jacob and the house of Joseph" to
signify the reunion of the Northern and Southern kingdoms, were
to act as the means of God's judgements upon "the house of Esau",
devouring it with fire.

v. 19: "The south ... the plain (lowland) ... the field" is a
reference to the original borders of the tribe of Judah (see Josh.
ch. 15). After the coming judgements upon the nations, the
Israelites of "the south" would control the "mount of Esau" and so
be secure on that border; similarly those of the Shephelah (the
coastal plain) would dominate the territory of the Philistines; their
possession of the fields of Ephraim and Samaria implies the
restoration of Jerusalem's dominion over the Northern kingdom;
and the fact that Benjamin, the remaining one of the two southern
tribes, should possess Gilead, the inheritance of Reuben, Gad and
Manasseh "beyond Jordan", asserts that the new restored Israel is
to occupy the full limits of the land promised to the fathers. A
remarkable feature here is the way in which Judah and Benjamin
are made to stand for the whole purged people of Israel.

vv. 20–21: The "captivity" are those Israelites carried away captive,
whether by Canaanites or later by Assyrians and Babylonians. They
are to take possession of Canaanite territory as far as "Zarephath"
(Sarepta, in Phoenicea). "Sepharad" is not mentioned elsewhere
and is unknown as a name—the Jewish tradition associating it with
Spain is a late one. Does not this suggest that it is most likely a
distant place? The "captivity" there would therefore represent
those Israelites transported to distant places, for example Assyria
and Babylon. On their restoration they are to possess "the South",
that is a location in exactly the opposite direction to "Zarephath",

Obadiah

an indication that they will control all the territory in between: the whole land of Israel and its surrounding peoples. But as in ancient times God had raised up "saviours" to deliver his people from their oppressors (as did Gideon for example from the Midianites), so again such deliverers shall "come up on" mount Zion; that is, they will not just return from captivity but will occupy positions of power there, as Isaiah represents the kingdom of the Lord as "exalted" above the mountains and the law going forth from Zion (2: 2–5). Edom will be subdued (and so by implication will "all nations"), but Yahweh will be supreme over all people in His holy mountain.

Concluding Reflections

If the devout Israelite saw in Obadiah's prophecy an allusion to the part probably played by the Edomites in the sack of Jerusalem by the Philistines and the Arabians about 848 B.C., then he may equally have seen a further fulfilment in the "judgement" of Edom by Israel under Amaziah about 795 B.C., or about 40 years later under Hezekiah. The brief references in the historical books cannot hide the drastic nature of Edom's punishment: "(Amaziah) ... went to the valley of Salt and smote of the children of Seir ten thousand" and "took Sela· by war and called the name of it Joktheel (God's reward by victory) unto this day" (2 Kings 14: 7). But Edom revived and eventually witnessed the utter destruction by Nebuchadnezzar of the city of Jerusalem, to which Obadiah's words must inevitably look forward.

In the days of the Maccabees the Edomites were a trouble to Judah, and were more than once conquered by the Jews, finally being completely subjugated by John Hyrcanus (135 B.C.), who "subdued all the Edomites and permitted them to remain in the country, on condition that they would receive circumcision and adopt the laws of the Jews", which they did (Josephus, *Antiquities*, Bks. 12, 13). Again the students of the prophets would see a fulfilment of Obadiah's prophecy of Edom's judgement by means of Israel. But the Romans came and swept away both Jews and what remained of the Edomites, and still the day of "the saviours on mount Zion" had not come. The final "day of the Lord" upon the nations now draws near; in it no doubt, the latter-day Edom, the modern Arabs, will join with the last oppressor, Gog, and come to their end with him, while a new kingdom of Israel will be established upon the ancient mountains and Yahweh alone will be worshipped there. In other words Obadiah's prophecy has the same unfolding character as Joel's.

Obadiah

One or two further features of the prophecy underline its comparatively early date.

It is noticeable that the picture of the future is painted in terms of *material* prosperity: Israel is to be delivered from their enemies, "the nations", who are clearly the peoples of Palestine: the Edomites, the Philistines, and the Phoenicians, and (as the mention of Gilead probably implies) the Ammonites and Moabites. Israel's future horizon is restricted in this prophecy to those limits which were the actual experience of those who heard it in the first place. There is no suggestion that the kingdom of the future will take in territories far beyond these confines; *that* was reserved for the days of the prophets like Isaiah, Jeremiah and Ezekiel, who saw the great powers of Assyria and Babylon becoming involved in the destiny of Israel, instruments of God's judgement, then subjects of it, and finally submissive subjects of the final dominion of Yahweh.

"The nations", too, come in Obadiah's prophecy under the temporal dominion of Israel, but there is no suggestion, as there is in the later prophets, that they are to become objects of the grace of God and able to enter into covenant relation with Him. Neither is there any explicit mention of the fact, so stressed later, that unless Israel undergoes a spiritual reformation and renewal in their worship of God, there will be no survival for *them* either. These interesting facts make clear that God always spoke to His people through His prophets in the language of their contemporary ideas, so that His message would be easily and instantly understood; but that the form of His words concealed wider issues at first unsuspected, so that the "nations" of the land of Canaan become in final fufilment the nations of the whole earth. Here then is the kind of "development" we may expect to find in the prophets. It is a development in the *understanding* of His people, who perceive that the purpose of God will eventually embrace all mankind, and that His service involves not merely political submission but a real "knowledge" of Him, transforming their heart and will.

5
AMOS
"PREPARE TO MEET THY GOD, O ISRAEL"

Introduction

After the uncertainties of date concerning Joel and Obadiah it is a relief to read the clear statement of Amos that he prophesied during the reigns of Uzziah of Judah and Jeroboam (the second) of Israel, "two years before the earthquake", and to discover that almost no one questions his statement.

The historical period, however, covered by these two reigns, which were largely contemporaneous, turns out to be most significant. The period of Syrian (*not* Assyrian) supremacy over Israel runs from approximately 850 to 800 B.C., under their kings Ben-Hadad and Hazael. Under Jehoash the tide of Israel's fortunes began to turn; by three victories he won back the cities of Israel which his father Jehoahaz had lost. But the real warrior was his successor Jeroboam II, whose reign of 40 years (783–743 B.C.) marked a great revival of Israel's political power. The brief statement in 2 Kings 14: 25, 28 that Jeroboam restored the border of Israel "from the entering in of Hamath (in the north) unto the sea of the Arabah" (in the south), and that he "warred and recovered Damascus and Hamath" implies that he extended the boundaries of his kingdom to limits not reached since the days of Solomon.

Simultaneously in the south Judah was benefiting from a similar political revival. Of Uzziah (769–739 B.C.) it is recorded that he conquered the Philistines and the Arabians, took tribute from the Ammonites (his father had conquered the Edomites), fortified Jerusalem, built walled cities on the boundaries of his territory; that he "made war with mighty power", having an army of over 300,000 men, apparently well equipped; and that "his name spread far abroad; for he was marvellously helped, till he was strong" (2 Chron. 26: 6–15). To both kingdoms this age of triumph must have been as sweet as it had looked unlikely only 50 years before.

Of course, political developments in a wider field, under the hand of God, were the real explanation. The period 800–750 B.C. was

50   *Amos*

marked by desperate Assyrian struggles with the fierce Urartu in the extreme north, and with Syrian coalitions in the west. The result was that the Syrians were too busy defending themselves to think of invading Israel; the Assyrians were prevented by their stubborn resistance from pushing into Canaan; and since Egypt was too weak through internal divisions to interfere, Israel and Judah under capable kings became the dominant powers in the land of Canaan, and enjoyed a political security and a commercial prosperity unequalled for 200 years past.

The effects of these successes were disastrous in both civil and religious life. Owing to increased control of important trade routes, wealthy classes emerged in the people of Israel. The worst features of their society appeared first in the Northern kingdom. Rich men bought up the lands of poorer Israelites, or oppressed them by extortionate rates of interest, or even sold them as slaves when they could not pay their debts. Their lives were full of self-indulgence: in their magnificent houses they feasted with wine and music, in which their women-folk joined. Civil justice was corrupted; the poor could not obtain redress, for the judges accepted bribes and favoured the powerful. A new commercial class in the towns, a product of the growth of trade and the decline of agriculture (how modern all this sounds!), were covetous and dishonest, trading with false weights and shoddy goods. Licentiousness was widespread. But the ruling class were indifferent to the decline in moral standards, intolerant of rebuke, devoted to the *outward* practice of their religion, offering sacrifices and observing new moons and sabbaths, convinced that Yahweh was with them—surely He *must* be! Had He not most signally delivered them from Syria? Such is the devastating picture of their own people, the covenant people of Yahweh, which is so vividly drawn by the prophets Amos and Hosea. In this society the noble message of the prophets shone like a light in a dark place.

It is not possible to state exactly when Amos prophesied. The earthquake is of unknown date, even though it was celebrated enough to be mentioned two centuries later by Zechariah (14: 5). Since Israel is portrayed as feeling politically secure, the prophecy was probably uttered in the latter part of the reign of Jeroboam, say 755–750 B.C.

Amos came from Tekoa in Judah, 12 miles on the east of Jerusalem; from his home the Dead Sea and the barren mountains of Moab stretched away into a dry and desolate region. It is somewhat surprising to learn that Bethel, the centre of the idolatrous worship of the ten tribes, was only 12 miles north of Jerusalem. Acquaintance with it for Amos would therefore be easy.

Amos 1 51

He is described as a herdman and a dresser of sycamore trees, which were cultivated for their fruit and their wood. The fruit was small and watery and eaten chiefly by the poor. Though Amos himself need not have been poor, it is clear that he was not one of the wealthy ones; his familiarity with the land and country life rather than with cities appears in every thing he wrote, and his contemplation of the barren regions of Moab may have encouraged in him something of the spirit of John the Baptist. Though his mission was primarily with the Northern Kingdom, many of his utterances are so worded as to make it evident that he was addressing both Israel and Judah and that both communities would have knowledge of his prophecy.

1. The Judgement of the Surrounding Nations (1: 1—2: 3)

1: 1-2: After brief biographical details Amos opens his prophecy with a direct allusion to Joel: Yahweh roars from Zion; in the divided state of the nation it is still from Jerusalem that God speaks. As a result the herdsmen lament and even fruitful Carmel is desolate. The allusion is such as to give the definite impression that it is Joel's prophecy which is the original and that Amos wishes to connect *his* prophecy with Joel's.

vv. 3-5: Then follow short judgements upon six of the nations of Palestine, all Israel's neighbours, with whom the people of Yahweh had become deeply involved in the business of war and trade. The repeated formula, "For three transgressions and (or, yea) for four" does not imply that there have been seven transgressions. In Hebrew a threefold repetition is final ("I will overturn, overturn, overturn it ...", Ezek. 21: 27). So three would have been a full transgression, and four is therefore an excess. In other words there is no question that these nations merit the judgement of God.

Damascus represents the *Syrians*, who are charged with treating the people of Gilead (an Israelite province beyond Jordan) as straw is chopped into little pieces under the iron teeth of a cart or sledge. About 40 years before Amos' day Hazael and his son Ben-Hadad had committed atrocities against Israel (2 Kings 8: 12; 13: 7). Now, in the fire of war, the Syrian line of kings was to be destroyed, Damascus itself was to be sacked, the fertile plain, "the vally of Aven", thought to lie between the two Lebanon ranges, was to become desolate, a particular palace of the Syrian kings was to be destroyed (Beth-Eden, the house of Eden—not the same word as the Eden of Genesis), and the Syrians themselves were to be taken captives far away into the unknown North. These judgements upon

52 *Amos 1*

Syria and Damascus were carried out by Tiglath-Pileser III about 50 years after the days of Amos (2 Kings 16: 9).

vv. 6–8: The cities of the *Philistines* are the next subjects. Gaza is charged with handing over to Edom a whole body of captives, who were almost certainly Israelites (though this is not explicitly stated). The allusion was no doubt to the invasion of Judah by the combined forces of the Philistines and the Arabians in the reign of Joram (2 Chron. 21: 16), already referred to by Joel (3: 3, ff.). The details of this judgement of the Philistines illustrate a feature of Bible prophecy, in that it is the *wall* and *palaces* of Gaza that were to be destroyed, the *inhabitants* of Ashdod, the *ruler* of Ashkelon, Ekron was to suffer generally, while Gath is not mentioned at all. The individual fates of these cities are meant to be added together to make a general judgement on *all* the Philistines. Gath may well not be mentioned because it was damaged by the Syrians under Hazael (2 Kings 12: 17). The Philistine judgement came to pass in the invasions of Sennacherib of Assyria, about 710 B.C., and later by Pharaoh Necho of Egypt.

Note 6: "THE LORD GOD": ADONAI YAHWEH

This name of God occurs 16 times in Amos' prophecy. Its use in the Old Testament generally is significant.

Adon means lord, master, possessor, and its plural form *Adonai* (like the plural *Elohim*) is frequently used of God. From its earliest use in the Old Testament can be seen its true sense. When God assures Abraham that He is his "shield and exceeding great reward", Abraham responds: "O *Lord God* (Adonai Yahweh), what wilt thou give me, seeing I go childless?" When God assures him again that He is the Lord (*Yahweh*) who brought him out of Ur "to give thee this land to inherit it", Abraham exclaims, "*Lord God,* whereby shall I know that I shall inherit it?" (Gen. 15: 2, 8). The impression created is that Abraham is using this particular form of address to God because he is conscious of the greatness of the Almighty and of his own insignificance, and is humbling himself before Him.

This impression is reinforced by later usage of the term. Moses twice uses it when he is prostrating himself before God. In his desire to be allowed to cross the Jordan and see the Promised Land, he "besought the Lord, ... O *Lord God,* thou hast begun to show thy servant thy greatness, and thy strong hand: for what God (elohim) is there in heaven or in earth, that can do according ... to thy mighty acts?" Upon the rebellion of Israel after the report of

Amos 1   53

the spies, Moses "fell down before the Lord ... because the Lord
had said he would destroy you. And I prayed unto the Lord ... O
Lord God, destroy not thy people and thine inheritance which thou
hast redeemed through thy greatness ..." (Deut. 3: 24; 9: 24–26).
In both cases there is the strong impression of the greatness of God
and of His judgement of human sin. So too with the one use by
Joshua; after the defeat of Israel before Ai, he "rent his clothes,
and fell to the earth upon his face before the ark of the Lord, ...
and said, Alas, O *Lord God*, wherefore hast thou ... brought all
this people over Jordan ... to cause us to perish?" (Josh. 7: 6–7).

David's use of the term, in his response to the great promise of a
son to reign upon his throne for ever, is remarkable: "Who am I, O
Lord God, and what is my house that thou hast brought me thus
far?" In the following eleven verses David uses this form of address
to God no less than six more times, clearly because his mind is
filled with the impression of God's utter majesty and his own
littleness; for example: "For thou art great, O *Lord God*; for there
is none like thee, neither is there any God beside thee" (2 Sam.
7: 18–29).

But the occurrences of this term in the prophets are even more
striking. In Isaiah it occurs 23 times (ten in the form of "Lord God
of hosts"), in the general context of majesty and especially
judgement. First occurrence in 3: 15: The Lord enters into
judgement with the elders, the people, and the princes: "What
mean ye that ye beat my people to pieces and grind the faces of the
poor, saith the *Lord God* of hosts?" In Jeremiah, 13 times: first
occurrence: Jeremiah, appointed by God a prophet to the nations,
says, "Ah! *Lord God*, behold I cannot speak; for I am a child"
(1: 6). And in Ezekiel, that prophet of final doom for rebellious
Israel, the staggering total of 120 times!

How significant, then, that a short prophecy like Amos should
contain no less than 20 occurrences of *Adonai Yahweh*; but not
really surprising, for there is much in Amos of Divine judgement on
human sin, whether of the Philistines as here in verse 8, or more
particularly of Israel. There is an important lesson here for us in
our generation, when human transgressions are excused and lightly
dismissed, and God's continuing grace is taken for granted. His
infinite mercy does not exempt us from "reverence and godly fear"
in remembrance of His holiness.

vv. 9–10: The charge against *Tyre*, chosen to represent the Phoenicians, is the same as that against the Philistines: delivering up to
Edom a large number of captives, whom they had probably bought
as slaves from some other invading power, perhaps Syria under

54   *Amos 1*

Ben-Hadad. In Ezekiel one of the charges against the Tyrians is that they "traded in persons of men" (27: 13). The brotherly covenant which Tyre had failed to honour must be an allusion to the close alliance between David and Hiram, king of Tyre, continued under Solomon: "they two made a league together" (1 Kings 5: 12), the word "league" being the same as "covenant" in Amos. Again there is no exact record of this offence against Israel, but Ezekiel represents Tyre as liable to the judgements of God because she had said "against Jerusalem, Aha, she is broken ... she is turned unto me: I shall be replenished, now she is laid waste" (26: 2). Tyre suffered at the hands of successive invaders of Palestine, being sacked first by the Assyrians under Sargon, then by Nebuchadnezzar, finally by Alexander the Great, who sold 30,000 of the inhabitants into slavery. From the days of Amos the judgement of God upon Tyre took 400 years to work out, but in the end the old city was utterly destroyed.

vv. 11–12: *Edom* is charged with pursuing "his brother" (see Num. 20: 14) with the utmost cruelty, keeping alive his anger and banishing all pity from his heart. The precise historical details referred to here are again unknown, but Edom was ever the first to combine with Israel's enemies, as with Ammon and Moab against Jehoshaphat (2 Chron. 20: 10). Joel charged Edom with having "massacred innocent blood in their land" (3: 19), that is helpless captives, an event which could have taken place when the Edomites revolted against Jehoram about 850 B.C. The exact location of the region of Teman is not known, neither is that of the city of Bozrah, but both names are frequently associated with Edom by the prophets. For the subsequent fate of Edom, see the commentary on the prophecy of Obadiah.

vv. 13–15: *Ammon* is charged with deliberate atrocities against the Israelites in Gilead, with the intention of permanently increasing their territory. Envy, jealousy and fear caused the Ammonites to hire Balaam to curse Israel, whose nationals dwelling in Gilead were always subject to Ammonite attacks. In addition to uniting with Moab against Jehoshaphat, the Ammonites joined Nebuchadnezzar in his attack on Jehoiakim (2 Kings 24: 2). Rabbah, capital of Ammon, was 25 miles N.E. of the northern end of the Dead Sea. There may be a double allusion in the word "king" of verse 15, for the Hebrew can be pointed to read Milcom (instead of "malcham", king), that is Molech, the idol notorious for its child sacrifices. Ammon was to be overrun by a foreign power; first the Assyrians, then the Babylonians oppressed the territory, and the Ammonites slowly disappeared from history.

Amos 2   55

2: 1-3: Finally, *Moab* is charged with "burning the bones of the king of Edom into lime". Any desecration of the bodies of the dead was regarded as a supreme humiliation in the ancient world; hence the great efforts of the Egyptians to preserve the dead, and the Assyrian atrocities in cutting off the hands of dead enemies. Since in the Scriptures no man has the right to kill another, except with Divine authority, to go beyond this and destroy the corpse is to assume an authority which belongs to God alone. The exact event referred to here is not recorded in the history of the Old Testament, but may well have taken place when Jehoram of Israel and Jehoshaphat of Judah waged war upon Moab with the king of Edom present (2 Kings 3). The location of Kirioth (the cities) is also unknown. The fact that it is the judge (rather than the king) of Moab who is to be cut off probably only means that it is an alternative term, as the corresponding "all the princes thereof" would suggest. Like Ammon, Moab disappeared from history after the aggressions of Nebuchadnezzar.

Note 7: THE JUDGEMENTS OF THE PAGAN NATIONS

The great passages of the Old Testament in which the judgements of God are pronounced upon the *heathen* nations, are: Isaiah 13-23; Jeremiah 46-51; Ezekiel 25-32. A brief review of these passages reveals the following as the charges made against them: 1. Worship of idols. 2. Pride, arrogance, trusting in their own strength and riches. 3. Inhumanity, revenge, rejoicing over the fall of an enemy. 4. Evil, iniquity; lying receives special mention. They are never condemned because they have not kept the law of the Lord.

The Amos judgements all concern those nations with whom Israel had already come into a close contact which still applied in the days of the prophet; there is *no* mention, for instance, of Assyria or Babylon, as there is with the later prophets. The message, in other words, was relevant to the practical situation, not just theoretical. The judgements, except in one case where Moab is charged apparently with impiety and sacrilege in burning the bones of an enemy, are all for barbarity, unmercifulness, general inhumanity. While four of the crimes were committed against Israel, and a fifth may have been so, the sixth definitely was not.

The best commentary is that of Paul in Romans 1:

"For the wrath of God is revealed from heaven against all ungodliness and wickedness of men who by their wickedness suppress the truth. For what can be known about God is plain to

56   *Amos 2*

them, because God has shown it to them. Ever since the creation
of the world his invisible nature, namely his eternal power and
deity, has been clearly perceived in the things that have been
made. So they are without excuse ..." (v. 18–20, R.S.V.).

Here "the truth" which men have "suppressed" is not the
Gospel, for they have not known it. It is the evidence of all creation
for the existence of an all-powerful God; hence men should have
realised that they are all "creatures", with obligations to one
another.

The Edomites, therefore, who "cast off all pity", and the
Ammonites who slashed pregnant women, should have known that
they were committing a crime. The rejection of the authority of
God ("ungodliness") and the practice of evil ("wickedness") merit
Divine judgement.

The argument is still as powerful today. Despite the plausible
arguments for materialistic evolution, as the man of common sense
feels in his bones "it stands to reason" that creation, in all its
variety and design, could not have come about by chance. It
requires a Cause adequate to explain the effects. Modern godless-
ness and wickedness are, in the same sense, "without excuse".

2.   How much more of Judah and Israel? (2: 4–16)

vv. 4–5: That the indictment of Judah is so brief is surprising. We
may explain it by the reflection that the religious life of Judah had
not yet fallen to such a low level as that of Israel, whose case was
therefore the more desperate and whose judgement the closer. It is
unreasonable, as some do, to charge Amos with being violently
anti-Israel and pro-Judah. His God-given mission was to the
Northern kingdom; Judah's turn was to come later through other
prophets.

Judah is condemned for despising the law of God; not just law in
general, but the *torah*, the revealed commandments and statutes;
and also for following idols, as "lies" certainly implies, for "walking
after" is the regular expression for idolatry. The fire upon Judah
and Jerusalem came 150 years later through Nebuchadnezzar.

vv. 6–8: If the surrounding nations were to be judged, how much
more should Israel come under chastisement? The remainder of
Amos' prophecy is largely a detailed account of the social, civil, and
religious sins of Israel, recounted with such vividness that we have
an unrivalled picture of the life of the time to supplement the
information of the historical books. In this the prophecy of Hosea
complements that of Amos.

Amos 2   57

The charges against Israel are that they pervert divine justice in oppressing the poor, and that they live in uncleanness and self-indulgent luxury. First, the Israelites sell God-fearing men for money. According to the law the Hebrew could sell *himself*, but his purchaser was to use him as a hired servant and not as a slave (Lev. 25: 39–40). The "pair of sandals" for which the "needy" were sold is to be connected with the practice of selling land by the transfer of a shoe (Ruth 4: 7). The Septuagint (LXX) of 1 Samuel 12: 3 reads: "Of whose hand have I (Samuel) received a bribe or a pair of shoes?" The shoe was the title deed of the poor man's inheritance, which the rich were taking at derisory prices. The poor are trampled into the dust of the earth, and the meek find no justice for their cause. Unchastity is rife. That "a man and his father" would "go in to the same maid" indicates widespread immorality; but it may allude to the sacred prostitutes attached to the shrines of Baal worship, both male and female (*kedeshim*, masc., *kedoshoth*, fem.). The masculine is frequently translated "sodomites" and the practice had been expressly forbidden in Deuteronomy 23: 17. By these immoral acts God's holy name was profaned, when the sins of His people were a reproach to Himself (cf. Paul in Romans 2: 24—"The name of God is blasphemed among the Gentiles through you").

These corrupt leaders took in pledge (for a debt) the garments of the poor and then laid down upon them in debauchery beside "every altar", that is Bethel and Dan and the "high places" where the worship of the Lord had been polluted with Baal rites. It was the upper garment, used as blanket and counterpane, and essential for warmth during the night. The law required that if a poor man needed to pawn his garment, it was to be returned to him by nightfall; and a garment so pawned was not to be slept upon (Exod. 22: 26–27; Deut. 24: 12–13). The wine drunk in these revels was paid for by those who had been "fined" (as "condemned" means). The whole picture in this section is of a self-indulgent society preserving the forms of religion, but intent on personal pleasure and gain, quite heedless of the clear commands of the Law to act in justice and mercy, especially to the "fatherless and the widow".

Note 8: THE POOR AND THE MEEK

The passage 2: 6–7 contains some very important terms for the right understanding of the worship of God in Old Testament times. The "needy" (poor, v. 6, A.V.) (*ebyon*) are those in want, oppressed, and wretched; the "poor" (v. 7) (*dallim*) are the weak or low; and the "meek" (*anawim*) are the afflicted and miserable.

58   *Amos 2*

They were at first the humble members of society, and the Israelite was required to treat them with mercy and kindness. As society grew more corrupt, they became identified, especially in the Psalms, with those who, suffering from the wickedness of men, saw no help but in God. Terms like poor, meek, humble, afflicted become descriptions of the faithful servants of God who wait for His salvation. Hence they are classed here with "the righteous" (v. 6). Only with this Old Testament foundation can we rightly understand Jesus' words, "Blessed are the meek" etc. The subject is fascinating. The reader is referred to the author's series "The Knowledge of God", article 8: The Faith of the Poor and Meek, *Christadelphian* 1967, Oct., pp. 444–7.

vv. 9–16: There follows now an appeal to Israel to remember that it was Yahweh ("Yet it was *I* ...", very emphatic) who had destroyed the Canaanites ("Amorite") before them, those giants in Hebron and those "men of stature" like cedars (Num. 13: 32) who had frightened the spies; "and it was *I*" (emphatic again), who had brought them out of Egypt and then led them 40 years (direct allusion to Deuteronomy) in the wilderness. Even then God had not abandoned them, but had raised up prophets and Nazarites to be their guides. Moses, Samuel, Ahijah, Jehu, Micaiah, Elijah and Elisha are obvious examples of prophets. It is remarkable that the Nazarites are here presented ("I raised up ...") as part of the work of God for His people, like prophets. The Nazarites who devoted themselves to the Lord (Num. 6: 1–12) did so of their freewill, yet they were the gift of God (like the prophets, pastors, teachers of the New Testament). If they were at all numerous, as they may well have been (e.g. the Rechabites), their influence could have been considerable as a protest against growing worldliness and self-indulgence. But Israel's only response was to persuade the Nazarites to drink wine and so be faithless to their vows, and to command the prophets to cease their irksome testimony. Israel, in short, were unrepentant.

vv. 13–16: As a result God's judgement will overtake them. Although the verb in verse 13 is rare, the sense must be: "I will press you down in your place, as a cart full of sheaves presses down" (on the earth) (R.V. and R.S.V.). The mighty men will be able neither to defend themselves, nor to find safety in flight, even when they flee "naked", stripped of all their armour. The only consolation for Israel is that so far the judgement, though severe, is not spoken of as final.

Amos 3 59

3. Israel Accused and Judged (3: 1—9: 10)

With the exception of the final five verses and a passage in chapter 7 describing the intervention of Amaziah "the priest of Bethel", the remainder of the prophecy is a sustained treatment of Israel's sins and of the judgements God will bring on His people, and is hence rather difficult to divide into sections. Since however chapters 3–6 consist of three appeals, each beginning "Hear this word ...", and two addresses beginning, "Woe ...", we shall treat these chapters as a separate section.

(a) *"Hear this word ... Woe ..."* (3: 1—6: 14)

3: 1-2: THE FIRST SUMMONS (3: 1-15) is addressed to "the whole family which I brought up out of the land of Egypt"; that is, to Judah as well as Israel. Clearly Amos' prophecy was designed to be known in the south as well as the north. (Is it not likely that the surrounding nations knew something of the divine judgements on *them* too?) God's appeal to the deliverance from Egypt as the evidence of His power and favour and as a reasonable ground for His people's service to Him, is constantly found in the prophets, and shows how much more than a mere historical episode it was intended to be. How wide of the mark therefore is the modern tendency to explain it by "natural" causes!

The Hebrew verb "know" means much more than the knowledge of facts; used of persons, it implies intimate, individual acquaintance. In declaring, "You only have I known of all the families of the earth", God is therefore asserting that only to Israel has He made a full and personal revelation of Himself because of His intense interest in their welfare and career as a nation; for no other community on "the ground" (*adamah*) has God done this.

But what follows must have come as a surprise to the people: "Therefore I will punish you for all your iniquities." Pagan worshippers considered that their god existed for the preservation of his people; his credit was inextricably bound up with them and he could not allow them to perish. No doubt many Israelites had come to think of their God in the same way. But Yahweh's way with His people is always to endeavour to raise them to *His* standard, never to lower Himself to theirs; hence His punishments are remedial, designed not just to chastise, but to redeem from sin.

vv. 3–8: There follow a series of figures taken from natural life. Their explanation is found in verses 7–8 which asserts that Amos' prophecies are the terrible judgements of God. So in the prophet's series of questions, there are ominous conclusions: Two people go to

60   *Amos 3*

a meeting place because "they have made an appointment". It is
God who has "appointed" His prophet and has sent him to Israel. A
lion only roars when it is about to seize its prey (Amos 1: 2 has
already declared, "The Lord shall roar from Zion"). A bird is
caught in a snare because it is unwary and the snare has been
prepared; so God's judgement awaits sinful Israel. When the
warning trumpet is blown, it means the city is in danger, and if
calamity ("evil": not sin, but the results of sin) befalls, it is God's
judgement. It has always been through the prophets that God has
given warning of His judgements: so He did through Noah before
the Flood, Moses in the presence of Pharaoh, Jonah in Nineveh,
and Jesus in Jerusalem. The "secret" which God will reveal to His
prophets is, however, much more than a so-far unrevealed fact; *sod*
implies friendly conversation, the council and counsel of friends; see
Jeremiah 23: 18–22, where the prophets are those who "perceive ...
and hear ... and mark" God's words, and thus "stand in His
counsel" (*sod*). Amos therefore feels that a pronouncement of God
is like the roaring of a lion; he can do no other than speak, like
Jeremiah over a century later (20: 9), who felt that the divine
judgement was in his heart like a fire within his bones.

vv. 9–12: The prophets are now to proclaim over the flat roofs of the
palaces of Ashdod and Egypt the Lord's judgement, thus summoning pagan nations to assemble on the mountains round Samaria
and to gaze upon the city. Samaria, itself built on a hill 1000 ft.
high, was situated in a natural amphitheatre of hills, five miles
across. Standing upon these hills even the idolatrous heathen would
be able to see for themselves the violence and the oppression going
on in the city; for the minds of this people of God were so corrupted
that they were devoted to robbery by force, having lost all
knowledge of right. The adversary, who was to "hem in the land",
soon appeared; in 734 B.C. Tiglath-Pileser swept over Gilead and
Galilee, in 724 the northern part of Israel, and in 722 Samaria fell
after a siege lasting three years. The remnant that were to escape
would be as insignificant as a couple of shin bones or the tip of an
ear, rescued by a shepherd from the lion devouring one of his flock.
In other words the rescue of these pleasure-loving Samarians,
lounging on their damask covered divans (see R.V.), would be no
rescue at all.

vv. 13–15: Now the Lord God (*Adonai Yahweh*, see Note 6, p. 52),
the Elohim of Hosts solemnly summons the assembled nations to be
witnesses against "the house of Jacob"; not just Northern Israel,
but Judah too, for her turn would come. His judgements will strike
at the corrupt calf-worship of Bethel, and "the horns of the altar"

Amos 4   61

in particular, because that is where the blood was placed when Aaron and his sons were consecrated (Exod. 29: 12). It would fall too upon the luxurious houses of the rich, like the ivory-panelled one Ahab had built (1 Kings 22: 39). They would all "have an end".

4: **1–5:** THE SECOND SUMMONS "Hear this word" (4: 1–13) is addressed to the "cows of Bashan". "Bulls of Bashan" was a traditional term for the mighty of the land (Bashan was lush cattle country). The deliberate use of the feminine here indicates the leading women of Israel's society, who continually "oppress" those of low estate, and "crush" the poor (the verbs are an echo of God's warning to Israel in Deuteronomy 28: 33). For the "poor" and "needy", see Note 8, p. 57. These women urge on their lords (husbands) to drunken revelry. The picture, devastating as it is, accords with historical and psychological truth, for it will generally be found that if the men of a society set a high standard, the women will respond; and if they adopt a low standard, the women tend to adjust their standards accordingly, speaking generally of course—there will always be individual exceptions.

But Adonai Yahweh has sworn by His holiness that judgement shall come. The holiness of God is first His utter separateness from man in quality, then His power and uniqueness, and *then* those qualities of righteousness, mercy and truth which are His, and must be His servants'. The same idea is found in the expressions: God swears by *His holy name,* and by *Himself* (Amos 6: 8). Because Israel have despised this holiness, they are to be taken away captive with hooks as was the Assyrian practice. Like cattle in a panic they will rush out through the breaches in the city wall, to be "cast into the palace". The translation "palace" is, however, pure conjecture, since the Hebrew term is unknown. The word could be the name of a place where Israel would be deported by the Assyrians (see R.V.).

Ironically God calls upon the Israelites to continue their transgressions at the idol centres of Bethel and Gilgal, both mentioned again at 5: 5, and three times in Hosea. There, nevertheless, they were sacrificing to the *Lord* after their own fashion. They were diligent in making thanksgiving offerings, and burnt offerings *with leaven* (according to the law leaven was not to be burnt: Lev. 2: 11), and in giving tithes. But they ignored the sin and trespass offerings, it would seem. The Lord God's final comment, "For so ye love it" (this liketh you, A.V.) shows how self-satisfied the people's worship was.

vv. 6–13: God now declares the judgements He has already brought

62   Amos 4

upon Israel; yet despite their sufferings, they have refused to change their ways. Widespread famine, lack of the "early" rain to ensure growth before harvest, scorching hot wind and blight (the terms "blasting and mildew" are taken direct from Deuteronomy 28), the locust plagues, the pestilence like that inflicted upon Egypt ("the diseases of Egypt", Deut. 28: 60), slaughter of their young warriors and of their horses (fulfilled in the invasions of Hazael and Ben-Hadad, 2 Kings 13: 7), and earthquake like the ruin of Sodom and Gomorrah (Deut. 29:22-23) till the escaped of Israel were like a brand snatched from the fire: all these had been the manifest judgements of God. Yet Israel had not returned to Him. The frequent allusions to the Pentateuch in this passage are striking; they show that the books of Moses were known not only by the prophet but also by those who heard him. They are a powerful witness to the antiquity of the first books of the Old Testament canon. The worshippers of Canaan attributed to their gods (Baalim) all power over natural phenomena, especially the fertility of the ground; but here Yahweh asserts that it is *He* who controls these things.

The fivefold refrain, "Yet ye have not returned unto me", leads to the solemn summons: "*Therefore,* prepare to meet thy God, O Israel". There comes a time when more drastic measures are required. For Israel must recognise that the Lord of the whole earth and of mankind in it is none other than Yahweh, the Elohim of hosts, the God of their covenant.

Note 9: THE PURPOSE OF GOD'S JUDGEMENTS

The clear teaching of Amos 4: 6–13 is that God controlled the natural phenomena of Israel's world—the rain, the wind, the pestilence and the earthquake—and used their effects to bring pressures to bear upon His people, with the aim of producing in them a change of attitude towards Him. But the same teaching had been found as far back as Moses' day, nearly 600 years before, in Leviticus 26. If Israel would not hearken to Him, in spite of the abundant blessings He had promised, God would bring a succession of judgements upon them: disease, famine, flight before their enemies, each one following the one before "if ye will not yet for these things hearken unto me". The purpose of it all is expressed by the phrase, "If by these things ye will *not be reformed unto me*" (Lev. 26: 14–26). So God's warning to Israel through Amos: I have brought these afflictions upon you, "yet ye have not returned unto me", five times repeated, was not a new one. If they had kept in mind His words through Moses, they should have known it well.

Amos 5 63

The principle occurs again in the later prophets: "In vain have I smitten your children; they *received no correction* ... O Lord, ... thou hast stricken them, but they were not grieved; thou hast consumed them, but they have *refused to receive correction:* they have made their faces harder than a rock; they have refused to return" (Jer. 2: 30; 5: 3).

Two important points arise from the Amos passage. First, God made repeated efforts to get His people to alter their ways. This was a sign of His mercy and love, for their ultimate blessing could only be found in their return to Him. The judgements of God, then, are not a sign of His vindictiveness, but of His earnest desire that His people should be saved from the consequences of their own sin. Second, if after repeated efforts it becomes clear that there can be no repentance—the people cannot be reformed—then God will put an end to that phase of their career: "*Therefore,* prepare to meet thy God, O Israel". So the Assyrian in due time will destroy the kingdom of Samaria. So with Judah: when repeated appeals through the prophets produce no response, the Babylonian will come to "overturn it", because there is "no remedy" (Ezek. 21: 25–27; 2 Chron. 36: 16).

These principles are important for us in these days. It is common today to think of God as taking no distinct action, but working solely through the interplay of natural phenomena. But if He could declare that in Amos' day He controlled them precisely to achieve His ends, it would be highly presumptuous to assert that He does not do so today, nor will He do so. And if God's servants were subject to His discipline in Old Testament times, must it not be so today? It is striking to discover that both the Old Testament and New Testament words for "tribulation" basically mean "pressure". As we seek to serve God in these days of our flesh, we are wise to accept all "pressures" which come upon us because of faithful service as the means by which God is preparing us for His fellowship.

5: 1–6: THE THIRD SUMMONS "Hear this word" (5: 1–17) is to the "virgin of Israel", expressing the purity of the service she should have rendered, declaring she shall be dashed down upon her land and not rise again (there would be no return from captivity). Her warriors shall be reduced to one tenth of their normal strength. This warning of judgement is addressed to the Northern kingdom, as the parallel "house of Joseph" (Ephraim) shows (v. 6).

Israel must "seek the Lord" and not resort to worship of idolatrous shrines: Bethel, notorious for its golden calf; Beersheba (four times as far South of Jerusalem as Bethel was North),

64 Amos 5

hallowed by its associations with Abraham, Isaac and Jacob; and Gilgal, probably not the place near Jordan but up in the mountains where was a school of the prophets in the days of Elijah and Elisha (2 Kings 2: 1; 4: 38). Bethel (the house of God) will become *Aven* (vanity, nothing); so Hosea calls it Beth-Aven (4: 15; 10: 5). The repeated call, "Seek the Lord and ye shall live" shows that repentance could even yet avert the fire of judgement.

vv. 7–13: Israel's leaders are charged with making the process of "judgement" like tasting wormwood (a bitter herb, often associated with gall), and with "casting down righteousness to the earth" (R.V.). "Judgement" and "righteousness" are key terms for understanding the law and the prophets. *Mishpat* (judgement) was the revealed will of God through His law, and *tsedakah* (righteousness) was the rightness of attitude and conduct shown in obedience to that will. That justice and righteousness existed as moral principles in their own right would not have occurred to the Hebrews, whose outlook was practical. Moral principles arose from the existence of God and righteousness consisted in doing His will. God was therefore charging His people, not with falling short of an abstract standard of righteousness, but of failing to carry out the just provisions of His law and to live in its spirit. (See "The Knowledge of God": Judgement and Righteousness, *The Christadelphian* 1967, Sept., pp. 392–5.) Israel had forgotten that it was Yahweh, their God, who had created the great constellations like Pleiades and Orion, that He controlled day and night, and had already brought a Flood in judgement upon the earth. He could destroy both the strong man and his fortress. But the Israelites hated the man who rebuked them publicly in the gate of the city. Perhaps this was Amos himself, since Jeremiah was twice told to rebuke king and people there (17: 19; 19: 2). The oppressors among them exacted presents of wheat as bribes from the poor, yet they built their houses of hewn stone instead of the old baked brick in their pride (see Isa. 9: 10), and planted vineyards to be able to stock their wine-cellars. But because of their unjust oppressions, their accepting of bribes, and their perversion of justice in the land, because "many are your transgressions and mighty are your sins", they should lose all in the evil time which was coming.

vv. 14–17: The exhortation which follows, "Seek good ... that ye may live ... it may be that the Lord will be gracious to the remnant of Joseph", shows that there is still time for repentance. Israel were comforting themselves with the thought that God was with them and that therefore they could not but prosper. That could still be true only if they abandoned their evil ways and re-established the

Amos 5 65

way of God in the land by seeking Him. But, it is implied, only a "remnant" will do this. So there would be lamentation in the streets and in the vineyards, for Yahweh will no longer "pass over" Israel but will "pass through" them as He passed through Egypt and slew the firstborn in the days of old (Exod. 12: 12).

vv. 18–20: The FIRST "WOE" ADDRESS (5: 18–27) is to those who wished for the coming of the day of the Lord, thinking it would mean their political salvation, their triumph over the Gentiles. (Other Israelites were scoffers, saying: "Let God make speed and hasten his work that we may see it", Isa. 5: 19). But for them it would mean darkness (cf. Joel 2: 1–2), calamity, judgement, and not triumph; and they would be unable to escape. They would resemble in fact a man who, running away from a lion finds himself confronted by a bear (reputed more ferocious than a lion in Syria), and who, fleeing then into a house, is bitten by a serpent from the wall. Whatever their precautions they should not escape. (See Note: 1, *The Day of the Lord*, p. 25)

vv. 21–24: Their special assemblies on feast days—the three annual feasts when all males were to appear before God—the abundance of their burnt, peace and meal offerings, were so repulsive to the Lord that He uses the following terms to describe His attitude: "I hate ... I despise ... I will not accept ... nor regard ..." "Take away from *upon me*" (as though it were a burden) is His command, "the sound of your singing and your string instruments", which evidently accompanied the religious exercises of Israel as though they were trying to imitate in Bethel the temple services in Jerusalem. Instead God required justice and righteousness, that right conduct resulting from attention to His revealed will; and that in abundance, like the waters of a perennial stream, not like the brooks which are only full after the rain and soon run dry in a thirsty land.

vv. 25–27: The next two verses contain some obscurities and have occasioned much discussion. The critics who believe in the late date of Deuteronomy have claimed verse 25 as proof that Amos did not know that a sacrificial system was in force in the wilderness. But the late date of Deuteronomy must be rejected on historical and internal grounds. God is saying to Israel that even in the wilderness, when they had but recently received evidence of His power and a knowledge of the right way to worship Him, the Israelites often preferred to worship idols. As Moses said: "They sacrificed to devils (idols) and not to God ..." (Deut. 32: 17); and Ezekiel concerning the wilderness period: "Their heart went after their idols ..."

66 *Amos 5*

(20: 16). Snaith (commentary on Amos) suggests that the names in verse 26 have been subject to the deformation which the Massoretic scribes commonly applied to the names of idols in Hebrew. They took the vowel points i-u of "shiqquts" (detested things), a word used of idols, or the o-e of "bosheth" (shameful thing), and applied them to the consonants of the idol name in the Hebrew text, so producing a deformed name in token of their abhorrence. Sometimes they substituted the name "bosheth" for "baal", as in Ish-Bosheth for Ish-Baal. By this system of vowel substitution Tephet became Tophet, and Melek became Molech.

In verse 26 here the word tabernacle is really Sikkuth, a deformation of Sakkut, the Assyrian god Ninib, whose *star* is Saturn in their system. Kuyyan is a deformation of Kewan, the name of the planet Saturn. The allusion is therefore to one Assyrian idol, a star-god, and the sense may be best rendered in the future, as the grammar permits: "You *shall* take up Sakkuth your king and (rather, even) Kaiwan, your star-god" (R.S.V.), the reference being to the time soon coming when God would cast them into exile beyond Damascus. When Amos wrote, the Assyrians were already in possession of Damascus, but here we have *prophecy* of the system of deportations practised shortly afterwards by the Assyrians, by which the Israelites were removed far "beyond Damascus", their land being given to captive Babylonians and Syrians.

6: 1-6: The SECOND "WOE" ADDRESS (6: 1-14) is directed to the "careless ones" in Zion and Samaria (one more indication that Amos was not forgetting the Southern kingdom), the "notable men of the first of the nations" (that is, Israel) "to whom the house of Israel come" for guidance and leadership (R.S.V.). These heedless leaders are commanded to consider three Gentile cities or powers: Calneh, one of four cities founded by Nimrod, 40 miles from Babylon; Hamath, originally conquered by Solomon, more recently by Jeroboam II; and Philistine Gath. These three Gentile cities may be cited because they had all recently suffered disaster, Calneh and Hamath at the hands of Assyria and Gath from Uzziah of Judah who broke down its wall (2 Chron. 26: 6). Since it is not certain that these conquests had actually taken place at the time Amos prophesied it is probable that the point is a straight comparison between the prosperity of Samaria and three Gentile cities. Have you, Samaria, been any less blessed with prosperity than they? The implied answer is, No. Yet the leaders of Israel are putting out of their minds the "evil day" of coming judgement in order to indulge their violence. They lie on ivory divans, sprawl on couches, feast on tender lamb and veal, amuse themselves by

Amos 6 67

"babbling to the sound of the harp" (the word "chant" is said to suggest a flow of trivial words in which the rhythm of words and music was everything and the sense nothing; the description has a modern sound). David had introduced instruments of music into the service of the temple, but these corrupt leaders debase them for their own amusement. The bowls in which they drink wine are really ewers, often translated "basons" (A.V.) as used in the service of the tabernacle. Silver bowls were dedicated to that service by the heads of the tribes (Num. 7). The finest ointments may have been in imitation of, or in rivalry with, the holy ointment appointed by God and forbidden to be copied. Both these features suggest that the Israelites were using holy things for profane ends. They were intent upon their pleasures, but they did not grieve for the "breach of Joseph"; as Joseph was heartlessly put in the pit by his brethren, so these Israelites care nought for the sufferings of the people.

vv. 7–11: Therefore shortly they shall lead the file of captives to be deported, their revelry (R.V.; the word translated "banquet" probably means "screech") shall come to an end. The action of "stretching themselves" upon divans (cf. v. 4) conveys their luxurious self-indulgence; dissolute attitudes betray dissolute minds. God makes clear His attitude to their self-indulgence by, "The Lord God hath sworn by himself." In 4: 2 it was "by his holiness", inseparable from "himself". When men turn away from God, they despise His holiness. The excellency of Jacob was first Yahweh Himself, then that which He had given them—His sanctuary in their midst, His law, and the knowledge of Himself. God now abhors this "excellency", and hates the strongholds of Jacob, who trusts in "his own strength" (v. 13) instead of in his God. In Israel bodies were buried, not burned, but the judgement is to be so severe that nearly all shall perish. To avoid the dangers of pestilence the corpses will have to be burned, and when a man's kinsman comes to take away the body, he shall find but a single man in the darkest corners of the house; and they will not dare *then* even to utter the name of the Lord, for fear that a worse judgement befall them. For great houses and small in Samaria shall be destroyed together.

vv. 12–14: Men do not attempt absurd tasks, like racing horses over rocks or ploughing the sea with oxen (R.S.V., based upon a different pointing of the same consonants). Yet Israel commit the equal absurdity of turning God's justice and righteous law into poison and wormwood (see note at 5: 7). They rejoice in Lo-Debar (a thing of nought) and say, Have we not captured Karnaim (horns) by our own strength. Both may here be names of places, referred to in Genesis 14: 5 and Joshua 13: 26. Both were in Gilead,

68   Amos 6

the recent battleground of Israel and Syria, where Israel had been
victorious, and were probably chosen for the play upon words. But
God is about to raise up against Israel a nation who shall not
merely take from them a couple of towns in Gilead, but shall ravage
their whole territory, from Hamath in the far north to the brook of
the Arabah, the southern boundary of Jeroboam II's kingdom on
the frontier of Moab, on the east of the Dead Sea. The Assyrian
power, like a great river, is about to overflow the land.

(b) *Visions of Judgement* (7: 1—17)

There follow three short visions of increasing intensity, cul-
minating with the destruction of Jeroboam's house.

7: 1–3: In the first Amos sees the Lord God forming locusts to
devour the greenery of the land at a particularly vital time; that
is, when the grass was growing fast after the spring rains, and after
the king's tribute in the form of a first mowing had been taken.
(Though there is no Scriptural reference to this custom, Amos'
words seem clear enough.) The subsequent growth would belong to
the farmer, but locusts came and devoured it. The prophet cries to
God for forgiveness for his people: "How shall Jacob stand?", and
God "repents" of the judgement, that is, He suspends it. For Note
on "How can the Lord 'repent'?" see Joel 2: 13, p. 30.

vv. 4–6: In the second vision the "Lord God" (see Note at Amos
1: 8, p. 52) calls the world before the bar of His judgement and
scourges it by fire. The "great deep" must ultimately stand for the
nations estranged from God, who are like the "troubled sea" (Isa.
57: 20). In the "burning up" of their works (2 Pet. 3) even the
"portion" (R.V.mg.) of Israel is about to be destroyed. At the cry
of the prophet that "Jacob is small" (for so he is compared with the
might of the Gentiles), God again halts the judgement.

vv. 7–9: In the third God is seen to stand upon the wall of a city
which had been built *straight,* because a plumb-line had been used;
but He declares that now He is going to measure *His people* with
the plumb-line, which will reveal their "crookedness"; He will not
"pass by", or overlook, their sins any more. The idolatrous
sanctuaries of "Isaac" (like Bethel and Dan) are to be destroyed.
The expression "Isaac" and "the house of Isaac" occurs only in
Amos, twice in this chapter (see v. 16). The parallelism with Israel
and the reference to Jeroboam show that it stands for the Northern
kingdom of Samaria. Can it be that Isaac is used because he would
have awarded the blessing to the profane Esau if he had not

Amos 7   69

subsequently experienced God's "fear", and Israel had gone all the way in that course? Israel is to be desolated and the "house of Jeroboam II" is to come to an end by the sword of an enemy: first, all Israel as the spiritual seed of "Jeroboam, the son of Nebat", and then the immediate dynasty of Jeroboam II. See 2 Kings 15: 8–12. This time the prophet makes no plea for mercy; it is understood that the judgement will be final.

These three visions of judgement could be prophecies of three Assyrian invasions which took place in the days of Amos. About 738 B.C. Pul (another name for Tiglath-Pileser III) threatened invasion, and Menàhem paid a tribute of 1000 talents of silver, raised by a levy from the richer Israelites (2 Kings 15: 19). A few years later in Pekah's reign Tiglath-Pileser invaded North Israel and Gilead and took many captives away to Assyria (v. 29). Finally in 722 B.C. Samaria fell to Shalmaneser; both kingdom and reigning houses were destroyed. The faithful few in Israel would see in these events the fulfilment of Amos' words and would be encouraged, despite their national affliction, in their faith that God was, despite appearances, in control of affairs. These short visions form an excellent example of the way in which the words of the prophets applied *first* to the immediate circumstances of their time for the encouragement of the faithful.

vv. 10–17: The next few verses are a break in Amos' series of visions and provide a valuable insight into the attitude of the authorities in Israel to a faithful prophet. Amaziah who was probably the head of the idolatrous system set up at Bethel, saw in the words of the last of these three visions a chance to get rid of Amos. The prophet had declared that God would "rise against the house of Jeroboam with the sword". Amaziah sent a message to the king charging the prophet with treason against him personally and *that* in public in the hearing of the people ("Amos hath conspired against thee in the midst of the house of Israel ... Jeroboam shall die by the sword"). The kingdom cannot allow this act of treason, said Amaziah; it will cause disaffection and revolt. Jeroboam did not answer the appeal of his high priest; he was a political realist and probably calculated that Amos' words would have little effect.

Amaziah then addressed Amos directly: "O thou seer ... "—the term was being used contemptuously—and ordered him to go back to Judah and there "eat bread and prophesy", that is, earn his living by acting as one of the professional prophets, of whom there were certainly many, both in Israel and Judah. He forbade him to utter any more prophecies in Bethel, because in Bethel was the

70   *Amos 7*

sanctuary (the religious centre, the golden calf) and the palace of
the king himself.

The nature of Amaziah's charges against Amos is highly
significant. He makes no attempt whatever to answer the prophet's
charges of spiritual corruption; his intervention was that of a
politician, anxious to maintain the status-quo, fearful of the
political consequences of "treason"; he never mentioned the name
of God, and regarded the "sanctuary" even not as the house of God,
but of the king. For him the prophets were just accessories of the
government. The intervention of Amaziah was an attempt to silence
a prophet of God by the authority of the state.

Amos in his reply defends himself from the charge of pro-
fessionalism: "No prophet I, no prophet's son, I; for a herdman, I",
as the Hebrew literally runs. Amos cannot mean that he is not a
true prophet; he must therefore mean that he is not a member of
the official guild of prophets, did not acquire his authority by virtue
of such membership, or "inherit" it by family tradition; rather by
occupation he was a keeper of cattle and sheep, and a grower of the
fig-mulberry (a kind of small fig, insipid and woody, eaten by the
poor of the land), and he derived his prophetic authority from the
Lord Himself, who had given him an explicit charge towards the
people of Israel.

Further, Amos refuses to be silenced. Amaziah had ordered him
to cease to prophesy: "Drop not thy word against the house of
Isaac", using an expression which is like that in Moses' song in
Deuteronomy 32: 2, "My doctrine shall drop as the rain", though
the original word here is different. It is used of God to Ezekiel:
"Drop thy word toward the holy places" (21: 2), that is, prophesy
against them; and of those who desired to silence the prophets in
Micah's day: "Drop not (the word)", they said (Micah 2: 6), and
the context shows that they found the word wearisome. Amaziah's
use of the expression indicates that he found Amos' prophesying
like a "continual dropping".

Amos however declares, in a direct message to Amaziah, that his
very family would suffer the severest ravages of war, that the chief
priest himself would die in a land where pagan gods were worshipped, that conquerors should divide up the land of Israel for
themselves by stretching across it the measuring line used for
allotting portions of the land, and that the people of Israel
themselves should be deported to a foreign land. So all Amaziah's
"political" calculations would be brought to nought.

Amos 8

(c) "The end is come" (8: 1-14)

8: 1-3: The first two verses illustrate admirably a prophetic device, that of driving home a message by the association of two words of similar sound, but of different meaning. The R.S.V. of Jeremiah 1: 11-12 makes the point clear: "Jeremiah, what do you see? And I said, I see a rod of almond (Heb. *shaqed*). Then the Lord said to me, You have seen well, for I am watching (Heb. *shoqed*) over my word to perform it." In an age when reading was the privilege of the few, the faithful Israelite, having *heard* the word of Jeremiah, would, every time he saw the almond, be reminded that God would surely do what He had said.

Amos, perhaps at the autumn festival in Bethel, which Jeroboam had fixed in the eighth month, instead of the seventh according to the law, saw in vision a basket of summer fruit, of *"kaits"* (from a Hebrew root meaning to cut); then God declared to him that "the end (*kets*) (a cutting-off) is come upon my people of Israel; I will not overlook (their transgressions) any more". When this word was known among the faithful, the sight of "summer fruit", the latest harvest in Canaan, would remind them that the judgement of God upon the nation was at hand. The songs of the idol's temple (or the word can equally mean palace) were to be changed into lamentation; the slain shall be everywhere; "He (the Lord) shall cast them forth, Hush!", as the Hebrew reads. Cease even your lamentation and remain silent in the presence of the judgement of God.

vv. 4-10: The next three verses give a vivid picture of the minds of these leaders of Israel, who "panted after the poor" (or the meek, the humble servants of the Lord; see Note 8, p. 57) like wild beasts after their prey, who observed the religious festivals (the new moon, the sabbath) but resented the interruption they caused in their commercial activities. (G. A. Smith, who in common with many critics regarded the "priestly system" as of late date, not earlier than the exile, finds the mention of the observance of the new moon here, two centuries *before* the exile, "interesting"! It is of course embarrassing to the critical theory.) Israel's traders were eager for the end of the sabbath so that they could "open" (set forth) the sacks of wheat and sell it with dishonest weights and scales, a practice explicitly forbidden in the Law. They acquired the land of "the afflicted" at a low price, and the wheat which they sold was "the falling", the thin grains which fell through the sieve.

There is a note of indignation in the Hebrew of this verse: "To buy the afflicted for silver ... to sell the falling of the wheat ...!" Yahweh declares, "by the excellency of Jacob", by His own great

72   *Amos 8*

Name (see Note 6, p. 52) that such works shall be punished. The
very land shall tremble (as evidently it had done or was shortly to
do in the famous earthquake), it "shall heave and sink like the Nile
of Egypt", for "the flood" is the Egyptian word for river, and the
Nile was said to rise 20 ft. at inundations and then subside. The
setting of the sun and the darkening of the land at noon was a
powerful figure for the sudden destruction of a nation in the full
light of its self-security. Great mourning would come upon the
Israelites: they would wear sackcloth next to the skin, they would
shave off their hair, and lament with that intensity common to the
East.

vv. 11–14: And now the greatest affliction of all was to overtake
them; to literal famine there would be added "a famine of hearing
the words of the Lord". As a result the Israelites would "reel (like
drunkards)" not just from Galilee to the Mediterranean, from the
North to the land of the Arabians in the East, but rather among the
nations of the earth, beginning with their deportation by the
Assyrians. The strongest and fairest inhabitants of the land would
die of thirst, and the habitual idolators who worshipped the "sin of
Samaria" (Hosea calls it "the calf of Samaria", 8: 5–6) and
exclaimed, "By the life of thy god, O Dan!" (an obvious perversion
of: "As the Lord liveth", 1 Sam. 20: 3), and "By the life of the way
of Beersheba", would fall for ever. Though we possess no Scriptural
information about the "way of Beersheba" (see 5: 5), expressions
like "the way of the wicked" indicate that there must have been an
idolatrous shrine there, probably even ostensibly devoted to the
worship of Yahweh.

The judgement following the vision of the summer fruits is then
to be complete; there is no call to repentance even. The nation is
evidently so corrupt that such a call is felt to be unavailing. "The
end" would come.

(d) *"Behold the eyes of the Lord are upon the sinful kingdom"*
(9: 1–10)

In chapter 9 the whole scope of Amos' prophecy widens. God
announces not just the fate of the Northern Kingdom centred on
Samaria, but the "house of Israel" (v. 9), the "children of Israel"
whom He brought up out of Egypt. Prospectively then, Judah is
included. The first ten verses of this chapter contain judgements
against "the sinful kingdom" (v. 8) so sweeping that the scattering
of Israel among the nations of the earth must be implied.

Amos 9   73

9: 1–4: So "the altar" of verse 1 and the temple building which is to be destroyed cannot just be those of the calf worship at Bethel, but must stand for the altar and temple at Jerusalem, which in turn represent God's manifestation of Himself to the whole people. As a result of the Lord's command, "Smite", the temple building comes crashing down upon the heads of the "worshippers".

There follows a series of illustrations to show how complete would be the retribution of God upon those who tried desperately to escape. They would be slain by the sword; those who tried to "break through to Sheol" by digging into the earth, or by contrast to climb up to heaven (cf. Psa. 139) by seeking safety on the tops of mountains (as doubtless some did in the Flood); those who sought to hide on Carmel, either in its thick woods or in its innumerable caves, 1800 ft. above the sea—all would perish. The dreaded sea-monster, leviathan, described in Isaiah 27: 1, would devour those who sought to hide themselves in the depths. Even those who would be deported into captivity would suffer extinction by the sword, for "I will set mine eyes upon them for evil and not for good". We reserve for final comment any observation upon this most stern of the pronouncements of the Lord.

vv. 5–10: In a brief passage the Lord God asserts His majestic power and supremacy: He touches the land and it melts as with fire, or heaves with earthquake and subsides like the Nile; He builds His chambers in the heavens (that is, He inhabits the heavens) and founds the vault of such building upon the earth; it was He who in time past called for the Flood of waters to engulf the ungodly: Yahweh is His name, Israel's own God, whom they had so tragically despised.

The children of Israel were become in God's sight of no more special concern than the Ethiopians, sons of Ham, the furthest removed from the promises of God, for whereas Shem was to be blessed, and Japhet's tents were to be enlarged, Ham was to remain a servant. The comparison in Jeremiah 13: 23—"Can the Ethiopian change his skin ...? ... Then may ye (Israel) also do good that are accustomed to do evil"—suggests that Amos' reference here means this: God's people were so far sunk in iniquity that reform was impossible. Although Yahweh had declared His choice of Israel in bringing them out of Egypt, yet He had also brought the Philistines from Caphtor (Crete) and the Syrians from Kir in the far North. Where was now their privilege? They were become a "sinful kingdom" which God would destroy, preserving only "the house of Jacob", an expression clearly to be classed with the numerous

74   *Amos 9*

allusions to the salvation of a remnant, who, being neither political
Israel nor sons of "Isaac", are the true sons of Jacob or Israel.

Meanwhile the iniquitous people is to be "sifted among all
nations". From Hosea's phrase, "They shall be wanderers among
the nations", and that of Jesus: "Satan hath desired to have you
that he may sift you as wheat" (Luke 22: 31), we may infer that
God's intention was to purge Israel by their sojourn among the
nations, so that the faithful who survived would be represented by
the grain that should not fall upon the earth. By contrast with this
"grain"* it is "the sinners" of God's people who should die by the
sword, especially those who, hearing the warnings of the prophet,
said in effect: "The evil *he* talks about will never take *us* by
surprise, indeed it will not come at all"; from which we perceive
that there were scoffers eight centuries before Christ as well as in
the days of the apostles; so there were to be in the last days. The
judgements of this chapter came about through the invasions and
deportations of the Assyrians and Babylonians, and later the
Romans. As a result Israel were indeed "sifted" among all the
nations.

4. Restoration (9: 11–15)

vv. 11–15: The prophecy closes with a short passage of hope and
consolation, promising restoration to the house of Israel. The
modern critics' habit of interpreting Scripture according to their
own preconceived theories is revealed in the treatment of these
verses, for it is argued on the one hand that Amos, the prophet of
the inflexible judgement of God, would never have written lines so
"out of character" as these; and on the other, that he could not
possibly have prophesied of restoration when the dispersion had not
yet taken place. Conclusion: Amos could not have written this
passage, which must be the work of a later hand. Let it suffice in
reply to say, first that there is not the slightest textual evidence for
rejecting this passage; second, that if its tenor is different from
much that Amos had written, it is *not* different from the general
prophetic writings; and thirdly, that if we accept Amos as a
prophet, receiving "the word of the Lord", there can be no
objection to his uttering a prediction.

What is to be restored is the "booth" of David, the simple hut of
branches erected by the Israelites at the feast of tabernacles, chosen
because at that feast Israel were commanded to forsake the

---

* So most translations. But the Hebrew term means "stone" (A.V.m.), or
"pebble" (Soncino Jewish V.); the figure could be that of sieving stones. The
parallelism of Jesus' words to Peter is very attractive, however.

Amos 9   75

dwellings of their *own* building and live in a temporary one, thus
signifying their dependence upon the Lord. The restoration of the
"booth" of David, and the repairing of its "breaches"—the unifying
again of Judah and Ephraim—conveyed the return of the glory of
the kingdom, under the Son of David, when all the surrounding
nations would become his possession and therefore the possession of
Israel's God. As in those "days of old", restored Israel would
possess the "remnant" of Edom—Edom being selected as the
relentless foe of Israel; and also "all the nations upon whom my
name has been called", as under the glorious dominion of David
and Solomon. To Amos and his contemporaries the promise
suggested therefore the restoration of Israel's dominion over the
Philistines, Phoenicians, Syrians, Ammonites, Moabites and
Edomites; the extension of this promise to include all the nations of
the earth appears in the later prophets. The prophecy continues in
terms of material blessings: favourable seasons producing abundance of corn and wine even on the mountains (it had been
promised in Leviticus 26: 5 that if Israel were obedient to God
threshing should reach unto harvest); a people returned from
captivity, rebuilding and replanting a desolate land and never more
to be removed out of it, for it was the land which Yahweh, their
God, had given them.

Amos and the faithful few in Israel doubtless hoped that the
Lord would raise up soon the Son of David who would achieve all
this; yet they must have known that affliction, and indeed captivity
(v. 14), were in store for Israel before this time of glory could come,
for when the prophecy was uttered the throne of David was firmly
held by Azariah, probably the strongest successor since Solomon.
Amos had already prophesied the destruction of the palaces of
Jerusalem. The time of joy was therefore not yet, but it would
surely come. Thus the faithful remnant was comforted in a time of
distress.

Note 10: JAMES AND THE "TABERNACLE OF DAVID"

In Acts 15 is the account of the council of Jerusalem, when the
Apostles and elders were called together to consider the question of
the admission of Gentiles to the Christian community upon their
belief of the Gospel: was it necessary for them to be circumcised
and to keep the law? Peter and Paul both testified that Gentiles
were receiving the Gospel of salvation in Christ, and that God had
shown His approval by the visible bestowal of His Spirit upon them.
The case of Cornelius was the clearest. James then quoted from
"the prophets" as witness to what they had observed:

76   *Amos 9*

"After these things I will return, and I will build again the
tabernacle of David, which is fallen down; and I will build again
the ruins thereof, and I will set it up: that the residue of men may
seek after the Lord, and all the Gentiles, upon whom my name is
called, saith the Lord, who maketh these things known from the
beginning of the world" (Acts 15: 16–18, R.V.).

Here James has commenced with an allusion to Jeremiah 12: 15,
then quoted Amos 9: 11–12 from the LXX version, and concluded
with an allusion to Isaiah 45: 21. The LXX version, which differs
chiefly in reading, "that the residue of men may seek after the
Lord" for Amos' "that they (Israel) may possess the remnant of
Edom, and all the nations that are called by name" evidently rested
upon a Hebrew text which differed in one or two small details from
that of Amos. (See F. F. Bruce, *The Book of the Acts*, p. 310.)

The interest of James' quotation is however in the way he applies
Amos' prophecy of the rebuilding of the tabernacle of David to the
manifestation, resurrection and ascension of Jesus of Nazareth, the
Son of David. Gentiles out of many nations were coming to
acknowledge him as Saviour and Lord, and were being called by
the name of God. So the fulfilment of Amos' prophecy of the
restoration of David's house had begun.

But though a few will listen even now, "all the nations" do not
yet acknowledge God, nor Jesus as Redeemer and Lord, nor do they
yet say, "Let us go up to the ... house of the God of Jacob ... and
he will teach us of his ways" (Isa. 2). The Son of David must come
again. Then not only Israel after the flesh but all the nations will
bow before him, and Amos' prophecy will receive its literal
fulfilment. And when the time comes for the Son of David to hand
back dominion of the earth to the Father (1 Cor. 15), his Spirit will
fill all the redeemed in the earth, taken out of all the nations, and
"God will be all and in all".

Concluding Reflections

Amos, one of the earliest of the prophets, was certainly not the
"innovator" he is sometimes alleged to be. As a reformer he
invented nothing, for he sought to recall the people to a Law and a
way of life which they had already received. His familiarity with
the older books of the Old Testament appears on every page; he
knows of the history of Jacob and Esau, he alludes to Balaam's
prophecy concerning Israel, to the 40 years wandering in the
wilderness, and to David the musician, to quote only a few cases.

Amos 9

His condemnation of the people's evil practices implies the existence of a ceremonial law of festivals and sacrifices, and of detailed regulations concerning them (for example it is a sin to offer leaven with a sacrifice on the altar); his judgement of their iniquitous conduct toward their fellows implies a knowledge of a divine moral standard. All this acquaintance with the holy writings, from Moses onward, is *assumed* by the prophet as a matter of course.

What does cause surprise are the almost unrelieved condemnations by Amos of Israel's sins with little suggestion of mercy, in marked contrast to the attitude of Hosea, who wrote about the same situation and at about the same time. It should be remembered, however, that God conveyed His own message by using His instruments according to their capacities and to their suitability for His purpose. Amos was evidently appalled in mind as he realised how gravely Israel had forsaken the God of their fathers in spirit, seeking only their own material satisfactions. By the Spirit of God he saw this iniquity as so evil, the situation of the leaders of the people as so incapable of reform, that nothing but the sternest condemnation and judgement would meet the case. His words are a useful corrective for us in this humanitarian age, for we too need reminding that the "Lord God" of Israel, who is also the Father of the Lord Jesus Christ, will not for ever tolerate sin, but will cause His holiness to prevail by the destruction of the sinner, if the sinner will not have it any other way. But to the repentant and submissive remnant His mercy was and is still everlasting.

The complete sovereignty of God in nature is another feature of this prophecy; Yahweh rules the storm, controls the earthquake, brings a deluge upon the ungodly; He also disciplines by means of natural affliction, the drought and the pestilence, selecting even the portions of the land which shall receive the rain and those which shall not (4: 7). This is an aspect we are in danger of forgetting, not to say discounting, in this "scientific" 20th century, when all things are so readily "explained". But the dominance of God in nature is only cited as an evidence of His complete supremacy, in the national as well as in the moral sphere. Israel's God will punish them for their iniquity, but will redeem His faithful remnant at the last and cause His holiness to prevail; beside Him all else, the gods of the nations, their arms and their promises of help, are but as nothing. To help *us* to recapture this deep sense of the all-embracing supremacy of God, as real today as it was 2700 years ago, is not the least contribution that the prophecy of Amos can

Amos 9

make to our needs; which inspires the reflection that writings whose spiritual lessons for the faithful are as valid 2700 years later as in the days when they were written, must be unique indeed. But of course: they are the words of God.

6
Jonah
MERCY FOR NINEVEH

Introduction

The book of Jonah is unique among the prophets in that it does not provide an account of his teaching, but rather of a very significant episode in his life. Apart from Jonah's prayer (ch. 2) it is entirely narrative, resembling the histories of Elijah and Elisha; yet the narrative was obviously intended to convey the most profound lesson, first to Jonah himself who discovered in the process that he was in need of learning it, and then to his contemporaries. The lesson is everlasting and has its point for us too.

The prophet tells us nothing of himself except that he was the son of Amittai, which suggests that he must have been identical with the "Jonah, the son of Amittai, the prophet" who foretold the restoration of Israel's borders achieved by Jeroboam II (780–740 B.C.). This date agrees with the traditional place of the book among the Minor Prophets, where it is grouped with Hosea, Amos and Joel (who prophesied before or during the reign of Jeroboam II) and before Micah who prophesied after Jeroboam's death. Pusey's verdict of a century ago was that the book is written in a "pure, simple Hebrew" which would agree with this date. The majority of modern critics allege the book to be of late date, exilic or post-exilic, partly for reasons of language, partly because they regard it not as fact but as an allegorical account such as is found in later Jewish literature, and partly because they have decided that the book's attitude to the salvation of the Gentiles could not have been written before Jeremiah.

As regards the objection to an early date on the score of language, a century ago Pusey made a thorough examination of the alleged vocabulary difficulties, and showed that some of the words cited were actually already in existence in the Psalms of David, and that others were special seafaring words which the Hebrew writers would have had no occasion to use before Jonah's day because he is the first really to deal with the sea; others again are natural terms to find in the mouths of foreign sailors or of Ninevites. E. J. Young, who was Professor of Old Testament studies at the Westminster Theological Seminary, America, a scholar respected by the critics

80   *Jonah*

themselves for his knowledge and fairness, dealt with more modern objections on the score of language when he wrote: "The presence of Aramaisms (in Jonah) cannot be made a criterion for determining the date, since they occur in Old Testament books from both early and late periods. Furthermore, the recently discovered texts from Ras-Shamra contain Aramaic elements (circa 1500–1400 B.C.)", that is before the date of the writings of Moses even. The internal evidence of the language of the "psalm" in ch. 2 is not without its importance. There are expressions in this chapter of two kinds: the first from already existing psalms of David; the second, found in other psalms which are *later* compositions, in which the authors made use of Jonah's psalm. "The internal evidence, therefore ... so far from proving a late era for the book, strongly favours the belief that at least *this* part of the book was written by Jonah himself" (*Speaker's Commentary*). As is so often the case, the linguistic objections of the critics to the authenticity of the prophecy, when subjected to examination by people competent to estimate their value, turn out to be nothing like so formidable as they sound to the ordinary reader. The frequency with which this happens is encouraging to the believer in the integrity of the Bible, as is also the manifest disagreement among the critics themselves as to date and authorship, for the book has been assigned by scholars to every century from the eighth to the second B.C.!

The majority of modern commentators take Jonah's prophecy as allegory and not as fact, chiefly because the incident of the great fish is just "incredible". The most ancient tradition, however, has always regarded the book as fact and its internal details support that view. The whole narrative is told with such a wealth of circumstantial detail—the action of Jonah in going "to Joppa", in catching a ship for "Tarshish", in "paying the fare", in going down to the hold to "sleep"; the distinctive character given to the "shipmaster" and the sailors; the recognition of the Ninevites that they needed to put away "violence" (consistently with the detailed charges of Nahum); the psychological realism of the whole narrative—all these speak of an action which the prophet had personally experienced. The swallowing of Jonah by the great fish and its casting of him upon the shore are only objections to the mind which refuses to allow the possibility of the miraculous. Of course it was a miracle, but so was the resurrection of Christ; if we accept that, we have no just grounds for disputing the experience of Jonah.

There is no need to cite the evidence of biologists that great fishes capable of swallowing a man exist, in the Mediterranean itself, and that the phenomenon is known to have occurred. The

Jonah

most important testimony to the reality of the action described in the book of Jonah is that of Christ himself: "The men of Nineveh shall rise in judgement with this generation and shall condemn it: because they repented at the preaching of Jonas: and behold, a greater than Jonas is here" (and you who hear me do not repent) (Matt. 12: 41). The reproach was based upon the assertion that "as Jonah was three days and three nights in the whale's belly, so shall the Son of man be three days and three nights in the heart of the earth" (v. 40). The comparison between his own case and Jonah's and his reproach of hardness of heart against his own people give real weight to Christ's words only if he was referring to an actual repentance.

The verdict that Jonah could not have been written before Jeremiah is based upon critical theory, according to which the teaching of the book could not have shown a merciful and welcoming attitude towards Gentiles until a "late" date. The theory is unsound, for the kind of "evolutionary development" in Israel's religion, as upheld by most modern critics, is a product of their own imagination. It should not be allowed any weight against the solid evidence of the traditional place of Jonah in Scripture and the internal evidence of the book.

It is also alleged that the record of Assyrian history found upon the monuments makes no allusion to the visit of Jonah. But Assyrian history has many gaps. There is nothing incredible in the fact that a prophet of Israel may have visited Nineveh during one of the periods of civil confusion which arose from time to time and created a remarkable effect there (no doubt only comparatively short-lived), without the rulers' having thought it was a fit subject for permanent record.

Remarkably, Jonah does not explain or defend himself, but tells what happened; the reader is left to draw his own conclusions. The Ninevites are even shown in a favourable light, and the prophet in just the reverse; a fact which should cause us to wonder that a Hebrew prophet could leave on record such a flattering picture of the enemies of his own people coupled with what is in fact a condemnation of himself, and then that people should have been so impressed with the authority of his words that *they preserved them among their inspired Scriptures.* Surely they must have known that the book came from a prophet of God, worthy to be ranked with the other great names.

The book is really prophecy in the form of history, and its purposes are at least four: it shows Jonah as a prophecy of the resurrection of Christ on the third day, the only passage of the Old Testament which predicts this detail and is so used by Christ

82   *Jonah*

himself; his experience was typical of that of his own nation, who
would have to pass like him through the waters of affliction before
a remnant was delivered; the rebellious nature of Israel is
emphasised in contrast with the repentance of Nineveh; and lastly,
Israel were being warned not to presume upon their state of
privilege so far as to believe that God would not look with favour
upon "the heathen" (even the enemies of Israel) and would not give
them a chance to repent. The mercy of God could not be confined
to Israel: that was the lesson which no doubt struck home the
hardest in the minds of Jonah's contemporaries, proud of their
God-given ritual and heedless of His spiritual service. It is also the
lesson which remains most topical for us.

1. The Flight of Jonah (1 : 1–17)

1: **1–5:** The first word in the Hebrew text is not "Now" but
"And", the traditional commencement for authors who wished
to signify that their work was to be connected with the already
accepted writings of Israel. The first four books of Moses are all
connected by this "And", as are Joshua, Judges, Ruth, 1 and 2
Samuel, 1 and 2 Kings, 2 Chron., Ezra and Ezekiel; and a similar
beginning after an introduction is found in Nehemiah, Jeremiah,
Hosea and Amos. The *Speaker's Commentary* remarks that this
shows a "continuous, literary consciousness". Jonah felt that he was
contributing to the writings of the prophets.

The direct command to go on a mission to a heathen city must
have been most striking to an Israelite. Nineveh, that "great city"
and capital of Assyria, was probably being used not only for
Nineveh proper, founded by Nimrod, but for a complex of four
cities with an area of 25 miles by 15 miles. Although Assyria had
not had direct dealings with Israel in Jonah's day, she had done so
with adjacent peoples, such as the Syrians; and Ahab of Israel had
(in 850 B.C.) actually played a prominent part in a coalition of
powers, aimed at preventing further Assyrian advance in Syria. The
reputation of the Assyrians for cruelty and the dread of their name
would therefore be well known in Israel; as would the name of their
capital city. Jonah was told to "cry *unto* it" or "against it",
suggesting a call to repentance from the great "wickedness". A
number of Old Testament allusions involving a cry to God: Abel's
blood that "cried" from the ground (Gen. 4: 10), the "cry" of
Sodom "because their sin is very grievous" (Gen. 18: 20–1), and the
allusion in Psalm 72, "he shall deliver the needy when he crieth",
all suggest that it is the oppressed whose "cry" God hears and
whom He desires to deliver.

Jonah 1

Jonah however found this astounding charge too much for his Israelite prejudice. Fearing also for his personal reputation as a prophet, for he felt sure God would eventually spare the city and *he* would be discredited, he took flight "from the presence of the Lord". He did not expect to escape from the presence of God, but rather by abandoning the land of Israel to avoid the duty of "standing before the Lord" as His prophet. He set off in the *opposite* direction from Nineveh, finding at the port of Joppa a Phoenician ship trading with Tarshish. Of Tarshish we learn that it supplied Tyre with all kinds of wealth, iron, tin, lead (Ezek. 27: 12); that its ships (probably not ships belonging *to* Tarshish but those trading *with* that place) were symbolic of the power of men and that their destruction by the "wind" of God would be a vindication of His power (Psa. 48: 7). By the 1st century A.D. the identity of Tarshish had been lost. Scholars generally identify it with Tartessus in Southern Spain, but the evidence is unsatisfactory. There is an independent tradition that the Phoenicians traded with the British Isles, and there is no reason why the word Tarshish may not have that sense. It is fair to say, however, that the identification of the Old Testament Tarshish with the British Isles rests upon inference rather than upon positive testimony.

The point for Jonah was, however, that the ship was going a long way away, to the end of the world, as it were. Why did he flee? The only explanation given by himself is that he knew Yahweh as a God of mercy, who would not carry out the judgement threatened. So Jonah would be discredited as a prophet, and the name of God would be dishonoured; and in any case how could he go and preach repentance to these uncircumcised Gentiles, the enemies of his people? So God allows Jonah to have his way—to a point. He "pays the fare" (realistic touch, but why mention it unless he was the only passenger and the fare was considerable) and goes down below. In v. 4 there are two very imaginative touches: God "casts along" a wind (the ship had probably not got very far) and in the ensuing "mighty tempest" the ship "*thought* to be broken". The crew were probably of mixed nationality; each man called upon his own god and eventually the decision was taken to throw the goods out into the sea, a desperate expedient because of the serious loss involved.

vv. 6–7: Jonah however was deep in the "innermost parts of the ship" (R.V.), fast asleep; a sure touch this, conveying his physical exhaustion after his perhaps long journey, but more significantly his "psychological withdrawal", his effort to escape from a painful situation, for of course his conscience must have been active. The "shipmaster" (lit. "chief of the pilots": it is interesting to learn that

84   *Jonah 1*

in the vocabulary of naval affairs given in Ezek. 27 there are two
words for sailors, both of which occur in this first chapter of Jonah)
seeks Jonah out (evidently he was the only passenger) and
indignantly asks him, "What ailest thou?" Why was he not doing
his best to ensure the safety of the ship by calling on his god like the
others? It is quite possible that at this point Jonah may well have
prayed; but the storm continues unabated (there was probably some
unusual feature about it, such as excessive suddenness or violence
which made the sailors believe it was a divine visitation) and it is
decided to cast lots.

vv. 8–12: When the lot, evidently divinely overruled, selects Jonah,
it is most striking that the sailors do not immediately cast him
overboard (a tribute to their character) but ask him the most
embarrassing questions about himself. To these he replies fully and
frankly, declaring himself first a Hebrew (the name by which the
Israelites were known to the surrounding nations), then a servant of
Yahweh for whom he makes the claim that He is the "God of
heaven", Creator of "the sea and the dry land" (tantamount to a
claim for Yahweh's supremacy over all other gods) and gives the
full reason for his flight. Jonah is now convinced that the storm is
on account of him, and sees no reason why these innocent men
should have their lives imperilled for his transgression. When they
enquire what they should do, he tells them to cast him into the sea
and assures them that the tempest will then cease. Two points here:
Jonah does not cast *himself* into the sea, but submits to the
judgement inflicted through others (as did Christ); and he obviously
had no idea that he was going to be saved, probably feeling utterly
unworthy, and was accepting the righteous judgement of God upon
himself.

vv. 13–17: But the ship was evidently not far from land and the
mariners were conscious that to cast a man into the sea was to
sentence him to death and to incur guilt, so they "dug" (vivid
phrase in the Heb.) in their efforts to row to land; but finding the
sea too tempestuous, they prayed direct to Yahweh, acknowledged
His power ("thou, O Yahweh, hast done as it pleased thee"),
besought Him that He would not hold them guilty for Jonah's
death, and cast the prophet into the raging waves. "And the sea
ceased from her raging"; the abruptness of the phrase suggests that
the calm was both rapid and sudden. The mariners were convinced
of Yahweh's power; they offered a sacrifice and "made vows",
implying their worship of Yahweh.
    Our version gives the impression that this was done while the
men were still on board, which is quite possible, for there would

Jonah 2

almost certainly be some animal on board fit for sacrifice. But in view of the facts, first: that the ship had lost its cargo (what point in going on to a distant port *empty?*); and second: that they were evidently not far from land, why should they not have returned to the port from which they set out—Joppa—or to some other nearby, and the news of what had happened immediately spread among the local population, and eventually to the Israelites themselves? Jonah the prophet, fleeing from a charge God had given him to go to preach to Nineveh (he had told the sailors this) had dramatically perished at sea in a storm created by Yahweh Himself. The more widespread was Jonah's reputation among the Israelites, the greater would be the shock at this signal judgement of Yahweh upon one of His own prophets.

But, unknown to the world, Yahweh had intervened and prepared a refuge for His erring servant: the great fish (not a whale, but a species of large shark which used to be common in the Mediterranean) was at the appointed spot when needed; this is the sense in which we are to take "the Lord had prepared a great fish". Jonah was in its belly for three days and three nights which were to be a type of another and more significant sojourn, that of Jesus "in the heart of the earth". We have here the simple declaration of the operation of the power of God on behalf of one of His servants; of course it cannot be explained by natural phenomena—neither can the resurrection of Christ. The simple answer is that it is not meant to be.

2. The Prayer of Jonah (2: 1-10)

There follows a prayer which the Scripture tells us explicitly was uttered "out of the fish's belly". It is important to note that Jonah is not praying to be delivered from the fish; this is a prayer of thanksgiving for *his deliverance from the ocean.* The prayer is full of allusions to the Psalms. It is not that Jonah quotes literally and exactly, but rather that his prayer has worked into it numerous idioms and phrases. This is just what would occur to a reverent Israelite familiar with the Scriptures.

2: 1-10: Jonah's prayer is "to the Lord his God", expressing his sense of Yahweh's presence and power even in his peril. He cried "out of mine affliction" and was heard by God "out of the *belly* of Sheol" (not the same word as in v. 1 of the fish). Cf. Psa. 18: 5-6, "The cords of Sheol compassed me: the snares of death prevented me. In my distress I called upon the Lord ... He heard my voice". For God had cast him "into the heart of the seas", the phrase which

86 *Jonah 2*

probably suggested the "heart of the earth" (the grave) of Matt. 12: 40. "All thy billows and thy waves passed over me" (notice God is in control) is identical with Psa. 42: 7, where the context is: "Why art thou cast down, O my soul? Hope thou in God ... Therefore will I remember thee ..." Feeling "cast out" from before God's face, like Adam from Eden—cf. Psa. 31: 22, "I am cut off from before thine eyes; nevertheless *thou heardest* the voice of my supplications when I cried unto thee"—Jonah resolves to look again toward His holy temple: he may mean the temple in Jerusalem, or heaven, as in Psa. 11: 4, "The Lord is in his holy temple, the Lord's throne is in heaven". As he sank in the waves, "the waters compassed me about"—the verb occurs only here and in Psa. 18: 4—"even to the soul", as in Psa. 69: 1. The weeds enveloped him—a vivid touch— and he sank "to the cuttings-off of the mountains", the dread depths where the great mountains had their foundations. It was as though the earth had barred him for ever—cf. "the lower parts of the earth", a synonym for Sheol, Psa. 63: 9. "About me" is the same Hebrew as in "the Lord shut him in", of Noah confined in the ark, and is always used of being shut *in*, never out. But God has delivered him from "the pit"—cf. Psa. 30: 3, "O Lord, thou hast brought up my soul from the grave ... that I should not go down to the pit". When Jonah's soul "fainted within" him—cf. Psa. 142: 3, "When my spirit was overwhelmed within me"—that was the moment when he remembered Yahweh and prayed towards "his holy temple"—an obvious reminiscence of Psa. 18: 6, "In my distress I cried unto my God: he heard my voice out of his temple". Those who worship idols ("lying vanities", see Psa. 31: 6 for same term; *Speaker's Commentary* translates, "nothingnesses of falsehood") forsake "their own mercy", or *chesed*, goodness. It is Yahweh who is primarily *chesed*, goodness and mercy, cf. Psa. 144: 2, "Blessed be Yahweh ... my *goodness* and my fortress". This mercy He extends to others, and thus becomes "their mercy", not a quality which they possess of themselves, but which they receive from Him, and then manifest in their turn. "But as for me", cries Jonah, "I will offer sacrifice with thanksgiving"; that is, he will give public testimony of his service to God, he will carry out what he has vowed (possibly a resolve to go to Nineveh, if the opportunity to do so should be granted him again in the mercy of God?). His prayer ends with the triumphant declaration: "Salvation (is to be ascribed only) unto Yahweh!" Cf. Psa. 3: 8, "Salvation (belongeth) unto the Lord! thy blessing (is) upon thy people".

The frequency of allusion to the Psalms in this prayer is eloquent proof of their existence in Jonah's day and also of their well-known

Jonah 3

character. They must have been frequently heard in the temple worship and perhaps in other less formal ceremonies as well. To them in his need for expression of his deep emotion Jonah turned instinctively and found the echoes and the assurance he sought. The most striking feature of the prayer, however, is that it is one of *thanksgiving* for a deliverance already accomplished, and *that* not from the fish but from *the sea:* "the deep ... the midst of the seas ... the floods ... the billows ... the waves ... the waters ... the depth ... the weeds ..."; these are the perils from which he never expected to survive. Finding himself still alive in the body of the fish, Jonah rèalises that he has been preserved and that it could only be by direct act of God. Hope and faith revive and he makes a renewal of his homage which he had owed before as a prophet of the Lord. As a result "the Lord spake unto the fish" and Jonah was deposited upon the land. God responded at once to his humble obedience and delivered him from his prison. His frame of mind was now such that God could use him for His purpose.

3.   Jonah's Mission to Nineveh (3: 1–10)

3: 1–2: The first verse of ch. 3 must conceal a considerable lapse of time. Jonah, exhausted from his harrowing experience, must have returned home to recuperate, may even have gone to Jerusalem to pay his vows. Since the next divine command to him commences with the word "Arise", he must have returned to some settled habitation, there to await the pleasure of the Lord. The interval of time between his "return from the dead" and his departure for Nineveh could have been several months; in other words there is every likelihood that the episode of his flight and miraculous deliverance had become well known in Israel, and, in view of the probably mixed nationality of the mariners, in other countries as well.

Jonah does not go of his own accord on his return from the deep, but waits for a renewal of his commission from God—a reaction which may have been due to a sense of his own unworthiness, but also to a secret hope that God would change His mind. In time the charge is renewed in terms ("Preach the preaching" or "cry the cry that I bid thee") which suggest he is being recalled to strict obedience; but otherwise there is no word of rebuke. "So Jonah arose and went to Nineveh": a simple statement which conceals an immensely long journey, probably 700 miles, every yard of which he probably walked, through difficult country and perhaps hostile tribes. We have no means of estimating the time he took—if he walked steadily every day he could have hardly taken less than a

88   *Jonah 3*

month and probably took much longer. We can imagine his
thoughts, especially in view of what transpired later; but he is now
resolved to carry out his task.

vv. 3–4: The statement in v. 3 that "Nineveh *was* an exceeding great
city of three days journey" has caused some to contend that the
book must have been written after the fall of Nineveh (612 B.C.).
Others agree that Hebrew tenses are not to be estimated by the
analogy of modern Western languages. The *Speaker's Commentary*
says that the last past tense here is not intended as an¯historical
notice, but is "relative to Jonah's sentiments regarding his mission ... He *went* to preach though he *knew* Nineveh *was* a great
city". The estimate of·its size as "three days journey" must be
based upon the measurement of the *circumference* of the city; "the
circuit of ... the mounds of Konjunjik, Nimrud, Karamless and
Korsabad, now generally allowed to represent ancient Nineveh, is
about 60 miles" (*Ell. Comm.*). Its population has been estimated at
700,000. Jonah went "a day's journey" into the city—a vague
measurement, for which Herodotus gives between 17 and 23 miles,
and the Assyrian inscriptions 14 miles. His cry: "Yet forty days and
Nineveh shall be overthrown" is in Hebrew a terse phrase of four
words and would undoubtedly be impressive. The word "overthrown" is that used for the destruction of Sodom and Gomorrah,
and may well have been better known to Jonah's hearers in that
sense than we think.

vv. 5–10: "So the people of Nineveh believed *in* God". Why?
Because, says Jesus in Luke 11: 30, Jonah was a sign unto them.
This must mean that his appearance among them was significant,
implying that they already knew what had happened to him. In the
same way the queen of Sheba (from the extreme South as Nineveh
is in the extreme North) the very next example quoted by Jesus,
already knew of the wisdom of Solomon before she journeyed to
commune with him. Communications in the Middle East were
good, though slow by our standards, and commercial contacts were
continuous; some considerable time must have passed between
Jonah's return from the sea and his journey to Nineveh, so there
would have been ample opportunity for the astonishing news to
spread. There is a very old speculation that the mariners themselves
went to Nineveh, in fulfilment of their vows, to tell what they knew.

The Ninevites' "belief" in God was like that of the mariners: an
acknowledgment of His supremacy over all other gods. At all events
they took action, proclaiming abstinence from food (for how long
we are not told) and the wearing of haircloth for their normal
garments, both signs of abasement in which the whole population

Jonah 3

joined. The "matter"—not just the news of Jonah's preaching but the whole affair of his experience in the sea—came to the king, who took off his "robe", a large and costly upper garment, the "goodly Babylonian garment" coveted by Achan (Josh. 7: 21), said to be the most magnificent part of the dress of kings; but remarkably the word is also used for Elijah's "mantle" (1 Kings 19: 13, etc.), and that of a prophet generally (Zech. 13: 4). The king put on sackcloth, with ashes on his head (the traditional signs of mourning in the East) and caused a "decree" to be published. The word is peculiar, occurring repeatedly in the Chaldean of Daniel for an order of the king of Babylon, and of Ezra for that of the Persian sovereign. Evidently it was the technical word actually used by the king of Nineveh; and far from being an argument for "late date", it is evidence of truth. The fact that the decree comes from "the king and his nobles" suggests that he was not the omnipotent monarch that the later rulers of Assyria were; the *Speaker's Commentary* notes "the remarkable deficiency in the records relative to just the very time at which we may most reasonably suppose Jonah to have visited Nineveh"; a time of civil strife then, we may infer, for the great rulers were not in the habit of leaving themselves without public testimony to their own glory.

The decree enjoined signs of mourning upon all, even upon the beasts, that is the domestic animals which shared the life of men (Herodotus IX.24 recounts a similar incident among the Persians and implies that it was a "barbarian" custom); it urged an earnest appeal to God ("cry mightily to God"). The fact that this repentance did not take the form of sacrificing animals or children suggests a Hebrew influence, probably from Jonah himself. The most striking feature of the decree, however, is the call to turn from an "evil way" and from the violence they were committing; it was a call for *moral* reformation in the Hebrew tradition, not just the satisfying of an angry god by the offering of appropriate sacrifices. The precise mention of "violence" is a mark of truth, since this above all others is the charge made against the Ninevites by Nahum and agrees with all that we know of their character. The hope that God would "repent" and "turn away from his fierce anger" is in the same form of words used by Joel to Judah.

The repentance was evidently translated into action: "God saw their works that they turned from their evil way". The aim of His dealing with the Ninevites was attained, for the object of God's warning was that He might *not* have to do what He threatened, as the figure of the potter in Jer. 18: 7–8 makes clear. The reaction of the city showed that it did not yet merit final judgement; God therefore "repented of the evil", adapting His measures to a

90   *Jonah 3*

changed situation, and the judgement was stayed. (See Note 3,
"How can the Lord repent?" at Joel 2: 14.)

4. The Rebuking of Jonah (4: 1–11)

4: 1–3: Jonah is very displeased, even angry, and expostulates
with the Lord: had he not said this would happen? Was not that
why he had fled to Tarshish? For he knew that God was gracious
and merciful, as He had declared Himself to Moses (Exod. 34; see
also Joel 2: 13). Jonah's expostulation with God is respectful ("I
pray thee, O Lord ..."), but his former rebellion is not repented of;
he prays for death, *not* as a punishment for himself but to put an
end to his own grief. He is more concerned with his own will for
Nineveh than he is with the Lord's.

vv. 4–9: So God teaches him a lesson a second time. "Are you very
angry?" The gentleness of the reproof is remarkable. Jonah goes
out on the east side of the city—*not* on the way home—and builds a
booth in the Hebrew fashion, with only incomplete shade for the
head from the fierce noon heat of the sun. And as he waits to see
whether God will send down fire and brimstone upon Nineveh as
upon Sodom of old, and doubtless feels afflicted by the heat, God
caused a "gourd" to grow up over his booth and afford him grateful
shade. The plant was probably the palmchrist, or castor-oil plant, a
perennial growing to the height of a small tree. It is said to flourish
even in the poorest soil, especially in the region of the Tigris. Its
growth is notoriously rapid, and its wide leaves afford good shade.
By the power of God natural process was accelerated and Jonah
found himself relieved from the affliction of the heat. But the plant
was attacked the next day by "a worm"; the word is in the singular,
though in Deuteronomy 28: 39 and Isaiah 14: 11 the same word is
translated "worms". It represents in other words a *class* of
creatures. An Eastern traveller (quoted in *Speaker's Commentary*)
describes how black caterpillars can swarm on the palmchrist and
devour all its leaves in one night. Then Jonah, deprived of his
protection, finds himself exposed to the sirocco, the suffocating
wind of the desert, so that his sickness returns and he wishes for
death, as Elijah had done, but for a different reason. Elijah felt he
had failed and therefore judgement would come upon Israel; Jonah
was grieved because judgement had *not* come upon Nineveh. To the
Lord's repeated remonstrance, gently expressed, "Are you very
angry on account of the gourd?", Jonah replies obstinately and
wilfully that he is, so much that it well nigh kills him.

vv. 10–11: Then comes the final lesson: Jonah has been "loth to

Jonah 4

lose" (A.V. spared) the palmchrist, which he had done nothing to produce and which had perished in a few hours; how should not God be "loth to lose" Nineveh, that great city in which there were more than 120,000 children unable to distinguish between good and evil? This description of children is found in Deut. 1: 39 and Isa. 7: 15–16, and the number given implies a total population of 600,000. The prophecy ends abruptly, without informing us what Jonah's reaction was and how he reached his home again. But from the fact that we possess his book, we may infer that he learned his lesson and spent some time among his own people afterwards, instructing them too.

5. Reflections

Conclusions need only be brief, since many of the lessons of this fascinating book are evident.

Despite his resistance Jonah's *faith* in God is never in doubt, nor his recognition of God's utter supremacy. Nowhere does this receive greater expression than in the psalm of thanksgiving. His error was that of rebellion: sensing injustice in a command to offer mercy to a nation of violent, uncircumcised Gentiles, the enemies of Israel, who were God's own people, perhaps resenting the fact that God would judge *Israel* for their sins nevertheless, Jonah disputes with God, respectfully but determinedly, rather like Job of old. "He would govern God's world better than God himself" (Pusey). And like Job of old, he had to learn the lesson of submission to the will of God, even when "the way ahead" is not altogether clear. It is a lesson we too, in common with all faithful servants, need to learn.

Among the other features of this book is the astonishing *gentleness* of God; Jonah, brought back to the way of obedience by his near approach to death and his astounding deliverance, is not even rebuked, but simply told to carry out his commission, with the reminder that it is God who bids him do it. When he cannot overcome his own bitter feelings at the "escape" of the Ninevites, God twice mildly interrogates him: "Are you *very* angry?", with the implied "*Should* you be?" This gentleness translates itself into mercy for the Ninevites who are still willing to repent, mercy for the thousands who know not yet the difference between right and wrong because of their tender youth; mercy for a population for whom He has "laboured", "willing not that any should perish, but that all should come to repentance" (2 Peter 3: 9).

Jonah found it hard to rejoice in the pardon of worshippers of idols, the enemies of his people. He had to learn that it is God's prerogative, and not that of his servant, to decide who shall receive

Jonah 4

His mercy. The lesson becomes pointed for us in these days of widespread evil, when we may feel genuine reluctance to desire the salvation of those whose lives are manifestly under the power of sin. Jonah may have thought the Ninevites to be most unlikely and undeserving converts; but God demonstrated to him that there is no predicting who may repent and who may not, and that His judgement is stayed when there is a possibility of repentance. Until the manifest day of judgement come, we must co-operate with God in seeking the repentance of men for whom He has "laboured", and find the strength to do this in realising the great riches *we* have received through "the word of His grace".

7

HOSEA

THE LOVE OF GOD FOR HIS PEOPLE

Though the ministry of Hosea was long, up to 70 years, the bulk of his prophecy seems to have been delivered a little later than that of Amos and a little earlier than those of Isaiah and Micah. Like Amos his words were directed almost entirely to the Northern Kingdom, first in the last years of the prosperous reign of Jeroboam II (780–740 B.C.) and then during the years of confusion and bloodshed which followed the death of that king (740–720 B.C.). In the first three chapters Samaria is not yet overthrown, Gilead still belongs to Israel, there is no mention of Pekah's alliance with the Syrian Rezin for the purpose of subduing Judah, and Assyria is an unreliable ally and not yet an implacable enemy. The later chapters of Hosea, however, paint such a picture of chaos in government, such disregard for human life, and such degradation in morals and religion, that they evidently suit that period after the reign of Jeroboam II when usurper after usurper waded through blood to the throne (of the six successors of Jeroboam, four died violent deaths). The discouraging effect of all this upon the faithful "poor and meek" still left in Israel is obvious, as is the test of their faith.

Hosea is with Amos our great source of information about the affairs of the Northern Kingdom in its declining years, before God made an end of it through Sargon's capture of Samaria about 720 B.C. Hosea's close acquaintance with Israel shows in his use of place names (Ephraim occurs 17 times, but Jerusalem not once) and in the variety of his knowledge of conditions and events; shows also in the yearning care he evidently felt for his own people in their tragic suffering, in contrast with the rather detached tone of Amos.

In Hosea there is the same knowledge of the writings of Moses as in Amos, the same kind of allusion which assumes complete acquaintance in the hearer or reader; the same conception of the covenant relation between God and His people; the same urgent need for the abandonment of injustice and bloodshed, corrupt worship of idols, and foreign alliances in place of trust in God. Each usurper tried to strengthen himself with foreign aid: Baasha with Ben-Hadad, Ahab with Tyre by marrying Jezebel, Jehu by sending

94   Hosea

tribute to Assyria (according to the Assyrian inscriptions), Pekah
by alliance with Rezin. "There was not one king found who would
risk his throne for God" (Pusey). The demand is for a return to
ways of justice and mercy, and to the knowledge of God. There is
the same promise of restoration, too, under the throne of David.

But while Amos is concerned with God's dealings with the
nations generally, Hosea scarcely mentions them, but concentrates
upon God's care for the remnant whom He will redeem out of His
people. This remnant, which is still a nation, is however treated
with such tenderness and yearning desire for its salvation, that the
way was evidently being paved for the time when God would speak
openly of the salvation of *individuals* irrespective of their membership of a national community, the distinctive feature of the
preaching of the Gospel itself.

It has been remarked that the case of Hosea shows great
similarity with that of Jeremiah, for as the former prophesied in the
declining years of the corrupt Northern kingdom, so did Jeremiah
in Judah 150 years later. Jeremiah was evidently well acquainted
with the prophecy of Hosea, for the allusions to it in his writing are
numerous. For us, so many centuries later, not the least of its values
is its astonishing revelation of the tender love of God towards those
who are His, His yearning desire that they "might not perish" but
might turn unto Him and be saved. This love is expressed in Hosea
with such earnestness, that if we had not had this sanction of the
word of the prophet himself, we might well not have dared to
presume that it could be so great. In the light of Hosea we may
enter a little better into the convictions of the apostle Paul that
nothing, literally nothing, can "separate us from the love of God
which is in Christ Jesus our Lord".

Hosea's prophecy falls naturally into two unequal parts.
Chapters 1-3 concern Hosea and Gomer as a type of Yahweh and
Israel; and the remaining chapters 4-13, (very difficult to divide up
into any logical scheme, as the varied results of those who have
attempted the task indicate), consist of mingled condemnation,
warnings of judgement, and entreaties, with a final appeal in
chapter 14. In our study we shall indicate the various sections which
the subject matter seems to require.

1. "YE ARE NOT MY PEOPLE" (1: 1—3: 5)

1: **1-9**: Hosea's prophecy, though delivered mainly to Israel, is
dated first by the kings of Judah, for the obvious reason that
future salvation for the people was to be through the Davidic line. It
is significant that no Northern king after Jeroboam II is mentioned

here; his successors were mostly usurpers and the kingdom came to an end within 20 years.

Hosea's name means "saving" or "deliverance" like Joshua and Jesus, and presents his basic message, that although God will reject an idolatrous nation, there is hope for the faithful and the repentant.

The record reads as if Hosea was directly commanded by God to marry Gomer who was a harlot, and to name his three children symbolically. When Gomer abandoned him in wild profligacy, the prophet sought her out (chap. 3), redeemed her from slavery, and set about the task of her reformation. The episode is clearly meant to be a representation of the relation of Yahweh with His own people, Israel, a relation frequently referred to under the figure of marriage: Yahweh was the Husband and Israel was His wife. Much has been written about the "moral difficulty" created by the apparent command of God to His prophet to take to wife a woman whom he already knew to be of impure life. It is hard to imagine such an order coming from God and difficult to see how such an action would not have done harm to the reputation of the prophet in Israel, among the very persons whom he was intended to influence. Even more, such a course would destroy the allegory, for as 2: 15 suggests, Israel was not faithless when God took her to Himself to begin with, but became so afterwards.

Some have sought to escape from the dilemma by regarding the whole episode as allegorical only, with no foundation in fact, but this is not the impression which the factual narrative produces, nor does it seem consistent with such an interpretation that, while the names of the children are unquestionably allegorical, that of the wife, Gomer bath Diblathaim, is not. The most probable solution is that Gomer was of apparently blameless life when Hosea married her for love, but that she was subsequently seduced by the licentious religious rites of the worship of the Canaanitish baals, sinking to the degradation of slavery, from which Hosea in love redeemed her by purchasing her freedom, and then kept her in seclusion until her repentant heart should realise her husband's affection and be ready to return it. Thus the prophet's own experience with Gomer ran exactly parallel to that of Yahweh with Israel, and he was the more able to enter into the feelings of God Himself, which are so graphically expressed in this book. When he looked back upon the whole episode afterwards, he would be able to see that the command to take Gomer to wife was indeed "from the Lord", according to His word and His will.

vv. 2–5: As the children were evidently not yet born when Hosea

96   *Hosea 1*

received the command to "take a wife of whoredom", prophetically
it is possible that Gomer was not yet openly dissolute when he
married her, but proved so afterwards. Although the narrative is
not absolutely clear, the expression "children of whoredoms"
certainly suggests that some of them at least were the fruit of
Gomer's adulterous unions; in fact only the first child is clearly said
to be Hosea's. The figure of a wife's unfaithfulness for apostasy
from God is found in the writings of Moses (Exod. 34: 15–16; Lev.
20: 5). It may have originated in the sacred prostitution practised at
the heathen shrines (the sin of Israel with the women of Moab at
Baal-Peor comes to mind) and then been used figuratively for the
abandonment of Yahweh in spirit. The transition from the woman
to the land in verse 2 shows the close link between the two ideas
which recur in the first three chapters.

The name Gomer bath Diblathaim does not yield any satisfactory allegorical sense; in any case none is given to it by Hosea.
The first child, unquestionably Hosea's, is to be named "Jezreel" of
which the first sense is "God will scatter". The "blood of Jezreel"
which God will avenge is not simply that of Naboth, destroyed by
Jezebel; it is the blood of the house of Ahab exterminated by Jehu.
Although Jehu had acted by divine command in destroying the seed
of Ahab, he had evidently done so not in a spirit of co-operation
with the righteous judgement of God, nor because he wholly
condemned the deeds of Ahab and Jezebel, but for personal
aggrandisement. He had afterwards used his position as a means of
evil-doing himself, for "he departed not from the sins of Jeroboam"
(2 Kings 10: 31). So judgement comes in its turn upon his house
too. (See in 1 Kings 14–16 the parallel case of Baasha who
exterminated the house of Jeroboam according to the prophecy of
Ahijah, and was later destroyed himself.) The phrase "yet a little
while" shows that the judgement had not yet been carried out;
Jeroboam II was therefore still on the throne.

The judgement, however, is to go further than the house of Jehu,
for it will put an end to "the kingdom and the house of Israel",
whose "bow" is to be broken in "the valley of Jezreel". The bow of
Israel was referred to by Jacob ("the portion ... which I took out of
the hand of the Amorite with my sword and with my bow", Gen.
48: 22) and was used by him in the blessing of Joseph or Ephraim.
It is often used in the prophets for the northern kingdom: "his bow
abode in strength, and the arms of his hands were made strong by
the mighty God of Jacob" (Gen. 49: 24) is an evident symbol for
the strength of the kingdom of God's people. The valley of Jezreel
had more than once seen the judgements of God upon the Gentile
enemies of Israel: Sisera and Midian had been destroyed there. But

Hosea 1

so had Israelite hosts too, like the armies of Saul and Ahab. There is a resemblance in the sound of names here: Yisrael, Yidsreel. No actual historical event involving an Israelite defeat in this plain and leading to the extinction of the Northern Kingdom is known, but such an event could easily have occurred in the invasions of Tiglath-Pileser, which ended in the destruction of Samaria (722 B.C.).

vv. 6–9: Gomer's second child is to be named Lo-Ruhamah, or "Not Pitied" as the R.S.V. translates; Paul, "not beloved" (Rom. 9: 25), and Peter, "hath not obtained mercy" (1 Pet. 2: 10). "Love and mercy are both contained in the intensive form of the verb ... (It expresses) deep tender yearnings of the inmost soul over one loved" (Pusey). The same verb is found in Psa. 103: 13—"As a father *pitieth* his children ..." (yearneth over). This is the first of many indications in Hosea of the earnest desire of God for His people's salvation. But their iniquity is now so great that "I will no more have mercy upon the house of Israel, that I should ... pardon them", v. 6, R.V. By contrast, however, Judah is to receive His mercy and to be saved, but not by relying on her own strength; it was a prediction which many of the faithful who heard Hosea's prophecy would live to see fulfilled in the destruction of Sennacherib's host in the days of Hezekiah.

In the East children are usually not weaned until the third year. The births of the three children were probably spread over a period of not less than six years. The name of the third child, Lo-Ammi, "Not my people" (R.S.V.) with the addition, "and I am not your God", implies the cancellation of the covenant made at Sinai and Israel's final rejection by God.

Restoration

v. 10—2: 1: By one of those abrupt transitions common in Hosea God turns immediately to the "end" which He has in view for His people; the Abrahamic promise is not cancelled, for Israel shall yet be "as the sand of the sea". In the very place where they are now rejected, that is in the land of Israel itself, they shall be called the sons of the living God. The two kingdoms are to be united under one king (the faithful would understand the son of David). The expression, "They shall come up out of the land" is ambiguous, for it is used of the return from exile in Ezra 2: 1 and Neh. 12: 1, and could signify here in the first place the return of representatives of the 12 tribes from Babylon under Zerubbabel; or it can signify marching as to war. The context seems rather to favour this latter

98   *Hosea 1*

interpretation, in which case the meaning is that united Israel will go up to battle (cf. Micah 5: 5–9) in the "great day of Jezreel", in which God will finally scatter the heathen and "sow" this people again. And so the message to Hosea's "brethren" and "sisters"—evidently a term for the faithful and purged remnant—is: Ammi, My People, and Ruhamah, She has obtained mercy. The dread judgement will be reversed.

"I will visit upon her the days of baalim" (2: 2–13)

2: 2–5: The allusions of the second chapter become much clearer once the religious ideas of the time are understood. "It was common to nearly all Semitic religions to express the union of a god with his land or his people by the figure of marriage" (G. A. Smith), a fact which explains the sacred prostitution carried on at the shrines. The fertility of a land and of its people was believed to depend on this union, from which a land became "possessed" or "blessed" by Baal. It is even possible that the term used by God through Isaiah, "Beulah" (possessed or blessed by the lord, Baal), may have been in common perverted use. For the grossly physical ideas of the Canaanites, the prophets of Israel expounded a spiritual union: the bride of Yahweh is not the land only with its physical fertility, but the *people;* and the relationship is a moral one, a holy people serving a Holy God.

From the appeal to the children to plead with their mother, despite the fact that the whole community of Israel (the mother) is being judged, it is evidently still possible for the individual faithful of Hosea's generation to protest against sins and to depart from them themselves. (Cf. the 7000 faithful in Elijah's time.) "Plead" (v. 2) should rather be "contend"; it is an appeal to Hosea's generation to recognise the sins of their community and to condemn them. The plain sense of God's declaration "she is not my wife, neither am I her husband" is that Israel's adulteries have destroyed the marriage bond with her Lord; it no longer exists. A new bond can only be created through the repentance of Israel (the remnant) and by the mercy of God (see 2: 19); Israel shall be punished as an adulteress by being stripped naked (see Ezek. 16: 38–9) and "fixed" helpless, (as "set" means), parched like a wilderness. The rapid transition from the "mother" to the "dry land" is remarkable. Israel turned away from the spiritual water of God's providing; she shall perish for lack of natural water.

Lo-Ruhamah, "I will not have mercy", is now repeated; by another of his swift transitions, Hosea next alludes to the children in the third person, after having addressed them directly: "Plead

Hosea 2 99

with *your* mother ... I will not have mercy upon *her* children". The harlot Israel has not only acted "shamefully", but does not wait to be seduced: "Let me go after my lovers". The strong expression of desire and the plural "lovers" show the sinful character of the act. Absorbing the idolatrous ideas of the Canaanites, Israel came to believe that all her material blessings—oil, wool, bread and wine—came from worshipping the "baalim" of the land. It is quite probable that many of the Israelites thought they were honouring Yahweh in celebrating these pagan rites; it was His name that they pronounced there. They transformed the *asherim* (groves) and the *mazzeboth* (images), for the worship of Yahweh, but in fact it was the rites and ideas of paganism which were honoured there. Hence the prophets can both denounce the people for idolatry and for observing the *form* of the worship of God, multiplying sacrifices and keeping feasts, while at the same time leading evil lives.

vv. 6–13: God's judgement on Israel's condition is significant: the remedy is not to be found through continued gentle treatment, which evokes no response, but through discipline. Confined by a thorn hedge, Israel will be prevented from finding "her way" (by contrast with the "way" of the Lord, Gen. 6). Although she eagerly pursues her lovers, she will not be able to find them, so that she will say: "I will go and return to my first husband". This is not the language of real repentance as it was in the case of the Prodigal Son, but only disappointment at her neglect and suffering, for there is no confession of sin: merely, "it was better with me then than now". "Then" would signify the time before Jeroboam I set up the worship of the calves in Samaria and Dan. "For she *would not* know" (not, "She did not know"; there was *no desire* to know) "that it was I (very emphatic)" who had given her *all* her material blessings, which she had attributed to the baalim and with which she endowed their shrines.

God would therefore withdraw Himself, and take away "in the time ... season thereof" the corn, and wine, suggesting that it would be done through famine; and He would "pluck away" (R.V.) from off His people the wool and flax, so leaving them naked and helpless under the gaze of her companions in idolatry. All her rejoicing ("mirth") would come to an end. Even the religious festivals supposedly in honour of Yahweh would cease: the three great feasts of the year, the observance of sabbaths and new moons, retained by Jeroboam for his own political ends. There would be no "joy and gladness" as was traditional at such times, because a great blight would come upon the land; the fruit trees would become a jungle and the wild beasts would roam there. So would apostate

100   *Hosea 2*

Israel be punished for all the festivals held in honour of the baalim, when she had burned incense to them, treated her prosperity as the "hire" she had received from her lovers, decked herself with ornaments in their honour; "she forgat me, saith Yahweh", thus affording us a warning insight into the process of apostasy, which rarely commences by deliberate disobedience, but is the result of "forgetting" some vital aspects of God's true worship.

"I will betroth thee unto me for ever" (2: 14–22)

vv. 14–17: The next section commences rather unexpectedly with the word "therefore" (cf. vv. 6, 9), conveying that the purpose of this chastisement is Israel's reformation. "I, even I, will allure her", expresses the intense desire of Yahweh for His people's salvation, and at the same time the difficulty of convincing a guilty conscience of the genuineness of His love. Israel is to be brought into the wilderness as after the Exodus; an allusion rather, however, to the 40 years during which God "humbled" and "proved" His people (Deut. 8: 2–6). The nation is to suffer the hardship of exile from its own land. But God would speak "*on* her heart" as though making an impression upon it ("on their heart will I write my laws", Heb. 8: 10, R.V.); and "from thence", that is on return from the chastisement of the exile, Israel would find "the valley of Achor", north of Jericho, no longer a valley of "troubling" (*achor*) as it was when Achan's sin (Josh. 7: 25–26) involved all the people in transgression, on their *first* entry into the land, but a door of hope. Israel should "make answer" (R.V.) again as she did on her deliverance from Egypt, by the Song of Moses and the people's profession, "All that the Lord hath spoken will we do" (Exod. 19 and 24). No longer would she use for the Lord the name "Baal", though that name seems to have been innocently used at first for God as Lord, to judge by some Israelitish names in the families of Saul and David, such as Meribbaal, Jerubaal, Ishbaal; indeed the words "ish" and "baal" were both used for "husband" in Hebrew, as witness 2 Sam. 11: 26, both applied to the same man, Urijah. Because of the corrupt associations of the "baalim" God would in future be to Israel only "Ishi", my husband. In this remarkable language the spiritual relationship of Christ and the body of his faithful (Eph. 5) is foreshadowed eight centuries before the days of the apostle Paul. Reformed Israel would never again go after idols, a feature often mentioned in prophetic passages dealing with restoration (Zech. 13: 2; Ezek. 36: 25; 37: 23).

vv. 18–23: The punishment of verse 12 is now to be reversed; the

Hosea 3   101

beasts of the field shall be at peace with Israel (cf. Isa. 11—"the wolf shall lie down with the lamb", etc.) and the land shall no more suffer under the warlike invader, nor shall its inhabitants need to make warlike preparations for their own defence, for they shall lie down like a flock secure. God will "betroth" Israel unto Himself. In the East the expression implies marriage; the verb form is applied only to the wooing of a maiden, not to the restoration of a wife divorced. In other words, the old union having been broken, this is an entirely new marriage. God's gifts to His bride will not only be material blessings, but "righteousness, justice, loving kindness, mercies, and faithfulness", all manifestations of Himself and the finest dowry He can provide. (For these fundamental terms in God's Old Testament revelation, see the series "The Knowledge of God", *The Christadelphian*, 1967.) And so the purged remnant (for it is only of a remnant that these things could be said, as we learn abundantly from the prophets), appreciating at last what these qualities mean, rejoicing in a righteousness with which God endows them, will truly "know" the Lord, instead of merely knowing *about* Him, understanding at last His love and acknowledging His holiness.

The result will be a great cycle of material blessings too, for as Israel cries unto the Lord, He will speak to the heavens, who will pour down their rain upon the earth, so that the plants spring up and produce the corn and the wine and the oil. Israel (Jezreel, God will sow) shall no longer be scattered (the first meaning of the word), but shall be *sown* unto God in the land (the first meaning of *ha-aretz*); with the revelations of the Gospel, ultimately the prophecy will involve the second meaning of the same word, the *earth*. The doom announced in the names of Hosea's children is to be reversed: the Not-Pitied is to obtain mercy and the Not-my-People is to be acknowledged as the people of God. As Paul shows in Rom. 10, the repentant Gentiles are included, but the conclusion reveals the essential basis, for this blessedness can only come when the people itself is ready to say: "Thou art my God".

"The children of Israel shall abide many days" (3: 1–5)

3: 1–3: By a swift return from the blessedness of the future to the hard realities of the present, Hosea receives a new command: "Go and love once more a woman beloved of her companion". There can be little question that it is Gomer who is meant; the term which is used for her ("woman" not "thy wife") suggests her degradation, for she is "an adulteress". The word translated "friend" could mean "husband" (in Jer. 3: 20 it is used of God

102   *Hosea 3*

Himself), but the parable behind the command seems to require the
idea of an illicit associate; for Hosea was being commanded to go
and seek to redeem Gomer by his love, while she was still an
adulteress, because that was what God was about to do with Israel.
God did not propose to wait for Israel to repent before expressing
His love, but would do it while she was still guilty. The nation was
still worshipping other gods with offerings of raisin cakes. Cakes
were frequently offered to idols (see Jer. 7: 18), the raisin content
being probably connected with thanksgiving for the *wine*, for
Canaan was pre-eminently the land of the grape.

But the love which Hosea was to show to his wife was to be
expressed through a discipline which aimed at her reformation.
First he redeemed her from a state of degradation by paying for her
what was evidently the price of a slave, 15 shekels in cash and 1½
homers of barley (the food of *animals*), or approximately 30 shekels
altogether (see Exod. 21: 32). He restored her to his home but not
to the full rights of a wife; she was not to be "for a man" (so the
Hebrew), not even "for her husband". She was to undergo a period
of seclusion and abstinence ("many days"), to give her opportunity
for repentance.

vv. 4–5: The parable is now explained. Israel also was to abide
"many days", deprived of her religious and royal institutions, with
neither king nor priest, but also without the idolatrous images and
teraphim. The prophecy can only refer to the long period of
banishment from their land which came to an end only in recent
times. A remarkable feature of their scattering has been the
faithfulness of Israel to their God after their fashion during all their
persecutions, and their freedom from the idolatry which had so
marred their national life in Palestine. Just the contrary might
confidently have been expected; surely a nation which had proved
so susceptible to the pagan worship of its neighbours while living in
their own land would prove even more so when they were scattered
among such pagan powers! Their refusal to worship "the gods of the
heathen" during the long centuries of their dispersion is a remarkable vindication of this prophecy.

But at the end of their period of discipline Israel would "turn
back" in heart toward Yahweh and acknowledge the rule of a new
David whom all the faithful expected to be "the son of David", the
Messiah. They would "come with trembling" to the Lord and His
goodness. Jeremiah 31: 12–14 suggests that the "goodness" referred
to is not an abstract moral quality, but a practical expression in the
form of wheat, wine and oil; so "my people shall be satisfied with
my goodness". This was to happen "in the latter days", the usual

Hosea 4 103

expression for the "day of the Lord", when He would make an end
of Israel's oppression by the nations and restore them to favour with
Himself. To the faithful the phrase meant the days of the Messiah;
and although they would have little idea in Hosea's time how far off
those days would be, they would realise that they could not come
until the period of exile and discipline was over.

2. MINGLED WARNING, JUDGEMENT AND ENTREATY (CHAP. 4–13)

It is very difficult to offer any satisfactory analysis of the second
part of Hosea's prophecy, since the passages move swiftly from
denunciation to reproach and appeal, and even sometimes to
consolation. It will be best therefore to accept the chapter divisions
as they stand, but in order to make this large section a little more
manageable the following subdivisions may serve as a general
guide:

    a. Israel's guilt (4–8): Priests (4); Leaders and people (5–6);
Israel's sins (7–8).
    b. Israel's doom; judgement inevitable and necessary (9–11).
    c. Past history of ingratitude (12–13).

The prophecy concludes with a remarkable final chapter which
we may call: Restoration after Chastisement (14).

Israel's Guilt (4–8)

4: 1: The "controversy" which God has with the seed of Israel, the
people of His covenant, is in fact an endeavour to *convict* their
consciences of wrong-doing. His charge against them is that there is
no "truth nor mercy, nor knowledge of God" among them. It is
dangerously easy for us to understand these terms in a superficial
sense, in harmony with modern thinking, as though truth were but
the opposite of error or falsehood, and mercy were just kindness.
They are in fact two of the most important themes of the Old
Testament, for they are qualities of God Himself. "Truth" is really
"unchangingness", and represents God's utter faithfulness to
Himself, that is He will never act out of harmony with His own
nature; then His faithfulness to His covenant people, whom He will
not abandon; and finally the faithfulness of that people to Him.
Mercy (*chesed,* a very important word) is that combination of
loyalty and love which God shows towards His people when He
redeems them (e.g. Exodus) and which His people should then show

104   *Hosea 4*

towards Him and towards one another (see Lev. 19) in gratitude for
the redemption they have received.

The recognition of all this by His people is what is meant by
their "knowledge of God"; not just an acquaintance with the
historical facts of this revelation, but an acknowledgement of
Yahweh in His personal qualities, and the working out of the
response to them in their lives. There can be no true "knowledge of
God" without first a reverent acceptance of what He has revealed
about Himself and His will, an appreciation of His truly Divine
qualities (He is a personal God, not an abstraction), a humble
submission to what He requires, and an endeavour to live in the
very spirit of His word. These conditions apply as much to us today
as they did to Israel in the days of the prophets. They reveal how
inadequate is both that knowledge which is "of the word" only, and
that which is based on feelings without instruction. (For fuller
treatment, see series "The Knowledge of God", *The Christadelphian,* 1967.)

vv. 2–3: When men turn away from this knowledge of God, they
develop a "reprobate mind" (Rom. 1), that is one incapable of
distinguishing between good and evil. In Israel their deeds were
gross; swearing profanely by the name of God, robbery, murder and
adultery. Since man was given dominion over the earth and the
creatures which dwell in it, when he turns to sin the animal creation
shares in the inevitable suffering.

vv. 4–10: Verse 4 is difficult. The text suggests that Israel were
rejecting the counsel of faithful priests, such as "keep knowledge"
(Mal. 2: 7) and were therefore condemned as those who "pre-
sumptuously" disobey (Deut. 17: 12–13). The passage, however, is
a denunciation of false priests. By a small alteration of punctuation
the R.S.V. renders: "Yet let no one contend ... for with you is my
contention, O priests!", which at least fits the context very well.
Priests, prophets (that is the false prophets) and people are to
perish together. The people perish because the priests have not
instructed them in the knowledge of God, which it was their solemn
duty to do; that knowledge is summarised as "the law of thy God"
(note the assumption by Hosea that it existed and could be known
by the people). The priesthood had increased in numbers (they were
recruited on the hereditary principle) and no doubt wealth; they
"feed on the sin of my people" (R.V.), by devouring their
sin-offerings as Leviticus 6: 26 entitled them to do, yet spiritually
sharing their sins. The extent of their evil is expressed by the vivid
literal sense: "to their iniquity they lift up their soul". They have
turned the glory of God—the instruments of His worship and

Hosea 4   105

especially the knowledge of His will expressed in the Ten Commandments—into shame. As the people are to perish, so shall the priest (despite his privilege). They are to eat of the fruit of their own way, being afflicted with famine and barrenness; and this because they no longer "wait upon" the Lord, enquiring what is His will.

vv. 11–14: As a result the people have lost all power of discernment, being drunk both with wine and with idolatry (when men fall under the power of their own sensual self-indulgence, their spiritual judgement and power are destroyed). They turn constantly to their images of wood instead of remaining under their God, as a wife is "under" her husband (Num. 5: 29). They preferred to offer sacrifices and burn incense on hill tops and under sacred trees, where the daughters and daughters-in-law (as the word rendered "spouses" means) prostituted themselves in licentious ceremonies in common with the Canaanite *kedeshoth,* profligates attached to the shrines. For punishment God would bring upon them the worst fate of all: He would abandon them to their fate, instead of bringing chastisement with a view to their reformation. (Cf. Hebrews 12: if men do not come under the chastening of God, then they remain "bastards, not sons".) Because they do not "understand" (the "knowledge of God" again) the people shall perish.

vv. 15–19: A warning is now issued to Judah, who still had the temple worship and some faithful priests and a knowledge of the law, not to resort to the idols of Gilgal or Beth-Aven (perversion of Beth-El, House of Worthlessness for House of God). The accusation that some were sinning in swearing "The Lord liveth", may be explained by Amos 5: 5, where Beer-Sheba (the well of the *Oath*) is associated with Gilgal and Bethel. Since Israel has behaved "stubbornly, as a stubborn heifer" (the word is used in Deuteronomy 21: 18 for the "*incorrigible* son"), how can God feed them as a lamb in a broad meadow? (The sense seems to require that this last phrase be taken as a question.) Since Ephraim (a favourite word with Hosea for North Israel) is "joined to idols", as a wife becomes the companion of her husband (the related word is used in Malachi 2: 14, "she is thy *companion* and the wife of thy covenant"), he shall be abandoned by God. The Hebrew of verse 18 is said to be obscure. It can be rendered: "Their carouse is over; they give themselves up to whoredom; their rulers (lit. "shields", that is the princes, priests and prophets) dearly love shame"; so a storm shall envelop Israel in its wings, a figure of which Zechariah 5: 8–9, the two women with "wind in their wings" and associated with "wickedness", may be an echo. The wind will sweep Israel

106   *Hosea 4*

away to exile, and there they will be put to shame because of their
idolatrous sacrifices.

5: 1–7: The whole community, priests, nation and rulers, are now
warned that they are to be judged who were accustomed to be
judges. Mizpah, the scene of the covenant between Jacob and
Laban when God protected His elect (Gen. 31: 23–49), was "the
mountain of Gilead", east of Jordan; Tabor, similarly a mountain,
rose out of the plain of Esdraelon. Both were probably centres of
idolatrous worship. The Hebrew of verse 2, called by one com-
mentator "an impossible combination of words", by the substitution
of one letter 't' for another produces the R.S.V. allusion to Shittim,
where Baal-Peor was worshipped. The series of allusions then
becomes: "a *snare* (at Mizpah), a *net* (spread upon Tabor)" and "a
pit" (in Shittim), all common means of catching wild beasts. Israel
had been ensnared in their idolatry, with which these places were no
doubt associated. But God Himself is their rebuke: "I, even I, know
Ephraim ..." and see that the nation is defiled like an adulteress,
so that their deeds will not *permit* them to turn to God; their
idolatry has so taken possession of their minds that they no longer
know Yahweh. Israel's pride, his "arrogance", consisting of his
sense of his own sufficiency with no need for repentance, based
upon trust in a ceremonial which he considered God-given, was an
open witness against him.

So Ephraim should fall, and (the first of a number of allusions in
this chapter and the next) Judah shall fall as well. Seeking Yahweh
with many sacrifices, they will not find Him, because He has
withdrawn from them. This significant verse shows that the
Israelites were still bringing offerings with the intention of serving
God, but "they have played false" with God ("as a wife
treacherously departeth from her husband", Jer. 3: 20); their
children are "strange", either because those of mixed marriages or
because the children worship strange gods; their idolatrous worship
at "the new moon" (see R.V.) would bring about the destruction
both of themselves and of their inheritance in the land (portions).

Note 11: THE PRIDE OF EPHRAIM
     The choice in the prophets of "Ephraim" to represent all the
tribes of the Northern Kingdom of Israel (as distinct from Judah)
arose from circumstances rooted deep in the history of God's
people. When the men of war were numbered in the wilderness, the
total of Ephraim and Manasseh (Joseph) combined was almost
equal to that of Judah, and when the people were encamped, the

Hosea 5   107

"standard of the camp of Ephraim" (comprising Manasseh and
Benjamin) was placed on the west, directly counterbalancing the
camp of Judah on the East. When Israel occupied the land of
Canaan, the tabernacle was at Shiloh in Ephraim, and the first
great prophetic leader, Samuel, was an Ephraimite. Thus Ephraim
acquired among the tribes a leadership which was sharply chal-
lenged when God deliberately chose David of Judah as king, a
choice which Ephraim with the other ten tribes resisted for seven
years, although they must have known that Samuel had anointed
David by command of God. The removal of the ark of God to Zion
instead of its restoration to Shiloh was another blow to Ephraim's
privileged position in worship. The "men of Israel" who willingly
followed Absalom's flattery and supported his revolt against David
must have had considerable support from Ephraim, and their sharp
contention with the "men of Judah", even at the moment of David's
restoration to his throne, indicated the rivalry always simmering
beneath the surface. When therefore Jeroboam revolted against
Rehoboam and set up a separate kingdom for the Northern tribes,
Ephraim accepted his rule and his false system of worship, knowing
full well that it was contrary to the law of God. The prophetic
choice of Ephraim to represent the rejection of God's will and
worship was therefore clearly significant.

vv. 8–15: The cornet, a curved horn, and the straight trumpet of
metal, both used at times of foreign invasion (8: 1; Jer. 4: 5; 6: 1),
were to be sounded as a war alarm in Gibeah, Ramah and Bethel,
all hill towns, the first two just inside Judah, the last near the
border. Benjamin is warned that the enemy is upon him. Evidently
the enemy has invaded Israel and now threatens Judah itself.
Though it is Ephraim who is desolate, *all* the tribes (including
Judah) shall experience God's judgement. Israel's princes have
removed the landmarks between God and idolatrous Baal. If under
the law a man removing his neighbour's landmark was condemned,
how much more those who remove the landmarks of God! So Judah
too shall suffer the utmost judgement of God, like a flood of water.
If Israel is as a result to be oppressed and crushed (by foreign
invaders), it is because they have been determined to obey the
command of Jeroboam to worship the calves.

Rottenness shall be at the heart of both kingdoms, for they have
both sought to save themselves by appealing to "King Jareb" (a
symbolic name for "an avenging King", or, as some pointing the
Hebrew word differently read, "the Great King"). The allusion
must be to the action of Menahem who sent a tribute to Assyria in
738 B.C., seeking to establish himself upon a throne which he had

108   *Hosea 5*

murderously usurped (2 Kings 15: 19); and to that of Ahaz, who did likewise a little later, seeking to deliver himself from the combined aggression of Pekah and Rezin king of Syria (16: 7–8). But the "sickness" and "sore" (both kingdoms were diseased) of Israel and Judah could not be cured by recourse to Assyria; for that power would be the destroying lion by which God would carry out His judgement upon them, without possibility of rescue. (For Yahweh as a lion, see 13: 7.) God will withdraw from His people, abandon them, so that they may be led to "acknowledge their offence" and so return to Him. Affliction will break their hard-heart (as prosperity never does) and soon they will repent.

6: 1–3: In these three verses, echoing the thought that Israel will "seek God's face", the prophet passes from judgement to restoration. Commentators who cannot believe in Biblical prophecy are forced to interpret them as insincere repentance. A 19th-century bishop like Pusey, who did not believe in the literal restoration of the Jews in any form, interprets them of the Christian Church. But as prophetic of the repentance of the remnant of natural Israel in days yet to come, they are consistent with other passages in the prophets. Their note is too genuine for an assumed sincerity.

First there is the acknowledgment that their chastisement had come from God, and then an expression of faith that He would heal also. No doubt the contemporaries of Hosea, especially the faithful remnant, looked for relief to follow quickly after repentance: in a short period expressed by "after two days ... in the third day". But by the Spirit of God the prophet has been led to use an expression which is remarkably apt of the resurrection of Christ on the third "day", and of the nation itself in the third millennium. The repentant faithful believed that God would "revive" or "quicken" the nation and "raise them up", both expressions being used for resurrection from the dead ("Thou shalt *quicken* me again and bring me up from the depths of the earth", Psa. 71: 20; "Thy dead men shall live; together with my dead body shall they *arise*", Isa. 26: 14, 19). The language aptly conveys the combination of national and spiritual resurrection, expressed by: "and we shall live *before His face*" (God had said they would seek His face, 5: 15) as faithful Abraham walked before God's face, conscious of His presence. Their former lack of the "knowledge of God" is to be remedied by their determination to "press on to know" Him; as a result the blessing of God would be as sure as the coming of dawn, and as refreshing as the October rain at seed-time and the spring rain to fill out the crops. To the faithful Israelite, grieved in soul for the

Hosea 6   109

iniquity of his people, this brief passage must have been as encouraging and refreshing as the rain itself.

vv. 4–6: With a note of infinite tenderness—"O Ephraim ... O Judah, what shall I do unto thee?"—God appeals to both kingdoms asking what He could righteously do to them, except chastise them; for their "goodness" (*chesed*, loyal love of God, see note at 4: 1, "Judgement and Mercy") had been as shortlived as a morning cloud, dissipated by the warmth of the rising sun, and as the early dew. They had soon begun to forsake Yahweh, so the words of His prophets had hewn them and slain them ("My word is like a fire ... a hammer that breaketh", Jer. 23: 29; "like a sword ... piercing soul and spirit", Heb. 4: 12) and His judgement upon them would go forth like the lightning. For God had desired mercy (*chesed* again) and the knowledge of Him and not just a service represented by the offering of sacrifices, like Saul who had thought that a great offering could compensate for a lack of obedience.

Hosea, of course, could not possibly have been saying that sacrifices were not required, as many critics, intent upon their theory of religious "development" from "ceremonial" to "ethical worship", wish to make him say. God Himself, who required the sacrifices after the Fall and from the beginning of Israel's covenant, never points a contrast between mercy and sacrifice but requires *both*; for the act of sacrifice represented the open acknowledgment of a duty towards God, and "mercy" was that duty expressed towards one's fellows. But when the Jews abandoned God in their hearts, their sacrifices, though according to the law, became unavailing and were often rejected by God (see Isa. 1: 11–13; Jer. 7: 22–23; Psa. 50: 8, 14, 16). Christ twice quoted this saying: "I will have mercy and not sacrifice", in each case to show that a scrupulous keeping of the law could not atone for a lack of mercy, truly based upon worship of God.

vv. 7–11: Like Adam (R.V.) Israel had proved false to her covenant with God. Gilead—the region used for the people—is stained with blood, as is Shechem where companies of priests lie in wait to commit the enormities of robbery and murder. Shechem (read in the R.V. as a place name for "by consent") was on the road from Galilee to Jerusalem; the allusion could be to the murder of worshippers going South to the temple by the priests of the calf sanctuaries. The whole aspect of Israel, in her idolatry and her corrupt violence, is "an horrible thing", calculated to make one shudder. The last verse of the chapter abruptly promises to Judah a harvest, apparently of joy, when the people should return from captivity, that is from Babylon. Since in this chapter the previous

110   *Hosea 6*

allusions to Judah have been for judgement, and the few subsequent
uses of "harvest" by Hosea are for punishment and not for reward,
some prefer to take the last phrase, "When I return the captivity of
my people" with the next verse. As applied to Israel (Northern)
however the phrase seems unsuitable; it is better to take verse 11
therefore as referring to the restoration of Judah from captivity and
to the harvest of the faithful (see R.V.).

7: **1-7**: God had made repeated efforts to "heal" Israel, through
the words of the prophets and His judgements upon them; the
result was not their repentance but the exposure of their iniquity:
lying, thieving, and armed robbery abroad in the land. Israel say to
themselves that God will take no action, but He sees them as
hemmed in by their own evil deeds, which He cannot overlook (cf.
the apostle's "close-girding sin", Heb. 12: 1).

The figure in the next five verses is taken from the actions of a
baker: the leaders of the people find the king and princes ready
accomplices in their evil designs, but as a baker heats his oven and
then waits till the bread be risen before putting it to bake, so the
princes of the nation conspire against the king by first making him
drunk ("make him sick with the heat of wine", v. 5, R.V.m.); then
when he is in convivial mood, in good fellowship with the mockers,
they bide their time (as the baker waits for the bread to rise) until
they can murder him. For all these princes have destroyed their
judges and got rid of their kings; in their lawlessness none of them
thinks of God. The allusion must be to the state of anarchy which
succeeded the reign of Jeroboam II. Omri's dynasty had lasted to
his grandson, Jehu's to the fourth generation; all the other kings of
Israel either had no sons themselves or left them the throne, only
for them to be slain. Nadab, Elah, Zimri, Tibni, Jehoram,
Zechariah, Shallum, Pekahiah, Pekah, were all murdered by their
successors. When the captivity arrived, it represented the tenth
change of régime since the division of the kingdom. In the light of
these facts the language of the prophets about their own nation
becomes vivid indeed.

vv. 8-16: The remainder of the chapter deals largely with Israel's
reliance upon foreign nations instead of upon their God. Instead of
preserving his separateness, as a people "not numbered among the
nations" (Num. 23: 9), Ephraim had "mixed himself among the
peoples" and naturally as a result had "learned their works" (Psa.
106: 34–5); he was like a cake (a thin pancake) baked on one side
only, neither a good servant of Yahweh nor of the baals, "halting
between two opinions" as in Elijah's day. Foreigners were sapping

Hosea 8 111

his strength by their demands for tribute. Ephraim's pride convicted him openly—he acknowledged no sin or need of repentance—yet he did not return to God. He was like the simple dove quite lacking in understanding, in his reliance upon Assyria or Egypt. But wherever they went in their faithless ways, God would pursue Israel and bring chastisement upon them, as had been declared to "the congregation of Israel" centuries before through Moses, when they had been so graphically warned of the dire consequences of disobedience (Deut. 28; Lev. 26). Their fate can only be woe and destruction, for their deliberate transgressions; though God on His part (very emphatic) had *continually* redeemed them and would fain do so again, they on theirs had only spoken lies against Him. Examples of these "lies" are to be found in Jeroboam's assertion about the calves: "These be thy gods which brought thee out of the land of Egypt"; Israel's assertion that it was the baals who gave them their corn and wine; and their conviction that God would not judge them because they were His covenant people. In other words they took away His honour and denied His righteousness.

When they lamented because of affliction, it was not for true repentance but only the "howling" of impatient, unconcerted suffering; their tumultuous assembling "for corn and wine" (an obscure phrase which may imply a demand for food and drink in time of famine or may refer to some idolatrous ceremonies) was just rebellion against God. Though it was God who had "instructed" (as "bound" means) and strengthened their arms, yet *they* (emphatic contrast) devise evil against Him. "Men would willingly dethrone God if they could, and since they cannot dethrone Him in the world, they do so in their own hearts" (Pusey). Israel's conversions are hypocritical, like a bow that cannot be relied upon. Because of the provocation of their tongue (the word is everywhere else used of the wrath of God; the idea is that their words provoke His wrath) their rulers shall fall by the sword and Egypt, in whom they trusted, would have them in derision.

8: 1-6: The warning trumpet is again to be blown, for the Assyrian vulture (a bird of prey often found on the monuments) is to come against the "house of the Lord", that is the people ("My servant Moses is faithful in all mine house", Num. 12: 7), not the temple. Israel cry to God: "We, Israel, know thee", thus claiming protection ("This people draweth nigh unto me with their mouth ... but their heart is far from me", Isa. 29: 13; and Jesus: "Many shall say unto me in that day, Lord, have we not prophesied in thy name ...", Matt. 7: 22). But they have transgressed His law, rejected His goodness, and shall be pursued by the enemy. From the

112   *Hosea 8*

days of Jeroboam they had ceased to consult God about the choice
of kings or princes, so that government had become a matter of
politics and not faith. God had neither commanded nor sanctioned
their 18 kings from 10 different families during their 250 years'
history. Their wealth they had used to make idols to their own
destruction. As Israel had "abhorred" the good (v. 3), so God
"abhorred" their calf of Samaria (see R.V.; "Samaria" for the
kingdom and "calf" for the worship); for His anger was hot against
them. How long would it be ere they would learn to "endure" the
pure worship prescribed in the Law? Their idol was actually made
by a workman in their own country! How could they be so senseless
as to regard it as a god? But the "calf of Samaria" was to be
"splintered" (suggesting it was a wooden image overlaid with gold).

vv. 7–14: The people have sown wind, that is vanity or nothingness,
but they shall reap a whirlwind (in the form of the foreign invader).
There shall be no standing corn. Here again is a play upon the
sound of words in the Hebrew: "The *tsemach* yields no *kemach*",
"the flower yields no flour" (*Speaker's Commentary);* and even if it
does, it will be devoured by the enemy. The Gentiles are to swallow
up Israel (not to destroy him, be it noted), but among them the
people will be like a vessel put to the basest use, fit only to be
broken in pieces. Dispersed Israel has followed the most despised
trades in their exile, and are said to have been regarded by the
Romans as offensive to the smell. Instead of "going up" to
Jerusalem, they prefer to "go up" to Assyria, like a wild ass, an
animal which had the reputation of being headstrong, unruly,
indisciplined, going his own way (Ishmael was a "wild ass man",
Gen. 16: 12). Israel had hired "lovers" by paying tribute, but God
will gather the nations hired by them. The R.V. of verse 10 reads:
"They begin to be minished by reason of the burden of the king of
princes", that is the king of Assyria, who boasted that all his
princes were kings (Isa. 10: 8).

Ephraim, who had transgressed the explicit command of the law
and multiplied altars, would find they were a cause of sin. God had
revealed the multitudinous things of His law, not only in the Ten
Commandments, but in the innumerable utterances of the prophets
since (note the implied existence among Israel of the detailed
knowledge of God), yet His people treated them as coming from a
stranger. The unacceptable sacrifices which Israel multiplied upon
God's altar were just "flesh", fit to be eaten like any other meal,
but no sanctified offering. For their sins they should "return to
Egypt", that is, go back into the condition of bondage from which
God had redeemed them in the first place. As Moses had sung

Hosea 9 113

prophetically: "Then he forsook God which made him and lightly esteemed the Rock of his salvation" (Deut. 32: 15), Israel now had forgotten his Maker and begun building palaces; even Judah had built fortified cities (an allusion to the work of Azariah, 2 Chron. 26: 10, about this time or a little earlier), trusting in *them* for safety. But both cities and palaces should be devoured by fire. Sargon at Samaria in 722 B.C., and Nebuchadnezzar at Jerusalem in 588, were to show that the word of the Lord was sure.

Israel's Doom (9: 1—11: 11)

The following two chapters deal largely with the particular judgements which are to come upon Israel because of their iniquity.

9: 1-6: At a time of general rejoicing, probably on the occasion of some religious festival such as a harvest, Israel are bidden not to exult like other nations, for they have loved "the hire of a whore" (*ethan*. See Deut. 23: 18; 10 times in Old Testament, always in this sense). The cornfloor had been the scene of their idolatry; either because the corn was regarded as a reward for serving Baal, or because it was associated with corrupt rites. But the corn and the wine they exulted in should not last, for "the new wine shall lie to her" as Israel had lied to their God. God had resolved they should no longer dwell in *His* land (the expression is noteworthy; cf. "the land is mine; for ye are strangers and sojourners with me", Lev. 25: 23). It is highly likely that some individual Israelites had already sought refuge in Egypt, or soon would do so, and the allusion here may be to such. But in view of 11: 5 ("He shall not return into the land of Egypt") it seems better to take the phrase symbolically here, signifying a return to *bondage*, for the literal deportation was to be to Assyrian territory, where they would eat "defiled" bread, because in a land defiled by the worship of idols (cf. Ezekiel 4: 13—"Israel shall eat their defiled bread among the Gentiles"). So "Egypt" takes on a symbolic sense, an anticipation of its use in the New Testament, cf. Rev. 11: 8.

Under the law drink offerings were to accompany all burnt and peace offerings and all feasts; because of the famine they would not be offered, and their very bread would seem like that consumed at a funeral. It could be used only as food for their natural lives, with no thought of offering it to God, because, being the food of a pagan land, it would be polluted. When they found themselves in exile, what would they do *then* to celebrate the festivals, such as the feast of tabernacles, that universal expression of joy and gladness? Those who flee to Egypt "because of the spoil" (the Assyrian)—no doubt

114   *Hosea 9*

some prominent members of the nation—would be "buried" by
Memphis, the celebrated seat of idolatry, the worship of Apis, the
original of Jeroboam's calf, and a vast burial place. Their dwellings
with their treasures should be invaded by thorns and nettles.

vv. 7–9: Israel have sought the false prophet and "the man that hath
the spirit" (v. 7, R.V.; cf. Micah 2: 11, "a man walking in the spirit
and falsehood" who lies; and 1 Kings 22: 22, "a lying spirit"). They
shall realise that the day of reckoning has come. The meaning of
verse 8 is obscure, but probably Hosea is identifying himself with
the "watchman of Ephraim" (see R.S.V.), and the translation:
"even the prophet, on all whose ways is the fowler's snare, even
rancour in the house of his God" (*Speaker's Commentary*) conveys
the unhappy lot of a faithful witness for God in the midst of a
faithless nation, who resented his rebukes. The present corruptions
of the nation are like that scandalous action of the dissolute
Benjamites, sons of Belial, who outraged the concubine of the
Levite (Judges 19) at Gibeah (one more example of an indirect
allusion to their past history); such iniquity can only bring God's
judgement upon them.

vv. 10–14: The fathers of Israel, Abraham, Isaac and Jacob, had
been as refreshing to God as grapes in the wilderness (see Deut.
32: 10) and as the early figs, renowned for their sweetness; but
Israel, for *their* part, instead of separating themselves *unto* God like
the Nazarites, devoted themselves to the shameful idolatry of
Baal-Peor and became as abominable as their idol. "The shame" is
bosheth, substituted for *baal* (Lord, master) in e.g. 2 Sam. 11: 21,
Jerubesheth for Jerubbaal, Judges 6: 32. (Note the second inciden-
tal allusion to Israel's earlier history within two verses.) Ephraim
the Fruitful shall become barren, and even when their children
survive, they shall be bereaved, because God has left them (as
Moses had warned them centuries before: "Ye shall be left few in
number", Deut. 28: 58, 62).

   Although verse 13 is obscure, the general sense seems to be that
"Ephraim was like unto Tyrus in her prosperity and security" (most
Jewish commentators)—Tyre's wealth and safe position on her
island off the mainland were celebrated—yet her children should be
slain. Of verse 14 there are two contradictory interpretations: the
first, that Hosea, in his pity for Israel, considers that since the
children are only to be slain, the greatest blessing Israel could
receive would be not to have any, so he prays therefore that they
may be barren; the second, that the prophet is so indignant at the
enormity of the corruption, that he prays for their barrenness as a
Divine judgement. The commentators who see Hosea chiefly as a

Hosea 10

prophet of mercy tend to favour the first interpretation, but it must be admitted that the second, stern as it is, better suits the context, which is one of unrelieved condemnation. In any case it must be borne in mind that in the ancient world failure to bear children was a disgrace and a calamity.

vv. 15–17: Verse 15 provides still another allusion to Israel's past history, for it was in Gilgal that they first gravely departed from God in desiring a king "like all the nations", and where He showed His displeasure at their "great wickedness" in the thunder (1 Sam. 12: 18). Other allusions to God's disapproval of their desire for a king are found in Hosea 8: 4; 13: 10–11. Gilgal had evidently now become a notorious centre of idolatry. Her princes were rebellious (there is a play upon words here also: their *sareyhem* are *sorim*, "all their rulers are revolters"); so they should be driven out of God's house like a child "not loved", no longer acknowledged as lawful offspring (contrast 11: 1—"When Israel was a child, then I loved him, and called my son out of Egypt"). Smitten with barrenness, Ephraim should be cast away by God (who never forsakes unless He is Himself first irrevocably forsaken) and His people would become "wanderers among the nations", fugitives and vagabonds in the earth like Cain, according to the warning given them through Moses 600 years earlier: "I will scatter thee among all people ... there thou shalt find no ease" (Deut. 28: 64–5). "Wanderers among the nations": this wonderful prophecy, delivered nearly 800 years before Christ, must not be allowed through familiarity to lose its unique power; for of what *other* nation has it ever been said, and of what other nation has it ever proved so true?

10: **1–8:** Israel, that "vine out of Egypt" (Psa. 80: 6–11) brought forth fruit luxuriantly (not "empty" as A.V.); but ascribing his prosperity to the baals, he multiplied idolatrous altars and pillars. Because their heart is "smooth" (cf. Ezek. 12: 24, "smooth (i.e. deceitful) prophesying"), they shall bear their punishment. God will break the necks of their altars (like the neck of an animal, perhaps a reference to calves' heads carved on the corners of the altars) and shatter their pillars. The time would come when they would realise that they had no king because they had abandoned God; and in any case, under the hand of the Assyrians, what use would a king be? They utter empty words of falsehood when they make agreements (instead of being faithful), and their "right" (*mishpat*, judgement, justice) springs up out of the soil like a poisonous weed, and *that* from cultivated furrows. The inhabitants of Samaria shall be afraid for the calves of Bethel, that

116   *Hosea 10*

House of Nought; Hosea uses a feminine form, cow-calves, probably in derision for there are no goddesses in God's revelation, only in idolatrous cults; the worshippers shall lament because of *it* (*masculine,* standing for "the idol"), as shall the *Chemarim,* a class of idol priests (2 Kings 23: 5; Zeph. 1: 4). The idol shall be taken to Assyria as a present to the Great King (see note on 5: 13). Although there is no historical record, there is no reason why the Assyrians, who boasted of the supremacy of their gods over the gods of the nations, should not have taken one of the calves to Nineveh. Israel would then share the shame of the idol, of whom they had asked counsel; and Samaria's king shall be cut off and carried away like twigs upon the surface of the water (for shoots "cut off", see note on Amos 8: 2). When destruction comes upon Israel's sin and its high places, then the thorn and the thistle shall overgrow their altars, as the ground was cursed for Adam's transgression. Only in Genesis 3: 18 is this combination of "thorn and thistle" found, and in the similar context of a curse: Hosea's familiarity with Genesis is evident. When these calamities come upon them, Israel shall desire death to put an end to their sufferings, in words—"They shall say to the mountains, Cover us; and to the hills, Fall upon us"—which were repeated by Jesus in Luke 23: 30, and in Revelation 6: 16; 9: 6, having evidently become proverbial.

vv. 9–10: That the shocking treatment of the Levite's concubine by the Benjamites in Gibeah was a significant episode in the nation's religious development is shown by the last verse of Judges 19: "All that saw it said, There was no such deed done nor seen from the day that the children of Israel came out of the land of Egypt unto this day." The suggested translation of the second part of verse 9: "There have they stood; shall not there overtake them dwelling in Gibeah the war against the children of crime?" (*Speaker's Commentary* and others), suggests that the Israelites have since pursued the same way of evil, and as the rest of the tribes banded together against Benjamin to punish the foul deed, so the same fate will befall Ephraim. Gibeah here takes on a "spiritual" sense, as does Egypt (see 9: 6), and Sodom and Gomorrah in Isaiah 1. Unrepentant as they are, they must be chastised by God, who will send the nations against them. The allusion to "furrows" is obscure. It has been pointed out, however, that the word occurs only here and in Exodus 21: 10, where it is rendered "duty of marriage". The idea would therefore be that Israel have bound themselves to two different husbands, Yahweh and Baal, an impossible situation.

vv. 11–15: Ephraim is now compared in her earlier years to a heifer

Hosea 11

broken in and delighting in the easy task of "treading out the corn", when according to the law the animal was not muzzled and could feed as it pleased. But God would now "assault the beauty of her neck" by putting a heavy yoke upon it; a rider would be set upon Ephraim, and Judah too; in fact the whole house of Jacob, should do the hard labour of ploughing (Jer. 31: 18 records Ephraim "bemoaning himself ... I was chastised as a bullock unaccustomed to the yoke", but now suffering the discipline of exile). Then follows an earnest appeal to Israel by Hosea to sow rightdoing in obedience to God's law and to reap the *chesed* (kindness, love and faithful mercy), which He would then show to them and they to one another. At present their ground is fallow, but there is *yet* time to seek the Lord, who would send the rain of His righteousness to bless their efforts. The word rendered rain frequently means to teach, so R.V. "teach you righteousness". The spirit of Hosea's plea to Israel in this verse is rather like that of Joel, "Who knoweth if (God) will turn and repent and leave a blessing behind him?" But Israel, trusting in their "own way" and strength, instead of God's, had ploughed wickedness and reaped iniquity and "the fruit of lies", an allusion to the worship of the "lies" of the nations, their idols.

A tumult (the word is habitually used of the confused noise of war) shall arise among Israel's "peoples" (the word used chiefly in the Pentateuch for the "tribes", Lev. 21: 4, 14; Deut. 33: 3) when their fortified cities are destroyed. The allusion to Shalman and Beth-Arbel is obscure, as no historical incident is known. It seems almost certain that Shalman must be an abbreviation of the Assyrian Shalmanezer and prophetic of the king who would bring about the fall of the Northern Kingdom (2 Kings 17: 3, 6). Beth-Arbel is hardly likely to be Arbela on the Tigris; perhaps more likely Arbela in Upper Galilee, mentioned in 1 Macc. 9: 2 and frequently in Josephus. But history is silent and we must confess our ignorance. One thing however seems clear: no forger would ever have bothered to insert so obscure an allusion! Whatever was the fate of *Beth-Arbel,* a similar destruction would come upon Israel, because of their devotion to the calves of Bethel; their king would be cut off just when least expected, early in the morning when the dangers of the night were thought to be over.

11: 1-7: The eleventh chapter forms a moving section of the prophecy, for in it God is pictured as a Father tenderly caring for Israel as His infant son, and though receiving nothing but rejection, determined that His love shall not ultimately be frustrated when correction has done its work.

The figure of Israel as the "son" of God is found in Exodus

118   *Hosea 11*

4: 22–3—"Israel is my son, even my first born. Let my son go ...";
and again in Jeremiah 31: 20—"Is Ephraim my dear son?" The
great deliverance from Egypt was to be seen by the nation,
therefore, as the expression of the love of a father. But as Moses
and the prophets appealed to the people, so Israel turned away after
the baalim. Yet it was Yahweh who had taught Israel to walk,
holding him by the arm and healing him when he fell, full of pity
for one helpless. (Cf. Moses, "In the wilderness thou hast seen how
that the Lord thy God bare thee, as a man doth bear his son ...",
Deut. 1: 31.) By a change of figure, God now says that though
Ephraim struggled against Him like a stubborn heifer, He drew
him with ropes not as if he were a beast but a *man,* with "cords of
love"; He eased the yoke off his jaws and put food before him.

But Israel desires only to find safety in Egypt (by intriguing with
King So in the days of the last king, Hosea); their efforts will fail
and they will become subject to the king of Assyria. Their cities
with their strong bars shall be consumed by war, because of Israel's
reliance upon such political counsels. They are so bent upon
deserting God that even the appeals of the prophets to return to the
Most High had no effect.

vv. 8–12: Then follows one of the most moving Divine appeals in all
the prophets: "How shall I give thee up, Ephraim? how shall I
deliver (surrender) thee, Israel?" By a strong expression God
conveys His yearning desire for Israel's salvation: "my strong
compassions are kindled". The verb is the same as in Genesis
43: 30: Joseph's "bowels did yearn over his brother" Benjamin; and
1 Kings 3: 26, where, in the test before Solomon, the real mother's
"bowels yearned upon her son". So God will not utterly exterminate
Israel as He had done the iniquitous cities of the plain, Admah and
Zeboim (Deut. 29: 23). Why are the lesser known Admah and
Zeboim preferred here to the notorious Sodom and Gomorrha?
Probably because this is an expression of mercy, not of judgement.
God is not a mere man to enter into a covenant and then go back on
it. His Holy Name had been proclaimed and His sanctuary set up
in the midst of Israel; He will not come among them as He had
entered into the city of Sodom, utterly to destroy.

For when chastisement has done its work, God will intervene for
them, roaring like a lion (familiar figure of Joel and Amos) as He
judges the nations; then His people (or the remnant of them, as we
know it must be) shall "go after" Him (cf. Isa. 52: 12—"The Lord
shall go *before* you and be your rereward", an allusion to the pillar
of cloud between them and the Egyptians at the crossing of the Red
Sea); when the distant ones hear His roaring, those who are really

Hosea 11   119

"sons" shall come trembling from the west ("the islands of the sea", Isa 11: 11), that is the Mediterranean; they shall come trembling and swiftly as a bird from Egypt and Assyria, to be settled, caused to dwell, in their houses. The passage is a remarkable prophecy of the restoration of Israel from the West, the South, and the North (the East was not a significant direction because of the desert), to be fulfilled in the latter days, on a scale which Hosea and his contemporaries could not possibly have foreseen.

"I am the Lord thy God from the land of Egypt" (11: 12—13: 16)

11: 12—12: 6: Although Israel multiplied lies in their service to God, Judah still honours God (El) and is faithful to the Holy One (lit. "holy ones": cf. Prov. 9: 10, where the parallel to "Yahweh" is the "holy ones"; Prov. 30: 3, where to "learn wisdom" is parallel to having "knowledge of the holy ones"). The contrast in favour of Judah is paralleled in Hosea 1: 7 and 4: 15, its basis being the possession of a Davidic king, Levitical priests, and temple worship, and *some* rulers who were faithful, as Hezekiah and Josiah were to prove to be. Ephraim however is merely pursuing the destroying East wind. His "lies", expressed in his seeking help from the Assyrians and offering his choicest product, oil, to the Egyptians, will bring desolation as a punishment; even with Judah God will have to contend; in fact *all* twelve tribes (Jacob) will have to be rewarded according to their ways.

The name Jacob recalls episodes in the life of that patriarch. At his birth he "supplanted" his brother Esau—the symbol was of God; by his faith, working powerfully in him, he prevailed in his wrestling with the angel of God at Bethel; so anxious was he to receive the blessing he sought, that he wept in supplication, knowing the distress of his natural situation in the face of his powerful brother. It was at Bethel that God thus made Himself known to Jacob, and through him spoke to *us*, who are his seed, first in the vision of the angels upon the ladder when he fled to Padan-Aram, then again on his return; and the God who so revealed Himself was Yahweh, who gave His name as an everlasting memorial to Israel. You, Israel, do as Jacob did; obey the law of God which has been declared to you, practise loyal love and justice *(chesed, mishpat)* one to another, and hope on Him continually for your salvation (cf. Micah 6: 8—"... do justly, love mercy, and walk humbly with thy God").

vv. 7–14: But, Ephraim, what in fact have you done? Look what significance *you* have given to *Bethel!* You are a Canaanite, that is

120   *Hosea 12*

a Phoenician (see Gen. 10: 15; Isa. 23: 11, R.V.), trading
dishonestly and abusing your power. You have become wealthy and
you regard your prosperity as a proof that you are without sin. And
yet your God is none other than I, Yahweh, who brought you out of
Egypt in the first place and will yet again (if only you will repent)
enable you to keep the feast of tabernacles with joy and gladness as
in the past, that feast in which Israel were wont to acknowledge
Yahweh as their God, their complete dependence upon Him as the
provider of all they possessed.

God had spoken repeatedly too, "*upon* his prophets" (cf. Ezek.
3: 14—"the hand of the Lord was strong *upon* me") by visions and
parables (such as Hosea's experience with his erring wife) by "the
ministry of the prophets". The verse suggests an abundance of these
communications in the past. From Gilead, the "heap of witness"
(Gen. 31: 25, etc.) in the east, to Gilgal, "heaping heap", on the
west of Jordan (that is, in all parts of the land) the idolatrous altars
are as *heaps* (of stones) in the fields.

Jacob, rather than become rich with the Canaanite inhabitants of
the land, fled to "the field of Aram", Syria ("an Aramite, Syrian,
ready to perish was my father", Deut. 26: 5) and earned his wife by
keeping sheep; and by the prophet Moses did God bring Israel out
of Egypt and preserved him like a flock (there are several textual
allusions to Genesis in these two verses). This is the example of
faith which Ephraim should have followed; but instead he has
provoked God's anger by blaspheming His name and by his acts of
violence. His guilt shall remain upon him.

13: 1-8: Continuing His allusions to earlier history, God
declares that when Ephraim used to speak in Israel, he was
heard with respect; but then he exalted himself in pride, and
transgressed in worshipping Baal. In Ahab's time we are informed
that there were 450 prophets of Baal, 400 of Ashtoreth; no wonder
Elijah thought that complete apostasy had come! As a result of this
idolatry Ephraim "died", that is spiritually, losing all contact with
God; or in imitation of the condemnation of Adam, "dying thou
shalt die", a process being set on foot whose end was inevitable. The
sin has in fact gone on developing, so that now Ephraim multiplies
idols "of silver" (it was a common practice in Egypt to gild images
of wood, stone, or bronze), all of them no more than the work of
some smith, made with the limitations of his own skill! How absurd
to worship a thing a *man* had made! Worshippers were commanded
to pay homage by kissing the image of the calf (cf. words of God to
Elijah: "I have left me 7000 in Israel, all the knees which have not
bowed to Baal, and every mouth which hath not kissed him", 1

Hosea 13 121

Kings 19: 18). The modern practice of kissing the toe of Peter at Rome has evidently an ancient origin! Because they have so offended, Ephraim shall be as evanescent as a morning cloud or the dew, dispersed by the heat of the sun; or driven from the threshing floor like the chaff; or disappear through the lattice like smoke.

In language reminiscent of Deuteronomy 32: 39—"I, even I, am he, and there is no god with me ... I wound and I heal"—God repeats the assertion of His unique power which He had made from the beginning of Israel's history; He alone can *save*, a declaration repeated through Isaiah ("a just God and a Saviour", Isa. 45: 21–2). (So the same claim regarding Jesus: "... Neither is there salvation in any other", Acts 4: 12.) The verse is really one more appeal to Israel to remember these things. For it was Yahweh who had acknowledged Israel as His people, and also made Himself known to them (the broad sense of the Hebrew verb to "know" is to be kept in mind); as a result they were fed even in the wilderness with food sufficient for their needs (again a reminiscence of Deuteronomy: "For the Lord ... *knoweth* thy walking through this great wilderness ... thou hast lacked nothing", 2: 7). But as a result they "waxed full", and in their pride they forgot God. Deuteronomy 8: 11–15 is the basis of this passage, ending with the warning "Ye shall surely perish", which corresponds with the judgement expressed in the next two verses in Hosea. Israel, having "waxed fat and kicked", are to become a prey to the ravening lion, the watchful leopard, and the ferocious bear bereaved of her young; the chamber of their heart (the breast) which they had closed against God, should be torn open.

vv. 9–16: Scholars agree that the A.V. of verse 9 cannot be defended; read rather: "It hath destroyed thee, O Israel, that against me thou hast set thyself, against they help", not so very different in ideas from the gist of the passage. God alone is Israel's king; where is the king that should save them in all their cities? And where are their princes of whom they desired to choose a king? The irony of this passage is strengthened by the reflection that the last king of Israel was called Hoshea, or Salvation! God had in fact given them what they wanted, a king like the nations; but the original should rather be rendered: "I *give* them a king in mine anger and I *take* him away in my wrath"; the allusion is not only to the granting of Saul and his downfall, but rather to a continuous process, illustrated in the succession of degraded dynasties in Israel's history and their removal. Ephraim's sin is "treasured up" as in a bag; an expression which recalls Deuteronomy 32: 32–4—"Is not this (iniquity) laid up in store with me, and sealed up among

122   *Hosea 13*

my treasures? To me belongeth vengeance ... their foot shall slide
in due time ... "; and Romans 2: 5—"After thy hardness and
impenitent heart *treasurest up* unto thyself wrath". For affliction
shall come upon Ephraim as pains upon a woman in travail; by a
swift change of figure, Ephraim, from being the woman, becomes
the child about to be born; a foolish child, for in hesitating to come
forth from the womb, he endangers both his own life and the
mother's (cf. Isa. 37: 3—"The children are come to the birth and
there is not strength to bring forth").

Verse 14 has been a great subject of controversy, for there are
two contradictory interpretations. The modern view maintains that
in Hebrew, "at its emotional heights, a sentence can be a statement
or an interrogative, and thus the meaning máy be positive or
negative" *(Century Bible);* "the Hebrew word *ehi* may be either the
adverb 'Where?' (as it was in verse 10), or a shortened form of the
future verb, 'I will be' " *(Speaker's Commentary).* So it is possible
to render the passage: "From the grasp of hell should I ransom
thee? From death redeem them? (implying, Far be it from me ...)
Where are thy pestilences, O Death? (Bring them forth ...) Where
is thy striking down, O Hell? Relenting shall be hid from mine
eyes". The verse is thus not a promise of redemption, but a calling
forth of doom. In favour of this interpretation is the general context
of the passage; both in the verse before and certainly in those after,
it is unquestionably that of judgement; and the concluding clause:
"Repentance shall be hid from mine eyes" (meaning that God will
not relent and withhold judgement) seems to tell against the idea of
redemption.

The traditional rendering must not however be lightly discarded.
While it may be possible to read the Hebrew as two questions, the
natural sense is as two statements ... "I will ransom them ... I will
redeem them" (A.V., R.V.). This is how the LXX translators
understood it, and is the sense in which the Apostle Paul used the
passage in 1 Corinthians 15: 55. The argument that the context of
verses 13 and 15 requires judgement, not redemption, seems
impressive, but in the prophets there are frequent switches of theme
in short passages, especially at points of high emotion. The
concluding phrase "repentance shall be hid from my eyes" proves
also not to be the obstacle imagined, for it could well mean that
God will not go back on His determination to bring final
deliverance (cf. "The Lord hath sworn *and will not repent*", Psa.
110: 4). We conclude therefore that it is right to take the passage in
the same sense of the A.V. and R.V., and as it is used in the New
Testament.

So, though Ephraim means fruitfulness, Assyria, that scorching

Hosea 14   123

sirocco from the desert, shall dry him up and destroy his treasured possession. Rebellious Samaria shall suffer the brutalities of invasion and shall become desolate, because she has not hearkened to "her God".

3. ISRAEL'S RETURN UNTO THE LORD (14)

14: 1–3: The prophecy concludes with a remarkable chapter expressing Israel's repentance and Yahweh's restoration of His people, not only materially but to His favour. The section provides such a striking contrast to the relentless doom pronounced in a large part of Hosea's prophecy (despite the brief passages of hope and promise) that many critics do not hesitate to deny it to Hosea and to ascribe it to some "later hand" (a favourite device, whose vagueness conceals ignorance and speculation). It is therefore encouraging to read the conclusions of Brown *(Westminster Commentary):* "This picture of the final triumph of Yahweh's love is so Hoseanic in language and thought that it can only be rejected on *a priori* grounds", that is without direct evidence and in the interests of a theory; and of G. A. Smith: "There is no phrase or allusion of which we can say that it is alien to the prophet's style or environment."

Hosea calls upon Israel to return *entirely* to Yahweh, for they have fallen down in their sin. Sin inevitably places stumbling blocks in the believer's way. They are urged to take with them not a multitude of sacrifices, but "words", the spiritual offering of their hearts, and to say: "*All* our iniquity do thou forgive" (cf. the psalmist: "Blot out all mine iniquity", 51: 9) "and accept good", the offering which we hope to present when we have received forgiveness. In the past we have offered bullocks only, but now we will offer the sacrifices of our lips. There follows in verse 3 a full confession of the sins which have led the people astray: first, reliance on Assyria; second, on their own armed strength (or the allusion to horses could be to Egypt, the country which supplied Israel with horses in the first place—see Deut. 17: 16 and 1 Kings 10: 28—and which in Isa. 31: 1–3 seems to have horses as a synonym); and third, reliance upon idols, now admitted to be only the work of their hands. None of these, but God only, can provide the mercy that the fatherless need, as Israel will have experienced to the full when the time for this repentance comes.

vv. 4–9: To this humble plea, God is quick to respond, as in Jeremiah 31: 20: "Is Ephraim my dear son? I do earnestly remember him still ... My bowels are troubled for him; I will

124   *Hosea 14*

surely have mercy upon him." So God declares: "I will love them
freely", that is without waiting for Israel to earn it, against their
deserts even (the resemblance to the love of God in the Gospel is
strong here: "being justified *freely*—without a cause—by his
grace", Rom. 3). Israel shall be as a number of natural growths of
great beauty and value: like the lily, renowned for purity and grace,
and the cedars of Lebanon for their strength and stability, and the
olive remarkable for the beauty of its dark green and silver foliage;
Lebanon was famous for the fragrance of its forests, due to a large
variety of aromatic shrubs. His redeemed people shall live under the
shadow of the Almighty (only the dwellers in a land of fierce heat
could appreciate the significance of a substantial "shadow" at
noon) and grow like the corn and the vine, the great symbols of
spiritual refreshment in Scripture; so their "renown" or "memorial"
shall be as Lebanon's scent.

Then follows a brief dialogue between the pardoned people and
God:

Ephraim: "What have I to do any more with idols?"

Yahweh: "I have heard and observed him."

Ephraim: "I am like a green fir tree."

Yahweh: "From me is thy fruit found."

And Hosea concludes his prophecy with a call to the "wise" to
consider these things. His question, "Who is wise ...?" does not
imply the impossibility of understanding, but the difficulty, and the
rarity; for in all ages the majority of men have been *too wise in
their own eyes* to understand. What they have consistently rejected
is that "the ways of the Lord are right", even when He requires
what they do not like, even when He judges human sin. The ways of
God imply not merely His commandments for His people but also
His dealings with them, His providence in the ordering of events.
The just shall live by submitting themselves to these ways, but the
rebels shall perish. So Hosea concludes by pointing the lesson of his
whole prophecy: God alone is wise. Whatever God does, toward
ourselves or toward others, let us accept it as right; whatever He
commands, let us believe without argument. True wisdom consists
in first understanding the principles of God's revelation, and then in
a willingness to apply that knowledge in practice. The verdict of
Jesus is no different, for it was the man who "heareth my words
and doeth them" who was blessed.

Hosea 14

Concluding Reflections

The impression inevitably produced upon the reader by Hosea's long catalogue of Israel's iniquity is one of astonishment that a people who had enjoyed so many privileges—the lessons of history, the instruction of a Divine law, the means of worship through tabernacle and priests, and the regular provision of prophets—could have allowed themselves to sink so far into thorough-going apostasy as Israel did. It is evident that some of the grossest crimes of the heathen were being imitated by this people who had so many reasons for knowing better. The example is a solemn warning of the unreliable character of the human mind and heart, once the sound basis of divine instruction is abandoned; a warning too of the helpless condition into which habitual sin delivers the sinner, who, caught in the toils of his own passions and appetites, becomes incapable of distinguishing between good and evil, and is eventually destroyed by that which he has coveted.

The result is the determination of God to chastise, and that thoroughly, when such a situation is reached on the national scale. The erring people are to suffer the desolations of drought and famine, the barrenness both of body and field, the agonies of foreign ruthlessness in invasion and deportation. But the chastisement of God always aims to lead Israel back to repentance, and the inevitable conclusion is that in God's view this was *the only way* to achieve that desirable result, even for a remnant. When repeated warnings have been consistently ignored, when corruption instead of being relieved grows ever deeper, God does not hesitate to take more drastic action; for the redemption of the few who will repent is of more consequence to the Divine purpose than the disappearance of the many who are hardened in their sin; and the enlightened are expected to see that the painful consequences are really the judgements of God.

Repeatedly in Hosea the apostasy is said to be the result of the lack of "the knowledge of God". The Hebrew *yadha*, to know, says G. A. Smith, "is a singularly supple word", conveying "many processes of knowledge: to perceive, to be aware of, to recognise, understand or conceive, experience, or be expert in. But ... nearly always ... a practical effectiveness and, in connection with religious objects, a moral consciousness." Israel, having learned of God from their fathers, through the law, and by the prophets, had not consistently sought to translate that knowledge into their own experience of life; they had not come to love God for the Being that He is, but only to expect favours from Him because He was "their God". They had not grasped the fact, so clear in the Law

126   *Hosea 14*

nevertheless, that since their God was holy, so must they be. The result was that they quickly "forgot God"; they rejected the knowledge of Him, believing that the multitude of their sacrifices would be adequate service (had not God commanded them?). So there was no truth nor mercy in the land. What a devastating commentary upon human nature that the rejection of the way of God should lead inevitably to this result; but so says Paul in Romans 1: "Ungodliness" (the rejection of God) produces "unrighteousness" (iniquity). Our own times provide a striking example. So Israel were "destroyed for lack of knowledge". But in the end the picture is brighter for the remnant, for they "shall know the Lord" and be ready to say to Him: "Thou art my God".

The whole subject is full of instruction for us, who live under the same laws of discipline, chastisement with the intent to reform, and submission to the way of God. Nothing is clearer than this: the necessary "knowledge of God" will not be attained by ritual of any kind, simple or complex; nor by the individual's efforts to devise his own way; but only by a willingness to "hearken", to receive instruction, and to walk in patience and faith.

But the really distinctive note struck by Hosea is found in the astonishing revelation of the compassion of God: "I will allure her ... and speak to her heart ... Thou shalt call me Ishi (my Husband) ... I will betroth thee unto me for ever ... O Ephraim, what shall I do unto thee? ... When Israel was a child, then I loved him ... I drew them with cords of a man, with bands of love ... How shall I give thee up, Ephraim ... I will heal their backsliding ... I will love them freely ..." We are made to realise that God feels intensely both grief and joy according to the response of His people, that His compassion toward them in their waywardness "as sheep having no shepherd" is infinite, that His love even toward the sinner (as long as there is a chance of redeeming him) is inexhaustible. So thoroughly is this aspect of God's character brought out by Hosea that the grace of God in Christ appears in its right perspective: not, that is, as something entirely new that God has done, and even as a little "out of character" perhaps, but as the consistent expression of the very same God who "spoke unto the fathers by the prophets" and has now spoken unto us by His Son. And the Son too appears in better perspective: not solely as the unique character *in his own right,* as some modern theologians seem prone to see him, but as the veritable expression of the Father who was Himself "full of grace and truth" from the beginning.

Hosea's prophecy is positively encouraging, despite its warnings. We may feel overcome by our own sin and pessimistic about our

Hosea 14

ability to find favour with God; but it is clear, since He is the same today as ever, that a real desire on our part to draw near to Him through His word, a real willingness to abandon our own ways and adopt His, a real cultivation of His "knowledge", will evoke the same response of love and mercy, the same "yearning" for our salvation. Truly this prophecy is a great example of the principle that the things that were written "aforetime" were "written for our learning, that we through patience and comfort of the Scriptures might have hope".

8
MICAH
"THOU WILT PERFORM THE TRUTH TO JACOB"

Introduction

After the strong government of Jeroboam II there succeeded on the throne of the northern kingdom first his son Zechariah in 743 B.C., then a rapid succession of five kings before Samaria went down in blood and ruin before the Assyrians in 722. Similarly in Judah the firm rule of Uzziah and Jotham was succeeded by the disastrous reign of Ahaz, a weak, unprincipled monarch who found himself attacked by the coalition of Syria and Israel. The invaders besieged Jerusalem, though without success, slew 120,000 men of Judah in one day and took vast numbers of captives, but they afterwards returned them. Ahaz also found himself attacked by the Philistines and the Edomites. He appealed for help to the king of Assyria who relieved him by attacking Syria's capital, Damascus, and then proceeded to relieve him of a considerable quantity of wealth, taken from the temple. Ahaz was a corrupt worshipper of false gods; during his reign "God brought Judah low" (2 Chron. 28: 19).

His successor Hezekiah (727–697 B.C.) was a remarkable contrast to his father. Jeremiah 26: 17–19 informs us that he was influenced by Micah's prophecy of destruction to come upon Jerusalem, and turned to God in entreaty. He instituted moderate reforms, restoring and rededicating the temple, celebrating a great Passover Feast, and removing high places. Hezekiah found himself involved in international politics. In his own country there were evidently parties favouring alliances with Assyria, Egypt, and later Babylon, while the prophet Isaiah represented another which urged him to put his sole trust in Yahweh. Three times between 720 and 700 B.C. it was the Philistine cities which bore the brunt of the Assyrian attacks, until at last Hezekiah and Judah were vouchsafed the wonderful deliverance from the aggression of Sennacherib which was such a sign to the faithful in Israel.

These, the days of Ahaz and Hezekiah, were the chief times of Micah and also of Isaiah. Micah must be distinguished from the

Micah

older prophet Micaiah, son of Imlah, who foretold the doom of Ahab in the presence of Jehoshaphat (1 Kings 22: 8). His name, an abbreviation of Micaiah (Jer. 26: 18), means "Who is like Yahweh?", a reminiscence of the exclamation of Moses: "Who is like unto thee, O Yahweh?" (Exod. 15: 11). He came from the village of Moresheth on the Philistine border and he was thus a countryman, who did not dwell amidst the corruptions of the larger towns; he was not involved in politics and makes no allusion to the conflict about political alliances, nor does he pronounce upon the fate of foreign nations. In this he offers a remarkable contrast to his contemporary Isaiah, who was an inhabitant of Jerusalem, fully conversant with the politics of the capital and of its rulers, capable of advising the king himself.

The use by God of these two prophets, so different in their particular gifts, personal experience and outlook, demonstrates remarkably that the spirit of prophecy did not destroy the individuality of the prophet, but rather used it. Yet, most significantly, the message of these two prophets, who were so diverse as men, is substantially the same. Both foretell deliverance from Assyria; both the captivity in Babylon, at a time when Babylon was subordinate to Assyria; and both promise the regathering of the people from lands where they had not then been scattered. Isaiah seems indeed to have made use of the prophecy of Micah for his famous passage 2: 2–5, "The law shall go forth from Zion ..."

In the prosperous reigns of Jeroboam II of Israel (783–743 B.C.) and Uzziah of Judah (778–740 B.C.) the expansion of the two kingdoms enabled them to command the main trade routes. The result was the growth of a civilisation based on great material prosperity, with extremes of wealth on the one hand and of poverty on the other which would have been impossible in an agricultural society based upon the land tenure of the Law of Moses. The result was greed, covetousness and oppression contrasted with poverty and suffering. This demoralising pursuit of wealth—ominously familiar to our modern ears—is fearlessly denounced by Micah, who attacks injustice and violence in Judah much as Amos had done for Israel.

In the days of Ahaz the religious corruptions also of the northern kingdom invaded the south. This dissolute king made molten images for Baalim, sacrificed unto the gods of Damascus, burned incense on the high places unto other gods, and even burned his children in the fire "after the abominations of the heathen" (2 Chron. 28: 1–4, 22–25). When the chief ruler of the nation engaged in such activities, the behaviour of the rest can be imagined. Micah is so conscious of the iniquity of the nation that he shows little hope

130   *Micah*

of a lasting return to God, an outlook which was justified by the
event, despite the reforms of Hezekiah.

The prophecy of Micah, though somewhat disconnected in the
arrangement of its material, falls into three parts, each commencing
with the call, "Hear ye ...", each reproaching Judah with sin and
announcing judgement, then promising future restoration. Modern
critics generally deny to Micah the authorship of large sections of
the book, on the ground that they contain ideas of a "later age",
such as the regathering of dispersed Israel and the deliverance of
Jerusalem by divine power. It is clear, however, that there is no
solid evidence for these conclusions which rest only upon the
preconceived ideas of the critic about the course followed by
"prophetic development". Horton *(Century Bible)* remarked that
"we are certainly justified in retaining the integrity of a book of
scripture, unless conclusive reasons can be advanced against it ...
There is no sufficient reason to deny Micah's authorship (of certain
disputed passages) ... unless it can be shown that the prophets
never predicted the future, or never had mingled visions of exile and
restoration ... The argument against the chapters is purely *a
priori*" (that is, it first assumes a basis, and then argues from that).

Concerning the disconnected character of the discourses, alleged
by the critics as a mark of composite authorship, Kirkpatrick
(Doctrine of the Prophets) remarked that "the question for the
student is not (as it is so often misleadingly put) whether the
sequence of ideas is 'what we should expect', but whether it admits
of explanation"; and E. J. Young wrote: "We cannot grant the
validity of any position which, for theological reasons, would deny
to the period of Micah the ideas of salvation found in the book.
There is no objective evidence to show that such ideas were not
present in Micah's day ... To insist, in the interests of a certain
naturalistic theory of the development of Israel's religious views,
that these (disputed) passages must also be ascribed to a later time,
is an utterly unwarranted procedure" *(Introduction to the Old
Testament)*. The *New Bible Dictionary*, referring to the custom of
modern scholars to ascribe Micah 7: 7–20 to a "post-exilic date" for
reasons of style and subject matter, comments: "Arguments from
style are never particularly strong at the best, since style can be
altered so easily with a change of subject matter ... There is
nothing in the context (of 7: 7–20) which is in the slightest degree
at variance with the language or the theology of the 8th century
B.C. prophets". It has been thought worth while to give some of
these quotations in full, as much of what is there said applies with
equal force to a great deal of critical judgement about the prophets
in our own day.

Micah 1   131

Micah makes frequent allusion to the Pentateuch: its history, laws, promises and threatened judgements. It is plain that he had the writings before him and expected his hearers to recognise his allusions. The land of Nimrod, the house of bondage, the miraculous deliverance from Egypt, Balaam, Gilgal, the mercies of God, the pledges to Abraham and Jacob: these are some of the references, unintelligible without a knowledge of the writings of Moses. In addition single expressions are frequently taken from the same source. Those who are prepared to look up the Biblical references will discover that Micah also quotes from, or alludes to, Joshua, Psalms and Proverbs; and that similar references to *his* prophecy are found in the prophecies of Habakkuk, Zephaniah, Jeremiah, Ezekiel, and in the Gospels of the New Testament. What a wonderful linking of inspired Scripture is this, and what light it throws upon the way "holy men of God" read with reverence the work of their predecessors! Can we do less?

Micah's leading ideas are the regeneration of Israel's remnant through judgement, the establishment of the Kingdom of Yahweh in the line of David, and the conversion of the nations through that kingdom. The conclusion of his prophecy is a triumphant expression of faith, which is seen in its true quality against the background of the materialism and the corruptions of the reign of Ahaz.

Micah's prophecy moves so swiftly at times from denunciation and threatened judgement to promises of the most remarkable restoration that it is difficult to make any analysis of it which would not seem piecemeal; however it is possible to divide it into three major sections, each beginning with the address: "Hear ye ..."

1.   Judgement of Jerusalem and her People (1: 1—2: 13)

1: 1-4: The reigns of Jotham, Ahaz and Hezekiah cover a period of over 40 years, the kings of Judah alone being named as only they represented a line appointed by God; but in the judgement Samaria is mentioned first. The call to the *peoples* (*ammim*, plural) might be taken as addressed to the 12 tribes (the term is so used only in the Pentateuch); but the addition of "O earth and all that is therein" shows that it is an appeal to witnesses against the people of God: first to the surrounding nations, then to the unchanging natural creation (cf. Deut. 32: 1; Isa. 1: 2). It is against Israel (not against "the peoples") that God is witness, as He speaks from His holy temple, heaven itself (Psa. 11: 4). Usually God "hides himself" (Isa. 45: 15), but in times of judgement He "comes forth ... comes down" (Psa. 144: 5) and subdues the earth, reducing the hills and valleys to wax in the fire of His wrath. (Cf. "Our God is a

132   *Micah 1*

consuming fire," Deut. 4: 24, where the context is judgement for
disobedience; and also the picture of the storm in Psa. 18: 7–15;
and, "A fire goeth before him and burneth up his enemies round
about ... The hills melted like wax at the presence of the Lord",
Psa. 97: 3–5.)

vv. 5–7: Jerusalem had now become as corrupt as Samaria, for had
not Ahaz burnt his children to Molech in Hinnom and "made altars
in every corner of Jerusalem" (2 Chron. 28: 3, 24)? Samaria would
therefore become desolate, like the heaps of stones gathered out of a
field in preparation for its cultivation; its stones would be "poured
down" (same word as v. 4) into the valley, exposing its foundations.
The Assyrians did not destroy Samaria, but Josephus records that
centuries later (approx. 128 B.C.) the Maccabean leader, John
Hyrcanus demolished what was left of the city and dug water-
courses there. The idols of Samaria should be beaten to pieces and
the gifts dedicated to her harlot's worship should go to another
harlot, even Nineveh.

Micah's Lamentation

vv. 8–16: Micah now utters a prolonged lamentation on hearing
these dire tidings: he will go "despoiled and naked" (like his people
into captivity, wearing only the undergarment), and howling like
the jackals and the ostriches, both notorious for their mournful,
piteous cries. Israel's wounds are beyond cure: the word literally
means "strokes", and is used in the Pentateuch for the "plagues"
which God would inflict in the event of disobedience, Deuteronomy
28: 59, 61. Israel's case is incurable by her own efforts, because she
is incapable of repentance; and the judgement, in the person of the
foreign invader, the Assyrian, will come right up to the gates of
Jerusalem itself.

There follows a series of lamentations for villages in the
Shephelah, or coastal plain, along which Sennacherib was to sweep
in his triumphal invasion. This section is to be compared with the
remarkable passage Isaiah 10: 28–32 where the prophet describes
the panic spreading from one town to another as the Assyrians
invaded from the north-east, whereas Micah describes the effect of
the invasion from the south-west, even as far as Lachish. The exact
meaning of some of these names in Micah is hard to determine, but
there is no doubt that they have been chosen generally with a view
to the judgement pronounced upon them; in other words we have a
play upon the significance of the names, as the following comments
will make clear.

Micah 1   133

The expression "Tell it not in Gath" was probably proverbial by Micah's day from David's lamentation on the death of Saul and Jonathan; the phrase can however be rendered: "Tell it not in Tell-Town". Following the Greek LXX Version we then have: "Weep not in Weep-Town" (only one Hebrew letter different from the text of our A.V.); "in the House of Dust *(Beth-le-Aphrah)* roll thyself in dust". Shaphir (Town of Beauty) is to pass away in shame; the inhabitants of Zaanan (abounding in flocks) have not gone forth (like flocks); the woe of Beth-Ezel shall take from them its resting-place (shall be no neighbour to them, but the etymology here is disputed). The inhabitant of Maroth (Bitterness) watched in anxiety, hoping for good; but it was evil (bitterness) which came from God, even as far as the gate of Jerusalem. In verse 13 the play upon words arises from the fact that the Hebrew for Lachish is the same as "to the swift steed", with the addition of one letter and the omission of another; *rechesh, Lachish.* Unless there is here a reference to some historical fact unknown (that Lachish was in effect the first city of Judah to adopt the idolatry of the North Israelites, for example), the "beginning of sin" is probably an allusion to the proximity of Lachish to Egypt and the centre she became for reliance on foreign alliances and in "trusting in horses". In verse 14 the presents are "bridal presents", given by a father to his daughter on her marriage as she went away to belong to another; the Hebrew word for "betrothed" is ~very like the name Moresheth, which means possession. Achzib shall be *achzab*, a winter brook, failing in time of heat, so unreliable. To Mareshah (Possession) God will bring "the heir" (Sennacherib) who shall inherit it; for the glory of Israel shall come even to Adullam, reduced to taking refuge in a cave like David, 1 Sam. 22: 1–2. The land is to "shear" itself, as a sign of mourning; to make itself bald like a species of vulture (which is bald on the top of its head), for its inhabitants have gone into captivity.

As regards the fulfilment of this prophecy, there must be in this passage some reference to the invasion of the cities of Judah by Sennacherib in 701 B.C., though the final captivity of Judah (v. 16) was only accomplished over 100 years later by the Babylonians under Nebuchadnezzar. But, prophetically speaking, the Assyrians would no doubt have carried it out, had it not been for Hezekiah's submission to God and his prayer of faith. As in other cases, it was a divine judgement capable of being delayed by repentance.

134   *Micah 2*

Judgement, yet Restoration (2: 1–11)

2: **1–5:** Instead of following the example of the psalmist: "Lord,
have I not remembered thee in my bed and thought upon thee
when I was waking" (Psa. 63: 6), the leaders of Judah think of
nothing but evil while they rest, and put their hands to it the first
thing in the morning. They are covetous and violent and seize the
property of others, not hesitating to oppress the persons of men (as
Jezebel did Naboth) in direct defiance of the commands of the Law
(Lev. 25: 17). Since they have devoted themselves to devising evil,
God too is devising an evil for them, which will be a yoke on their
necks as on animals doing hard labour; for the time is evil, both in
the works of Israel and in the punishment God will bring upon
them. When the judgement comes to pass, a song of lamentation
would be sung for and against them (there is a remarkable
alliteration in the original, *nahah nehi niheyah*, expressing repeated
lamentations): God has taken away from His people the inheritance
(portion) which He gave them in the land, so that they can no
longer divide up the fields by lot as they had been accustomed for
so long to do around their villages.

vv. 6–11: The people say to the true prophets like Amos (7: 16) and
Micah, "Prophesy not", impatient of their warning judgements (the
word is "Drop not", the term used by Amaziah to Amos, 7: 16,
quite a regular word for the prophet's utterance). But the true
prophets *shall* prophesy, says God, but "not to these", that is to this
godless people, who will not listen to their words; "shames shall not
depart", that is the people will not put away their false gods and
their evil ways. God then addresses His people "named the house of
Jacob", upon which Isaiah's words are an illuminating commentary: "House of Jacob, ... called by the name of Israel ...
which make mention of the God of Israel, *not in truth* or in
righteousness. For they call themselves of the holy city, and *stay
themselves* upon the God of Israel" (Isa. 48: 2). Judah were relying
on their original calling to guarantee their safety despite their
works, like the Pharisees before Jesus: "We be Abraham's seed ...
never in bondage to any man", John 8: 33. Is the Spirit of the Lord
shortened (straitened)? Is He really any less long-suffering than of
old? Are these calamities really the doings of the Lord? (The
prophet may here be repeating some of the protestations of the
unrepentant Jews.) To this God asks in reply: Do not my words
always do good to the man who walks in uprightness? Note the use
of "the Spirit of the Lord" (v. 7) to express both the moral nature
and the power of God.

Micah 2

But even now (Heb. yesterday) "my people" (the acknowledgment by God that the connection still exists is to be noted) indulge in acts of violence: they are vehement in pulling the cloaks off peaceful citizens who are passing by. Having robbed (and perhaps murdered) the head of the house, they oppress their widows and their children, the very ones whom the Law commended to their care, and take away the glory of God from them, by causing them to be exiles in a foreign land. Their present sojourn in the land is not the "rest" which God had in view for them, as He said by Moses: "Ye are not yet (in the wilderness) come to the rest and the inheritance which the Lord ... giveth you. But when ye go over Jordan and dwell ... when he giveth you *rest* from your enemies ..." (Deut. 12: 9–10, where the same word is used). The land had been "defiled" by the abominations of the Canaanites; therefore God had caused Israel to drive them out. But now Israel themselves had defiled the land; it should therefore "spue them out" (Lev. 18: 28) and destroy them. The only prophet who would please this disobedient people would be one who prophesied about "wine and strong drink", the false prophets who had not "the Spirit of the Lord", but "walk after their own spirit", "prophets out of their own hearts", "of the deceit of their hearts" (Ezek. 13: 3. 17; Jer. 23: 26). This unchanging reaction of human nature to the divine righteousness is illustrated equally in our own day. Modern men and women too welcome a false teaching which aims to satisfy them without calling upon them for any self-sacrifice. The one thing the modern, just like the old, false prophets avoid doing is to point out to the people their sins. They know they will lose their audience unless they prophesy "smooth things". It is a result which the true prophets have always been willing to accept.

vv. 12–13: The last two verses of the chapter provide one of those rapid changes of subject which are common in the prophecy of Micah, and not uncommon in all the prophets. The passage assumes that Israel (the *whole* nation now, not just the northern kingdom) is scattered in captivity, and describes their deliverance. Although "Jacob, all of thee", is addressed, it is clear that only *some* of them, "the remnant of Israel" of the next phrase, is meant (see similar use in 4: 6). The use by the apostle Paul of the idea of a remnant "according to the election of grace" who would be at the same time "all Israel" is similar, the conception of the call of the Gentiles remaining, however, much of a "mystery" in Micah's day.

The remnant is to be "gathered", the characteristic word, taken from Deuteronomy 30:3–4; it implies the gathering of a flock, and became the regular one for the regathering of Israel (see Jer. 31: 10). Bozrah was famous for its sheep (Isa. 34: 6). The parallel

136   *Micah 2*

between "sheep" and "men" is explicitly brought out in Ezekiel
34: 31 ("Ye, my flock ... are men") and 36: 38 (" ... Flocks of
men ..."). Verse 13 describes their deliverance: they are evidently
imprisoned, and are led to freedom by the Breaker-Through, a term
which later became one of the recognised titles of the Messiah
among the Jews; they follow him through the breach in the walls
and through the gate. The one at their head is their king, who is
equated in the very next phrase with Yahweh Himself, an anticipation by over 100 years of Jeremiah's ascription of the title "The
Lord our Righteousness" to the king who was to reign on the throne
of David.

This prophecy of the restoration has been largely denied to
Micah by the critics and ascribed to the period of the exile (written
by an "unknown hand" of course: the literary fertility of this
"author" must have been something to marvel at! Strange his name
has not been preserved). The reason is simple: the passage assumes
the exile and the captivity. Horton in the *Century Bible* remarks
that the critics' reasons are "purely subjective" and there is in fact
not a scrap of linguistic or internal evidence for denying it to
Micah. Such rapid switches from threats of judgement to promises
of restoration are common in the prophets. They form in fact the
prophet's answer to those of his contemporaries who complained
that he had no message but that of judgement.

2.   The Coming Kingdom of the Lord (3: 1—5: 15)

3: 1–4: The third chapter is a denunciation of the leaders of the
people, princes, priests and prophets, for wanton neglect of their
duties to the nation. These princes of Israel (Isaiah calls them
"rulers"—same word—of Sodom) rejected "judgement", that is the
just administration of the law of God, and pursued evil, so that
instead of being shepherds caring for the flock, they had become
butchers, slaughtering the sheep and feeding upon them (cf. "Have
all the workers of iniquity no *knowledge* [of God] who *eat up* my
people?" Psa. 14: 4). But in the day of *their* judgement, when they
cry to God, He will turn His face away from them and refuse to
hear. The same rejection is expressed in Jeremiah 11: 11—"I will
bring evil ... they will cry unto me and I will not hearken unto
them." Clearly the "cry" which produces this reaction from God is
not one of genuine repentance, but of angry, self-pitying morti-
fication at their sufferings.

vv. 5–8: The prophets are next condemned. They make the people
"err", by comforting them with the assurance that they are the
people of Yahweh, so the result must be "peace". But in fact they

Micah 3   137

"bite" with their teeth (the word is mostly used of snakes; cf. Amos 5: 19; Gen. 49: 17), and they "sanctify war" (that is, denounce in the name of the Lord) against any who do not pay their fees or bribes. But the sun (of salvation: Amos 8: 9) will set and the darkness (of judgement: Amos 5: 8) will descend upon these false prophets, who shall no longer "divine" (a word always used in a bad sense); having lost all contact with God, they shall "cover their lips" as the lepers in their uncleanness were commanded to do (Lev. 13: 45) and as a sign of mourning (Ezek. 24: 17, 22).

But, unlike these prophets who "walk after their own spirit", Micah, by contrast, is "filled with power by the spirit of the Lord", with the result that he boldly declares God's righteous judgements, and does not hesitate to point out to the people what their transgressions are. The false prophets gave no moral leadership to the people, for they never pointed out to them their sins, since they spoke only "out of their own heart"; their utterances must have been in the same vague, indecisive terms which many of the leaders of popular religion use even today. How different are the utterances of the prophet of the Lord, who feels himself mightily moved by a word that is not his, to such an extent that he can assume a righteous authority and denounce sin. In the same way the apostle Paul desired prayer on his behalf, "that utterance may be given unto me, ... that I may speak boldly as I ought to speak" (Eph. 6: 19–20).

vv. 9–12: The last section of the chapter returns to the attack upon the rulers, who abhorred the "judgement" which the Spirit of the Lord had impelled Micah to declare, and practised extortion and even murder that they might have enough wealth to "build" in Jerusalem for themselves. The priests and the prophets both take money for their services and delude the people with false promises: "Yahweh is with us; no evil can befall us", a sentiment repeated over a 100 years later in the days of Jeremiah: "The temple of the Lord ... are these", described as "lying words" by God; and "neither shall evil come upon us ... neither shall we see sword or famine" (Jer. 7: 4; 5: 12). In fact the judgement was to be so severe that the very site of Zion was to be "ploughed like a field" and the city reduced to heaps of stones.

Micah was the first of the prophets to foretell so bluntly the literal destruction of the city of Jerusalem and hence of its temple. With what sense of shock the Israelites of his day, both profane and God-fearing, would hear his words! The God-fearing Hezekiah heeded the warning and by his example of humble faith, averted the first stage of the judgement through Assyria. A century later profane princes of the people sought to persuade Jehoiakim to put

138   *Micah 3*

Jeremiah to death because he had pronounced a similar judgement;
but "elders of the land", citing the case of Micah's prophecy and
Hezekiah's example, succeeded in saving his life (Jer. 26: 19–25).

This awe-full judgement on the Holy City began to come to pass
in the destruction of Jerusalem through Nebuchadnezzar in 588
B.C., then through Antiochus in the 2nd century B.C., and finally
through the Romans in A.D. 70 onwards. Nehemiah describes the
desolate ruins in 2: 17 and 4: 2; Josephus declares that the Romans
"effaced the rest of the city" (B.J., vi, 9: 1). Pliny in A.D. 77 called
Jerusalem "a city which had been and was not". The actual
ploughing is declared to have taken place under Hadrian in the 2nd
century A.D., and Origen 100 years later describes the site as
desolate and ploughed. A temple devoted to the worship of
Ashtoreth was erected on the site of the sanctuary, a Roman colony
was founded, and Jews were prohibited from entering Palestine,
though this ban was later limited to the city of Jerusalem. Thus was
fulfilled the fearful judgement pronounced by Micah 700 years
before; and such is the fearful power of the word of God, inexorably
being fulfilled over a span of many centuries. Of what words of men
could this be said?

A Marvellous Restoration (4: 1–13)

4: **1–3:** By an abrupt contrast with the preceding prophecy of
destruction, but picking up the allusion to "the mountain of the
house" in 3: 12, Micah passes to the restoration of the future,
seeing the time when the house of God will be a place of pilgrimage
for all nations, who, recognising the God of Jacob as the sole source
of truth, will actually desire to go up to Zion to be instructed of
Him. It is a vision of "the last days", the time when God would
have carried out His work of Israel's redemption and the judgement
of the nations by the coming of the seed of David. Nineteenth-cen-
tury commentators like Pusey or Wordsworth could see nothing in
this passage but the prophecy of the admission of the Gentiles into
the Christian Church by the preaching of the Gospel. Taken in
harmony with Bible prophecy generally, however, it must be
understood of an abrupt climax in the career of the nations of the
earth, reached not through the willing cooperation of those nations,
for they will have "set themselves against the Lord and His
anointed" and "walked after the imagination of their evil heart"
(Psa. 2; Jer. 3: 17), but by the direct intervention of Divine power
(Dan. 2). That the rule will be firm is shown by the assertion that
Yahweh will "act as a magistrate" among the nations and "decide
concerning" them (A.V. judge, rebuke); in other words they need

Micah 4 139

discipline still. The beneficent effects of this rule are expressed in the striking transformation of weapons of war into tools of peace, so that war is "sanctified" no more, that is, the mistaken ideas which have led men to proclaim "holy wars" in the past will be removed.

Verses 1–3 are found also in Isaiah (2: 2–5), but a study of the context of the two prophecies suggests that it was Micah who wrote the original passage; for in his prophecy this section stands in close relation with the preceding verse, where it is declared that the "mountain of the house of the Lord" was to be "as the high places of the forest" (that is, wild and desolate), and Zion was to be "ploughed as a field". Micah then immediately proceeds to set forth the great contrast which the future will bring eventually, when "the mountain of the Lord's house" is to be "established" and "exalted" and from Zion the law is to go forth. In Isaiah's prophecy the passage stands in no such intimate relation with what precedes or follows, the likelihood being therefore that Isaiah was familiar with Micah's writing, was struck by the passage, and incorporated it into his own work.

vv. 4–5: The picture of prosperity, when every man was to sit under his own vine and fig tree, is a combination of two passages: Leviticus 26: 4–6, in which blessings were promised "if ye walk in my statutes": the land was to be fertile and Israel would dwell safely in their land, none making them afraid; and 1 Kings 4: 25, in which the prosperity of Israel under Solomon is thus described: "(Israel) dwelt safely, ... every man under his vine and under his fig tree ..." The restoration of the future will be a return to the strength of the Davidic kingdom in its most prosperous days; and the certainty of fulfilment is assured, because "Yahweh of hosts hath spoken it". Verse 5 is best read as: "(Though) all peoples walk in the name of their god, (yet) we will walk in the name of Yahweh our God for ever"; in other words, since it is difficult to take the verse as referring to the time of the first imposition of the dominion of Christ over the nations (surely then they will not be allowed to walk in the name of their gods), it must be taken as an expression of the faithful in Micah's day, who, hearing what the mouth of the Lord had spoken, declared their firm intention of remaining faithful to Him.

vv. 6–8: "In that day" of verse 6 links with "the last days" of verse 1, when the "law shall go forth from Zion". Before that day comes however, Israel will "halt", (that is be like sheep lame from wandering), be "driven out" and "afflicted" by God; see Zephaniah 3: 19 for similar language. This was a plain warning to the nation that there would be suffering before the glorious climax. But God

140   *Micah 4*

would assemble the wanderers, even though they were but a
remnant, and make a strong nation of them, with the result that His
reign over them "in mount Zion" (from which it had just been said
that His law should go forth for the nations) would from that time
be unbroken. Jerusalem is now addressed, as the "tower of the
flock". Israel is the flock and the dominion to be established there
will be its protection. The "stronghold" of Zion is Ophel, a hill in
the South of Jerusalem, near the temple area and the priests'
district, where David evidently built a tower "for an armoury"
(Song Solomon, 4: 4). The "first" dominion which is to come to
Jerusalem is the *former* dominion in its glory, that of David "the
shepherd" who had been called to become the shepherd of Israel.
The prophecy directly implies the idea of *restoration*, when God
sets His king "upon my holy hill of Zion" (Psa. 2: 6; see also Isa.
24: 23).

v. 9—5: 1: Looking forward in time, the prophet foresees Judah
lamenting because she has neither king nor counsellor (the very
titles to be assumed by the son of David: "his name shall be called
Wonderful, Counsellor, ... upon the throne of David ..." Isa.
9: 6)) and is in pain like a travailing woman (see Hos. 13: 13). The
people will indeed suffer, for they are to abandon the city and dwell
in tents like the captives of war, and be transported even to
Babylon. Modern critics cannot believe that Micah could have
foreseen the Babylonian captivity; yet 2 Kings 17: 24 tells how
Sargon had brought captives from there to Samaria after the fall of
that city in 722 B.C., and Isaiah 39 describes how an embassy came
from Babylon (probably about 710–705 B.C.) ostensibly to con-
gratulate Hezekiah on his recovery from illness, in fact no doubt to
try to form a political alliance against Assyria. At this very time
Isaiah was commissioned to tell Hezekiah that his people would
eventually go into captivity to Babylon (39: 6). The existence of
Babylon as a power and her political rivalry with Assyria were
therefore perfectly well known. But of course the decisive point is
that if we allow the possibility of prophecy at all in the sense of the
prediction of that which had not yet occurred, there can be no valid
reason for rejecting Micah's words here. The prophet does not stop
however at foretelling the captivity in Babylon, he goes even further
to foretell Israel's *deliverance from there* by the hand of Yahweh.
The attentive hearer of the prophets would know therefore what to
expect, though he would not know that the Babylonian captivity
was still over a century ahead, and the limited return under
Nehemiah nearly two centuries.

The time would come when "many nations", the surrounding

Micah 5   141

traditional enemies of Israel such as the Edomites, Ammonites and Moabites, would ally themselves against Jerusalem. Expressions of such concerted action by the nations against Jerusalem can be found in Psalms 83 and 74, prophecies which had a basis in fact in history and will doubtless have one again when the last great spoiler seeks to work his will "on the mountains of Israel" (Ezek. 38). But these nations, intent on the destruction of Israel, a traditional enemy, do not know that they are being gathered by God for their *own* destruction, as sheaves are gathered for threshing; and that Yahweh will carry out the threshing by means of the restored remnant of His people, making "their horn iron and their hoofs brass"; the enemies of Israel shall be trodden underfoot as the oxen trod out the corn. But the wealth of those nations will not go just to enrich Israel, but will be "devoted" to Yahweh, who will be recognised as the *adon* of the whole earth, that is its Possessor and Lord.

5: 1: The fifth chapter opens with a verse which in the Hebrew Bible is the last of the fourth; it is in fact a reference back to the theme of 4: 9, the travail of the nation when Jerusalem is besieged. The word "troops" is said to have two senses: marauding bands, or a crowd pressed together from fear. Jerusalem is "the daughter of troops" because of the bloodshed and violence within her; but by a play upon the same word her inhabitants are seized with fear when the enemy besiege the city, and her "judge" is smitten "on the cheek". The rod is a symbol of judgement and smiting on the cheek is an insult, contemptuously inflicted. While "judge" could mean ruler generally, the use of the word here may imply the absence of a real king, especially in view of 4: 9—"Is there no king in thee?" The earliest historical fulfilment of this prophecy would be the Babylonian invasion and destruction of the city, when the monarchy came to an end; but the circumstances would fit the Roman invasion equally well, with the interesting fact that the Roman soldiery did actually smite in the face the great future Judge of Israel, the Messiah (Luke 22: 64). The verse is one more example of the way in which a prophecy, originally given in a particular situation and having significance for those who heard it, is found to have a wider and more prolonged sense than could at first have been expected, even extending to the final onslaught of the nations upon Jerusalem.

The Coming King (5: 2–13)

v. 2: By contrast again the prophet now turns to Bethlehem

142   *Micah 5*

Ephratah (House of Bread, Fruitfulness), the place where Rachel
was buried (Gen. 35: 19) and associated with the family of David
(Psa. 132: 6). This small place, unable to muster a full tribal unit
(the thousand) and being therefore united with other small places
to make up the number, is yet to be the birthplace of the future
Ruler of Israel *for God* ("he shall come forth *unto me*"), to do *His*
will and to fulfil *His* purpose. The unique status of this ruler is
stressed by the assertion that "his goings forth (are) from of old,
from the days of eternity (from the days of that which is hidden)".
The terms are used of the eternity of God: "The eternal God is thy
refuge and underneath are the everlasting arms" (Deut. 33: 27);
"... From everlasting to everlasting thou art God" (Psa. 90: 2);
"... His mercy is from everlasting to everlasting" (Psa. 103: 17).
But they are used also with special reference to God's dealings with
His covenant people, Israel: see Micah 7: 14 and v. 20: "Feed thy
people ... as in *the days of old* ... Thou wilt perform the truth to
Jacob and the mercy to Abraham which thou hast sworn unto our
fathers from *the days of old* ". *Their use here therefore signifies
that the origin of the future son of David would have a close
connection with Yahweh Himself, and with His active purpose for
Israel, though the precise detail of the connection is not explained.*

This outstanding prophecy supplies one more link in the remarkable chain of Old Testament witness to the coming Messiah: the
seed of Eve was to come of the family of Shem, of the seed of
Abraham, of the tribe of Judah, in the line of David, and his precise
birthplace is now named: lowly Bethlehem; only the identity of the
mother and the exact time, plus the manner of his Divine origin are
now lacking, to be supplied in the New Testament. The great
significance of this prophecy is demonstrated by the fact that before
the birth of Christ the Jews unhesitatingly interpreted it of the
Messiah, as Matt. 2: 4–6 is witness; but after his crucifixion they
sought to change their interpretation, without however finding one
satisfactory to themselves. The efforts of sceptical modern critics to
take the sting out of it by attributing the "goings forth from of old,
from everlasting" to the previous history of the line of David (G. A.
Smith, for instance) only reveal the immense difficulty of finding
any other satisfactory interpretation for this prophecy than the one
contained in the New Testament record of Jesus Christ.

Note 12: MATTHEW'S QUOTATION FROM MICAH 5: 2

It has been objected that in Matthew 2: 5–6 the passage in
Micah 5: 2 is not accurately quoted, either according to the Greek
LXX or the Hebrew text.

Micah 5   143

It should be noted that Matthew is reporting the reply of the
priests and scribes when Herod "inquired of them where the Christ
should be born". In Bethlehem of Judaea" they said, "For thus it is
written by the prophet, And thou Bethlehem, in the land of Judah,
art in no wise least among the princes of Judah: for out of thee shall
come forth a governor, which shall be shepherd of my people
Israel." It is practically certain, however, that Matthew was
recording this reply with approval, since it harmonises with his own
insistence on the fulfilment of Old Testament prophecy in this part
of his Gospel.

The version in Matthew is a paraphrase, giving the sense of
Micah's prophecy for a Greek speaking audience with no knowledge
of Hebrew. The distinctively Hebrew "Bethlehem Ephratah", now
known only to students of the Hebrew Scriptures, is changed to
"Bethlehem ... Judah", easily intelligible and the very term used in
1 Samuel 17: 12 with reference to David. The "thousands" *(al-
laphim)* is replaced by the "princes" *(alluphim)*, where an obsolete
organisation of large groups would be best understood through the
leaders of those groups; and Micah's "Bethlehem ... which art
little to be ..." becomes "art in no wise least ...", because it is the
glorious fulfilment which is now in view, by which the name of
Bethlehem would be celebrated all over the earth. Matthew thus
testifies to the common expectation among the Jews at the time of
Christ's birth, and without doing any violence to the *sense* of
Micah's prophecy, makes clear its significant fulfilment.

v. 3: Meanwhile God would deliver up His people into the hands of
their enemies (because there was "no remedy", 2 Chron. 36) until a
certain birth: "until the time that she which travaileth hath brought
forth". The last mention of travail was in 4: 10—"Be in pain and
labour to bring forth, O daughter of Zion, like a woman in travail",
whence it seems natural to interpret the son to be born as the
remnant of Israel. Isaiah speaks in the same strain: "... as soon as
Zion travailed, she brought forth her children" (66: 7–9). But
Micah speaks here of an *individual:* "the remnant of *his*
brethren ... *He* shall stand and feed ... *He* shall be great unto the
ends of the earth ... *This (one)* shall be the peace ...", allusions
which make it inevitable to see in verse 3 a prophecy of the birth of
the son of the virgin of the house of David (Isa. 7: 13–14; 9: 6). The
word "then" in verse 3, which seems to link the time of this birth
closely with the returning of the remnant, does not necessarily do
so, since it should be "and". "The remnant (a term used of those
rescued after judgement: Zeph. 2: 9; Zech. 14: 2) of his brethren
shall return unto (along with) the children of Israel" would

144   *Micah 5*

probably mean to Micah's contemporaries that the faithful remnant
of Judah would be joined to the faithful of Israel, so that there
should be one true Israel once again. But the prophecy contains in
its fulness the call of the Gentiles, the redeemed among whom
become "brethren" of the Lord by doing his will (Matt. 12: 50),
from being "aliens ... strangers" are "made nigh" (Eph. 2) and so
become members of "all Israel" which shall be saved (Rom.
11: 26). To Micah's fellow Israelites much of this, however, would
remain hidden, as a "mystery" which the apostle Paul expounded in
the New Testament (Eph. 3: 1–7).

vv. 4-6: The prophet now turns to the glorious days of Messiah's
power, when he shall abide (stand) and feed his flock. The duties of
shepherd and ruler are often combined in the Old Testament. David
was raised up by God "to feed Jacob his people" (Psa. 78: 70–73);
Isaiah speaks of the arm of God which "shall rule for him ... He
shall feed his flock like a shepherd" (40: 9–11); and consistently
with the unfolding purpose revealed in the intention of God to call
the Gentiles, the Good Shepherd speaks of his "other sheep which
are not of this fold", for whom there must be "one fold and one
shepherd" (John 10: 11–16). This ruler will be endued with the
strength of Yahweh and will be upheld in the "majesty of the name
of Yahweh". He will not only uphold His reputation among the
heathen ("I will be sanctified in the eyes of many nations", Ezek.
38) but will manifest the spiritual quality of His attributes, of
which His Name is a summary. The result will be that the remnant
of Israel shall "abide", no more to be dispersed, and their ruler's
fame will be in all nations.

This (emphatic) man, this unique ruler, shall be Israel's peace in
the day of the Assyrian invasion. The connections between Messiah
and peace are numerous: as son of David, he would be the Prince of
Peace; as ruler he would "speak peace unto the nations" (Zech. 9);
in the New Testament he becomes the preacher of peace with God,
and even more the embodiment of the peace of his saints ("He is
our peace", Eph. 2: 14).

Micah saw him as the Saviour of Israel, under whom they would
raise up "seven shepherds and eight princes". There is no need to
take the numbers literally; seven is the complete number, eight is
therefore an abundance (cf. "for three transgressions ... and for
four", that is because of utter transgression, Amos 2); the phrase
suggests a complete and utterly sufficient body of priests and rulers,
who should so organise the nation, under the Messiah of course,
that they would actually be able to "eat up" the land of Assyria

Micah 5   145

with the sword and also the cities ("the borders") of the land of Nimrod, that is Babylon.

Assyria and Babylon were closely linked in prophecy as representative of the great Gentile opposition to the people of God, the instruments and yet the subjects of His judgements; in prophetic application to the time of the end they stand for the power of the nations arrayed against Jerusalem. The remarkable feature of this prophecy is its plain forecast of the desolating of Assyria by Israel, an event which must have seemed incredible even after the Divine deliverance from Sennacherib; it has not yet happened in any subsequent period. The commentators, unable to credit the direct intervention of God in the affairs of the nations, can only see in this passage an allusion to the way in which the preaching of the Gospel of Christ has overcome the power of Satan; indeed some of their 19th-century pronouncements now appear ludicrous in the light of the 20th-century decay of religion, with growing materialism, corruption and violence. The Bible, having represented God from the beginning as interfering in the affairs of *His* world in order to direct them according to His will, does not hesitate to do the same for the events of the great climax which is yet to be revealed; God is emphatically a God who manifests Himself through the history which He controls.

vv. 7-9: In the next three verses the activity of Israel towards the nations takes two different forms: first a refreshing one, as "a dew from the Lord". "My doctrine shall drop as the rain, my speech shall distil as the dew", says Moses (Deut. 32: 2). When Israel are healed, God says He will be "as a dew" unto them (Hos. 14: 5). Israel as dew for the nations will be that "word of the Lord" which shall proceed from Jerusalem, through the work of the remnant; and this work of blessing will not "wait for the sons of men", that is will not wait until *men* can accomplish it (as some people in our day even now expect) but will be "from the Lord".

The second activity however will be one of judgement among the nations "as a young lion among the flocks of sheep, ... who ... teareth in pieces and none can deliver". This is to be accomplished by "the remnant of Jacob" who shall be in a position to dominate their adversaries and cut off their enemies. The linking of these two ideas of mercy and judgement for the nations through Israel in the age to come calls to mind the apostle Paul's phrase: "The goodness and severity of God." Evidently as Israel have experienced this in their time of probation, the Gentile nations will do the same during the rule of Christ, and the very literal nature of this pronouncement

146   *Micah 5*

suggests that the purged nation of Israel will have quite a part to
play in the process.

vv. 10-15: The chapter concludes with a section describing that
purging of the remnant of Israel, which must take place before they
can play their part in the subjugation of the nations. God will "cut
off" the horses, chariots, and fortified cities in which they had
trusted, the soothsayers with all their multitude of idols and imges,
now seen to be merely the work of their own hands: His
"vengeance", that is righteous retribution, is to come also upon the
nations "which hearkened not". So Israel will be purified and fit to
serve the Lord for ever and the nations will hearken to Israel's God.

3.   The Controversy of God with His People (6: 1—7: 20)

In the third section the prophet turns from the comforting
contemplation of the glories of the future to the shortcomings of the
present, but finally expresses his complete faith in the fulfilment of
Yahweh's purpose for His people.

God's Appeal to His People (6: 1-8)

6: **1-5:** The passage opens with an appeal from God to the great
unchanging features of the earth, the mountains and the hills, to
act as His witnesses against His people, who have abandoned Him.
Exactly the same appeal is made by Moses in Deut. 32: 1 and
through Isaiah in 1: 2. God's controversy with Israel takes the form
of a "pleading", not wholly in the modern English sense, but also in
the legal sense: He will expound His charge against them and then
give them an opportunity to say what they can in their own defence.
The charge commences on a very compassionate note: "O my
people ..." showing that God still acknowledges Judah. It continues in terms of sorrow: "What have I done unto thee? Wherein
have I wearied thee?" In fact as Isaiah and Malachi testify, it is
Israel who have "wearied" God and become weary of Him: "Thou
hast been weary of me ... thou has wearied me with thine
iniquities" (Isa. 43: 22–24; Mal. 1: 13).

Putting aside all His prerogatives however, God invites Israel to
bear witness against Him, and reminds them of what has been
accomplished for *them* by His power and favour: redemption from
slavery in Egypt, provision of proper leaders like Moses, priests like
Aaron, and prophets like Miriam; the turning aside of the evil
designs of their adversaries when Balaam was obliged to bless Israel
instead of cursing them as Balak wished. Shittim was the last

Micah 6   147

encampment of Israel outside the Promised Land, where the sin with Baal-Peor took place, while Gilgal was the first *in* the land after the miraculous crossing of Jordan and the re-dedication of the people by a renewed circumcision. The address in verse 5 maintains the tender note of verse 3: "O my people, do remember ...", the word "now" making the attitude one of beseeching rather than of commanding.

All these facts are brought before Israel so that they might recognise the "righteousness" of the Lord: not here the abstract sinlessness of God, nor even the quality which the New Testament assures us God will impute to the redeemed, but His faithful acts of deliverance on their behalf, called "righteous acts" in Judges 5: 11 and 1 Sam. 12: 7. God had in fact carried out His covenant by repeated acts of mercy and aid. If then Israel have abandoned Him, surely they have acted without cause?

In these first five verses the implication very clearly is that God's dealings with His people are always just, since He never goes back on His word; and always reasonable, since He never expects from them a service which they cannot give. The appeal He makes is full of verbal allusions to the Pentateuch, to evidence then which the Israelites should very well know.

vv. 6–8: The same note of reasonable appeal is continued in the very important section verses 6–8. Here Micah impersonates the earnest Israelite, who in a time of confusion wishes to know how to approach God, and at the same time comments upon the ways in which many of God's people were wrongly answering the question. Does God require the most expensive offerings, such as vast numbers of rams or large quantities of oil, which accompanied the burnt offerings?

Does He require the most delicate offerings like veal? Is it any good offering their *own sons* (as was done in the pagan rites of Molech, in which Ahaz king of Judah had joined and as many others were even then doing)? All these suggestions, no doubt representing what Israel were regularly offering to God, betray the assumption that it is satisfactory to offer God a *thing*, something external to themselves, something that can be acquired for money with little effort and which therefore represents but little in the way of offering. But Micah suggests the true need when he asserts that the real fault is "the sin of *my soul*", for which no external offering can atone. Intent on bringing *things*, Israel had failed to offer *themselves*.

But, after all, Israel should have known: "He hath showed thee, O man, what is good". Echoing a passage from Deuteronomy,

148   *Micah 6*

"Now, O Israel, what doth the Lord require of thee, but to fear the
Lord, to walk in his ways, and to love him and to serve the Lord thy
God with all thy heart and with all thy soul ...?", Micah outlines
the way of service: "What doth the Lord earnestly seek (require) of
thee but to do justly and to love mercy and to walk humbly with thy
God?"

The verse is striking because of the contrast it seems to offer
between the ritual service of God and the service of the heart and
soul, but it must be read in the light of the whole of God's
revelation. There is nothing in Micah's pronouncement which is in
any way contrary to the spirit or requirement of the law. Samuel
could reproach disobedient Saul: "Hath the Lord as great delight in
burnt offerings ... as in obeying the voice of the Lord?" This
conviction did not prevent Samuel, a tower of faith in his
generation, from offering sacrifices. Neither did the convictions of
David: "Thou desirest not sacrifice ... The sacrifices of God are a
broken and a contrite heart ..." prevent him from concluding his
psalm: "*Then* (when the worshipper comes in the right spirit) shalt
thou be pleased with the sacrifices of righteousness ... with burnt
offerings" (Psa. 51: 17–19), nor from establishing a ritual system in
the temple. But to conform to ritual is always easier than to
discipline the heart and soul, and Israel as a whole had long chosen
the more attractive congenial path. Micah's warning to them is of
everlasting worth for worshippers of all ages.

Note 13: "WHAT DOTH THE LORD REQUIRE OF THEE ...?"

A shallow view, however, of the terms of this verse (verse 8) has
led in modern times to a serious misinterpretation of Micah's
meaning. He has been made to say that religious ceremony and
belief have little value, and indeed had little in the sight of God for
the Israelites in his day; all that God requires is a "good" life,
consisting of honesty and kindness towards one's fellows (humility
before God being rather ignored). The passage is a permanent
warning against taking Bible terms in their modern English sense
and so constructing a "theology" of our own. What we need
urgently to know is not *our* unaided understanding of "doing justly"
and "loving mercy", but Micah's under the inspiration of God.

Now a true Israelite did "judgement" *(mishpat)* when he
acknowledged the will of God as expressed in the laws He had given
to His people, and acted towards his fellows in a spirit of justice;
and he loved "mercy" *(chesed)* when he acknowledged the great
deliverance God had effected for Israel from Egypt, God's faithful
mercy in remembering His covenant with the fathers, and

Micah 6   149

recognised that he had an obligation to act with a similar mercy to his fellows; in this way he showed *his* faithful adherence to the covenant; and all this sprang out of his humble submission to God.

Micah, then, is not uttering a vague pronouncement about human conduct, but is going right back to the root of the Israelite's religion: his dependence upon God's mercy and truth *(faithfulness)* for his existence as a nation and as an individual. The intimate phrase "thy God" shows the closeness of the relation. The matter is a warning to us in our day, where so many would claim to be acceptable to God because they tell the truth and are kind. As in Micah's day, so in ours: a humble walking before God—the essential basis—will enquire what His revelation to us is, and what He requires us both to believe and do. Paul puts the matter briefly to Timothy: "Hold fast the pattern of sound words ... in faith and love" (2 Tim. 1: 13, R.V.). The pattern consists of the principles of God's revelation in belief and conduct; the faith and love are the spirit in which these are to be "held". We should not mistake the one for the other, or imagine that either can be dispensed with. (For justice, mercy, etc., see "The Knowledge of God", *The Christadelphian*, 1967).

Meanwhile, Judgement for Sin

vv. 9–16: The prophet now turns again to a vivid description of Judah's sins. In Jerusalem the voice of the Lord cries, like Wisdom in Proverbs 8: 1, 3, 4; as a result the "man of wisdom" shall "see" the Name of the Lord. The expression is unusual, but the meaning must be the same as "know" the Name, in all the fulness of its "goodness, mercy and truth" (Exod. 34, etc.). God has prepared a rod of correction for Judah, even the army of Assyria ("O Assyria, *the rod* in thine hand is mine indignation", Isa. 10: 5). The wise man must "hear" this rod, that is accept the correction brought by it, and recognise that it has been "appointed" by God for that very purpose (as God "appointed" the sword for Askelon, Jer. 47: 7).

The need for such correction is exposed by the fact that *even yet* (that is, after so many warnings which should have brought about a reformation) there are treasures gotten by evil means, short measure ("an ephah of leanness"), and false balances with incorrect weights in the houses of the rich. "Shall *I* be pure" with such things? asks the prophet, putting himself in the place of the Israelite, who knew very well that such practices were explicitly condemned in the law (Lev. 19: 35–36; Deut. 25: 13, 15, 16, the last verse ending: "All that do such things and all that do unrighteously are an abomination unto the Lord thy God"). Because the rich, in

150   *Micah 6*

addition, were given to lies and deeds of violence, God will make
their wound incurable (as later He was to make that of Nineveh,
Nahum 3: 19), for their sins shall bring desolation. Everything they
have rejoiced and trusted in shall be taken from them: in the very
place where they have justly amassed wealth, there shall they fall,
their desperate efforts to retain something from the ruin being in
vain.

As the law had warned them (Deut. 28: 38–41) the fruits of the
earth which should have been for their gladness ("wine that maketh
glad the heart of man, and oil to make his face to shine, and bread
that strengtheneth man's heart", Psa. 104: 15) shall be taken from
them; for it is not the "statutes and judgements of the Lord" that
they have kept as they undertook to do at Sinai, but "the statutes of
Omri ... and all the works of the house of Ahab". No doubt some
special transgression of Omri is alluded to here, though it was his
son Ahab who, through his marriage with the Tyrian Jezebel, gave
such powerful encouragement to the worshippers of Baal; and
Athaliah, the murderess of her own children, is called the
"daughter of Omri", her grandfather. The sacred historian's
judgement of Ahab is devastating: "There was none like unto Ahab,
which did sell himself to work wickedness in the sight of the Lord"
(1 Kings 21: 25). So the title "people of God", which should have
been a title of glory, would become one of reproach among the
surrounding nations, as the psalmist says it did: "We are become a
reproach to our neighbours, a scorn and derision to them that are
round about us" (79: 4).

7: 1–6: Micah now laments, on behalf of the faithful remnant, for
the sins of the people, rather like Daniel in Babylon, or the
apostle Paul, who had "continual sorrow" in his heart on account of
the plight of Israel after the flesh (Rom. 9: 2). He compares himself
to one who finds all the grape harvest already gathered, the most
delicious of the figs already picked. Israel had lost the "first-ripe
fruits" of righteousness which some of her people had shown in the
service of God (cf. Hos. 9: 10). The "good" man is the *chasid* (from
chesed, mercy: see Note 13, p. 148), that is, he recognises the
merciful deliverance God has accorded him, and acts towards his
fellows in the same way.

Such godly men have perished (apparently by violent means)
from the land, for men are hunting one another as they would wild
beasts. Princes and judges demand bribes, conspiring to accomplish
their "mischievous desire" (lit. the desire of the soul) by "weaving
together" their evil purposes ("so they wrap it up"). The moral life
in Judah is now so low that the prophet can compare "the best of

Micah 7
151

them" and "the most upright" to a briar or thorn hedge for
sharpness, for they have neglected the words of their watchmen, the
prophets, who urged them to heed the warning of "the trumpet",
that alarm-signal of invasion and calamity (Jer. 6: 17) and to hear
the words of warning from God (Ezek. 3: 17). "The day of thy
watchmen" is therefore the "day of the Lord" which they foretold,
and will be "the day of visitation" or judgement which they had
refused to believe in.

Judah's neglect of the uprightness of life required by God is now
so complete that a man cannot trust his companion, his intimate
friend, nor even his wife, words which are adapted by Christ to
describe "the latter days" (Luke 12: 53; 21: 16, etc.). Members of
the same family "dishonour" one another; the word means "lightly
esteem" and was used by Moses of Jeshurun (or Israel) who
"lightly esteemed the Rock of his salvation" (Deut. 32: 15); it is of
interest to note that in the age to come it will be the *sinner* who will
be "lightly esteemed" (A.V., cursed, Isa. 65: 20).

vv. 7–10: That Micah had been thinking of the passage about
Jeshurun from Deuteronomy 32 seems indicated by the fact that he
now turns to declare his faith in "the God of my salvation". The
"But as for me" (R.V.) which opens this verse provides a wonderful
contrast of attitude with that of the godless multitude; he will "gaze
intently upon the Lord", "wait for the God of my salvation",
confident that God will hear him. Verse 7 thus reveals in a few
words what was the faithful attitude of the prophets: in the midst of
national and religious corruption the prophet has *faith* in Yahweh;
he will submit to (wait for) the correction which God will bring on
His people, confident that in God alone is salvation (not in the
pursuit of material prosperity, nor in foreign alliances), and that
God will certainly hear him. The title "God of my salvation" is
frequently found in the Psalms (see 18: 46 and 25: 5) and the
expression "I will wait for God" is a Hebrew term almost
exclusively used for this patient submission to God and expectation
of His mercies, one of the most revealing of Old Testament terms to
describe the devotion of the faithful remnant. Its lesson remains
significant and powerful for us today.

The enemy, be it Assyria, Edom or Babylon, or later even Rome,
is bidden not to rejoice when Israel falls and sits in darkness like a
mourning widow; the faithful remnant whom the prophet represents
here, are resolved to bear the judgement of God because they
recognise it is the result of sin. But the time will come when the
desolate shall arise, light shall drive away the darkness, and the
"righteousness" of Yahweh shall be made manifest; not a purely

152   *Micah 7*

abstract quality, but the demonstration of His righteous judgement, this time upon the heathen. They, having been first the instruments of His wrath upon His sinful people, become themselves the subjects of judgement because of their unrighteous deeds, and especially because of their unmerciful treatment of His people. So those Gentiles who had contemptuously exclaimed: "Where is Yahweh thy God?" (Sennacherib was to be the first example after the time of Micah's prophecy), shall themselves be reduced to shame and be trodden under foot (as was Nineveh). But God's "righteousness" also signifies the forgiveness and restoration to favour of the faithful remnant. So this significant passage expresses the vindication and salvation which shall come for those who accept in submission the righteous judgements of God, in the spirit of Daniel who, in similar circumstances exclaimed: "The Lord hath watched upon the evil and brought it upon us; for the Lord our God is *righteous in all his works which he doeth*", even when they are works of judgement (9: 14).

vv. 11–13: The interpretation of verse 11 presents certain difficulties (contrast the A.V. and R.V., for instance). Since however the word rendered "wall" is never used of a city wall, but always of the wall or hedge of a vineyard, the prophet is thinking of Jerusalem (and so Israel) as the "vineyard of the Lord" (Isa. 5: 1–7; 27: 2–4; Psa. 80: 8–10) and so of its re-cultivation under His favour. And as the peoples of Assyria and Egypt (see R.V.) are to "come unto thee", the removing of the "decree" (a difficult word meaning possibly "boundary") must signify the breaking down of the barrier between Israel and the Gentiles. So Assyria and Egypt represent the coming of the Gentiles to the God of Israel in Jerusalem, much as in Isa. 19: 18–25. Isaiah and Hosea (Isa. 11: 11; Hos. 11: 11) both prophesy the return of Israel from Assyria and Egypt; the rule of Messiah from sea to sea had already been prophesied in Psa. 72, and the coming of the Gentiles from these lands in Micah 4: 2. Yet (with another of the swift changes of view so common in the prophets) despite the certainty of this glorious future the land should be desolate, because of Israel's sins; in other words the Divine retribution must take its course, for it will be the instrument by which the remnant will be truly prepared to become the "heritage" of the Lord.

vv. 14–17: Micah now prays for this "inheritance", that "flock" who need the Shepherd to feed them, albeit He must use His rod when necessary for chastisement; for Israel dwell "alone", as Moses had said: "Israel then shall dwell in safety alone" (Deut. 33: 28), and Balaam: "... The people dwell alone ... they shall not be reckoned

Micah 7

among the nations" (Num. 23: 9); as the flock of God they shall dwell in the fruitful field (Carmel) and in the rich pastures of Bashan and Gilead (cf. Jer. 50: 19). The idea of Israel as "the inheritance" of the Lord was evidently a recollection of the words of Moses: "Destroy not thy people and thine inheritance, which thou hast redeemed through thy greatness, which thou hast brought forth out of Egypt with a mighty hand" (Deut. 9: 26); and of Solomon: "For they be thine inheritance, which thou broughtest forth out of Egypt ..." (1 Kings 8: 51). It is therefore very understandable that Micah should next refer to the deliverance from Egypt and to the mighty works which accompanied it; a plea for their repetition in times of calamity had been expressed by Gideon: "Where be all his miracles which our fathers told us of, saying, Did not the Lord bring us up from Egypt?" (Judges 6: 13), and was to be so again by Habakkuk (3: 2).

Micah's prayer for his people as the "inheritance" of the Lord, had not been on account of their merits, but because they were called by His name, which was dishonoured by them. God answers the prayer in declaring that He *will* perform again the great deeds of the past, with the result that the nations shall be reduced to shame because of the failure of their own might; they shall put their hand upon their mouth in sign of silent submission; they shall "tremble out of their closed places", their strongholds, humbled to the dust like the serpent (see Psa. 72: 9), in which figure there must surely be an allusion to the condemnation of sin (Gen. 3); they shall "come trembling to the Lord our God and shall be afraid because of *thee*", that is because of what God has done again for the remnant of His people as He did it for them in the days of the Exodus.

vv. 18–20: So Micah, encouraged by his contemplation of what God will eventually do for His faithful, exclaims: "Who is a God like unto thee ... ?", alluding to his own name (Micah—Who is like the Lord?) and shows the depth of his spiritual understanding by proclaiming that the greatness of Yahweh consists not merely in the "mighty works" which He performs, but in His moral character: He "pardons iniquity" and "delights in mercy" (reminiscences of Exod. 34: 6–7 and Psa. 103: 9). Although this mercy can only be poured upon "the *remnant* of his heritage", yet for them the Divine favour will accomplish the utter removal of their sins, which shall be "subdued" (something which Israel as a people had been unable to accomplish) and "cast into the depths of the sea", again an allusion to the deliverance from the Egyptians, who sank into the "depths" of the Red Sea.

154   *Micah 7*

The prophecy concludes with a triumphant declaration that God's covenant would be realised: His "truth" (again, not an abstract quality, but His faithfulness to His promise), and His "mercy" (the gracious provisions of the covenant), the subject of an oath which God had made to the fathers Abraham and Jacob, would be performed, despite present appearances of corruption and national humiliation. The faith of Micah is the faith of all servants of God. We of a later age have been privileged to understand how "Jesus Christ" was made a "minister of the circumcision for the *truth* of God" (that same faithfulness to the covenant), "to confirm the promises made to the fathers, that the Gentiles might glorify God for his *mercy*" (Rom. 15: 8).

Concluding Reflections

There is much in Micah's prophecy which is similar to the features we have already underlined in the prophecies of Amos and Hosea. Although Micah does not stress the sin of idolatry as the Northern prophets do (evidently the calf worship of Jeroboam had produced a disastrous effect upon Israel from which Judah had in part escaped), he has the same condemnation of social corruptions—commercial dishonesty, lying, robbery by violence, bribing of judges and rulers, and even murder. Micah is at one with Hosea and Amos in proclaiming the inevitable judgement of God upon such deeds. Micah makes too the same numerous references to the writings of Moses, proving not only that these existed but also that they were well known among the people; and the same Divine appeal to the reality of the deliverance from Egypt as a ground for faith. There is the same conviction that the dominion of Yahweh will eventually be established, despite the certainty of the Divine judgement of the nation, that Israel will be delivered and the nations subdued.

There are however in Micah some emphases which were not so noticeable in the earlier prophets. Israel are to be taken in captivity as far as Babylon (4: 10), whence they are to return. The establishment of the dominion of Yahweh will involve the "wasting" of the lands of Assyria and Babylon (5: 10), an operation which will be performed by means of Israel. Obadiah had prophesied that judgement would come upon Edom through Israel, but Micah's forecast of the future activities of the people of God is much more extensive: "they shall waste the land of Assyria with the sword ... the remnant of Jacob shall be among the Gentiles as a lion among the beasts of the forest ... Arise and thresh, O daughter of Zion: for I will make thine horn iron and thy hoofs brass: and thou shalt

Micah 7 155

beat in pieces many people ..." (5: 6, 8; 4: 13). Since there has
been nothing in Israel's history which could even begin to fulfil
these predictions, we are evidently meant to see in them a prophecy
of the operations of the new Kingdom of Israel under the Messiah.

It is in his revelation of the person of the Messiah that Micah has
more to say than the prophets who had preceded him. Amos had
prophesied that "the tabernacle of David" was to be restored, but
Micah tells of the actual birthplace of the son of David, of his close
relation with God, of his career as deliverer, ruler and shepherd of
his people. The way is thus being prepared for the great prophecies
of Isaiah and Jeremiah, who speak of him as "the Prince of Peace"
and as the "king who shall reign in righteousness" and whose name
will be "Yahweh our righteousness". As we compare these later
pronouncements with the simpler declarations on this theme of the
earlier prophets like Joel, Obadiah, and even Amos, it is clear that
God has progressively revealed details of His great design to His
people in proportion as they have been able to receive them. It
would not have been much use, for instance, foretelling a
restoration from Assyria or Babylon when those powers had not
even begun to play a decisive part in the experience of His people.

Micah has no expectation that the bulk of the nation will be
brought to repentance; he foresees that judgement on the community is inevitable, but comforts his people with the assurance
that there will be redemption for a remnant: "I will surely gather
the remnant of Israel ... God ... passeth by the transgression of
the remnant of his heritage ..." (2: 12; 7: 18). He joins to this the
assurance that the redemption of the remnant will involve also the
return of the nations to the God of Israel: "Many nations shall
come and say, Come, and let us go up to the mountain of
Yahweh ... He will teach us ... We will walk in his paths ..." (4:
1–2). Israel are being accustomed to the idea that the Gentile
nations will not merely be subdued by the God of Israel but will be
reconciled to Him, so that in some measure Israel would lose their
exclusive privilege: an idea which was doubtless as unwelcome to
the Israelites of the prophets' days as it was to the Jews when the
Gospel was preached.

For us in these far-off days Micah is an inspiration in his attitude
to his task as a practising servant of the Lord. Three points may be
selected as illustration: his deep sense of the spiritual nature of true
religion, expressed in his best-known verse, "What doth the Lord
require of thee, but to do justly, and to love mercy, and to walk
humbly with thy God?" (6: 8); his sense of the righteousness of
God's judgements and his willing submission to them: "I will bear
the indignation of the Lord, because I have sinned against him ..."

156   *Micah 7*

(7: 9); his profound faith that God's purpose of redemption would not be frustrated: "(God will) plead my cause and execute judgement for me: he will bring me forth to the light and I shall behold his righteousness"; for the God of Mercy would find a way to heal Israel of their sins and so justly to "perform the truth to Jacob and the mercy to Abraham" (7: 9, 20). Here is the priceless value of Old Testament example, for these attitudes of Micah must also be ours.

9

THE OVERTHROW OF
ASSYRIA AND OF JUDAH

The 7th century B.C. witnessed some striking changes; by its close
the "old lion" Assyria was no more, having been replaced in the
politics of the Middle East by the new empire of Chaldea, or
Babylon; Judah was first subdued and then carried away captive by
Babylon, and Jerusalem was laid waste. New forces had begun to
operate and new conditions to prevail. For the faithful among the
people of God all this meant new problems to face, new adjustments
to make. The echo of these changes is found in the prophecies of
Nahum, Zephaniah, and Habakkuk.

Assyria's Decline

To understand what was happening in Judah it is necessary to
outline events in the international sphere. After the deliverance
from Sennacherib in 702 B.C. Judah was left in peace for about 20
years, since the Assyrian King was involved in long and exhausting
conflicts with his northern and eastern neighbours. After the defeat
of Merodach-Baladan, that tenacious Chaldean opponent of the
Assyrians, Sennacherib completely destroyed Babylon, in 690 B.C.
His son Esarhaddon, however, reversed his policy and rebuilt the
city (680–678 B.C.), but had to fight off a serious threat to his
empire from the Kimmerians and the Urartu in the North. He
succeeded, yet the growing power of these enemies was ominous for
the future.

Meantime Egypt, under the vigorous Taharqua (693–668 B.C.),
was meddling once more in the politics of Palestine, in fermenting
revolts among the lesser states. In 670 Esarhaddon carried out the
first of three expeditions against Egypt, in which he burned the
celebrated capital Memphis (No), took great spoil and tribute and
divided up the country under 20 subject princes. Further revolts,
however, led to more expeditions, and in 661 his son Ashurbanipal
(668–626 B.C.) again sacked Thebes and exacted an enormous
tribute.

The last years of Ashurbanipal are shrouded in obscurity. While
it is known that he had to wage further struggles against Northern
invaders and against Elam, and that in 645 he carried out a

158   *The Overthrow of Assyria and of Judah*

punitive expedition against the kings of Arabia for rebellion, taking at some time Manasseh, king of Judah, captive to Babylon, we have no information as to the end of his reign. His empire collapsed, however, with startling suddenness: in 640 it seemed at peace, yet from that year the records abruptly cease and within 20 years the Assyrian power was fighting for its life against a number of foes intent on its destruction.

The Fall of Nineveh

The fall of Nineveh was brought about by two new factors: first, the invasion of the Assyrian Empire by a new power from the North, the Scythians, of whom not much is known. About 630 they crossed the Caucasus and by 626 they were at the gates of Egypt, where they were bought off by a large tribute. The whole of Palestine seems to have been in a state of terror. Judah, in her mountain retreat, largely escaped direct invasion, but Herodotus declares that the Scythians dominated Palestine for over 20 years. Their arrival marked the end of the Assyrian control of that land. The Scythians seem, however, to have withdrawn as abruptly as they had come.

The second factor was the rise of a new power in Babylon, in the person of Nabopolassar the Chaldean, who was subservient to Assyria to begin with, but asserted his independence and soon began to combine with the Medes against her. After a war extending over 15 years Nineveh was finally sacked in 612 and the great empire, built on oppression and cruelty, was at last over-thrown, to the manifest joy of the peoples who had suffered her yoke for so long.

Pharaoh Necho, who had taken advantage of Assyrian weakness to dominate Palestine again, went up with an army to interfere in the Assyrian-Babylonian war, no doubt to obtain what he could of the spoils, but in 605 he was decisively defeated by Nebuchad-nezzar (son of Nabapolassar) at Carchemish on the Euphrates and from that moment the dominant power in Palestine was Baby-lonian.

The Role of Judah

It is against this background of international change that the significance of events in Judah must be seen. After Hezekiah's death, the long reign of Manasseh was marked by the return of all the evils which had defiled the reign of Ahaz: worship of baalim, installation of idols and an image in the courts of the temple itself,

The Overthrow of Assyria and of Judah 159

passing of children "through the fire", resort to wizards and necromancers, and the "shedding of innocent blood". 2 Kings 21: 11–16 tells us of a special message delivered to Manasseh by the prophets (not named), announcing the coming total rejection by the Lord of His heritage. "The Lord brought upon them the captains of the host of the king of Assyria" (the co-incidental truth of this statement is to be noted, for it is known that Ashurbanipal preferred to send his *generals* to fight his wars, whenever possible, and to stay at home himself). Manasseh was taken to Babylon, though the precise date cannot be determined. Rather surprisingly considering his earlier record, he repented there and returned to the service of God, when he had been restored to his kingdom. But despite his cleansing of the temple and re-establishment of the worship of the Lord, the people still continued their sacrifices on the high places.

' After the murder of Manasseh's son Amon, Josiah was made king by a spontanous movement of the "people of the land", probably led by a few faithful priests. In 621 (in Josiah's 18th year, but it must be remembered that he came to the throne at the age of 8) the "book of the law" was discovered in the temple. It must remain a subject for astonishment that it could ever have been "lost", yet so it evidently had been in the corrupt and idolatrous reign of Manasseh. Josiah was immediately struck by the remarkable prophecies of judgement upon Israel for disobedience, and commenced a policy of reform by removing idols and priests, by cleansing the temple and the land of images, and by holding a great passover. These energetic measures must have rejoiced the hearts of the faithful, yet the mass of the people were but little influenced by them, for they continued to worship upon the high places.

The interesting question concerning Josiah is: why was he so determined to oppose the northward march of the Egyptian army, which had no quarrel with *him*? (2 Chron. 35: 20–24). Perhaps Josiah thought he saw a chance of uniting the whole house of Israel under the sceptre of David in obedience once again to the God of Israel; the fact that he could oppose the Egyptians as far north as Megiddo shows the influence he already had over the former territory of the Northern kingdom. He presumed to anticipate the purpose of God and evidently was full of faith that God would support him. His death must have been a grievous blow to the devout party in Jerusalem.

The Fall of Jerusalem

After Josiah Palestine fell first under the power of Egypt, then

160   *The Overthrow of Assyria and of Judah*

following the victory of the Babylonians at Carchemish over the Egyptians, under the dominion of Nebuchadnezzar. Under the wretched succession of kings Jehoahaz, Jehoiakim, Jehoiachin, and Zedekiah, from 609 to 588 B.C., Judah, which might have survived as a separate kingdom if she had remained faithful in her servitude to Babylon, slid from one shifty act of treachery to another, until the final debacle in 588 when a large section of the population was deported and Jerusalem was laid waste. Thus came to an end the temporal kingdom of the Lord.

Of the Minor Prophets Nahum, Zephaniah and Habakkuk fall in this period. Nahum, the prophet of the overthrow of Nineveh, probably wrote about 640 B.C. or perhaps a bit later, foretelling the righteous judgement of God upon the wicked oppressor. Zephaniah writing in the reign of Josiah, reveals that judgement upon the nations generally, and especially upon the chosen people for their sins. Habakkuk, writing after the death of Josiah, seeks to understand how God can use an ungodly nation like the Chaldeans for the punishment of His people. In the emergence of another Gentile oppressor to follow the hated Assyrian, in the death of a righteous king like Josiah apparently when opposing the enemies of God, in the imminent destruction of the kingdom of God in Judah, lay problems for the faithful who still waited for that "day of the Lord" which would be not only a day of judgement upon Israel, but at last the day of *their* deliverance.

10

NAHUM

JUDGEMENT ON NINEVEH

Of Nahum, whose name means Consolation or Comforter, or of his
place of birth, nothing is known, though there is a Jewish tradition
that he came from Galilee. His prophecy bears no date, but there
are two indications which enable us to fix it at least within certain
limits. From the allusion to Thebes as having already suffered a
judgement (3: 8) it is clear that the prophet must have been writing
some time after 660 B.C., when that Egyptian city was sacked by
the Assyrian Emperor Ashurbanipal on his second invasion of
Egypt. On the other hand, though the fall of Nineveh is spoken of
as certain, and indeed imminent, it evidently has not yet occurred.
Since Nineveh was finally destroyed by the combined attacks of
Babylonians, Medians and Scythians about 612 B.C., we are
confined to the period 660 to 612. But the gap may be narrowed a
little, for it appears from Nahum's prophecy that Judah had
suffered quite recently from an Assyrian assault. Now in the
historical record the long reign of Manasseh, 697 to 642 B.C., is
almost one long blank, but it is known that Ashurbanipal's brother,
whom he had made king of Babylon, revolted against him about
648 B.C. If, as seems probable, this rebellion against the hated
Assyrian was a signal to the Palestinian powers to revolt also (they
were usually quick to take such an opportunity) and if Judah joined
in the revolt and it was quelled by an Assyrian expedition, that
would explain how Manasseh came to be taken in chains to Babylon
as 2 Chronicles 33: 11 tells us, and would explain also the allusion
of Nahum to an Assyrian onslaught. These suggestions are purely
conjectural, but they have the effect of locating Nahum's prophecy
rather more narrowly between 640 and 620 B.C. In view of the fact
that Assyria is spoken of as still powerful and feared, the earlier
part of the period is the more likely.

Some find evidence in Nahum's prophecy that he was actually
living in Nineveh when he wrote. The following points are urged in
support of the idea: Nahum seems well acquainted with Nineveh
and things Assyrian; he uses Assyrian words to denote certain
officers, speaks of the brick-built walls and the river-gates; he even
refers to the "mantelet" or the portable shelter for the soldiers
manning the battering ram (the word is found on the monuments);

162   *Nahum*

he speaks of the temples and images, and of the palace in the centre
of the city as the last refuge of the defenders; he is aware of the
large crowd of merchants with vast stores of wealth, of the princes
with their tiaras, of the marshals and nobles. These details are
depicted with such vividness as to suggest that the writer must have
been an eyewitness. While it cannot be proved that Nahum had
seen Nineveh, it is a natural inference from the forcibleness of the
language.

On the other hand his acquaintance and concern with Israel and
Judah appear in 1: 4 and 1: 13—2: 3. Conditions in Judah are,
however, not described in detail, and there is no reference to the
sins of the people or to the need for repentance. It has been
conjectured that Nahum may have been a descendant of the
captives removed from Northern Israel in 720 B.C. on the sack of
Samaria, or that he was carried to Babylon in company with
Manasseh. But of these points we cannot be certain.

One thing is clear: the prophecy was a written composition from
the first, not just a record of oral discourses. It is remarkably
single-minded, for while the destruction of the kingdoms of the
nations, based on pride and military might, and the establishment
of the kingdom of the Lord are regarded as certain, the recognition
(found in other prophets) that the Assyrian oppression had been
due to Israel's sins, that it would be followed by the Babylonian,
and that Judah was in urgent need of repentance, is absent. As
Assyria had filled the political horizon of the Middle East for
nearly 150 years, so her destruction was to the prophet the greatest
event of his time and a striking vindication of the honour of
Yahweh, whose name had been reproached by Sennacherib. And
this time there is no possibility of repentance or of reprieve for the
"city of blood".

The prophecy may be conveniently treated in the three sections
formed by its chapters. The first expresses the majesty of God in
judgement and His goodness to His people; the second describes the
overthrow of Nineveh; and the third consists of a reflective
lamentation upon that overthrow.

1.   God's Majesty and Goodness (1: 1–15)

1: 1–7: Nahum's prophecy is first called "a burden", that is a
threatened judgement, of Nineveh; and then a "vision", a
revelation of events yet to happen. Evidently, after the repentance
effected by the preaching of Jonah the Ninevites had fallen back
again into their former sins. Though appointed by God as the
means whereby He would chastise His people, the Assyrians had set

Nahum 1   163

out to uproot Israel and Judah in satisfaction of their own pride.
Nahum's name means Comforter, but not evidently for the
Ninevites; only for the faithful of Israel who still waited for the
"day of the Lord".

The name of Yahweh occurs three times in verse 2, His titles
rising in awesomeness. He is first "jealous"; jealous of the
reputation of His name among the peoples, that is, and of the way
in which His own people either honour or are a reproach to that
Name. In the case of Nineveh a long series of wrongs causes Him
to be an Avenger. In the Law the Lord had expressly forbidden His
people to take revenge, for "vengeance belongeth unto me" (Deut.
32: 35; Lev. 19: 18), thus asserting His right and His will to deal
with men according to their deeds. Of unrighteous Israel He later
said: "Shall not my soul be avenged on such a nation as this? ...
Shall I not visit for these things?" (Jer. 5: 9, 29; 9: 9). As we take
into account the numerous cases where the opposite is said of God
("Will he reserve his anger for ever?", Jeremiah 3: 5; "He will not
always chide, neither will he keep his anger for ever" Psa. 103: 9),
we perceive the necessity of keeping the exact situation in mind
before judging of such sayings. Here it is a question of an unrighteous city, evidently beyond the possibility of redemption.

The second verse repeats the declaration of His own character
given by God to Moses: "slow to anger" recalls the result of Jonah's
message to Nineveh, and is the same phrase as "longsuffering" in
Exodus 34: 6; "he will not at all acquit the wicked" is the "he will
by no means clear the guilty" of Exodus. The whirlwind and the
storm are the familiar figures of judgement, as in Psalm 18: 9–14.
His "rebuking the sea" and "drying up the rivers" are allusions to
the crossing of the Red Sea and Jordan, the evident demonstrations
of His power. The desolations of Bashan, Carmel and Lebanon,
celebrated for pastures, grapes and cedars, are cited as evidences of
the judgements of God upon His own people.

Yet despite the terror of His "indignation" (a word *almost only*
used of the wrath of *God*), when the mountains are shaken as by
earthquake and "his fury is poured out like fire" as in the
destruction of Sodom, yet it remains a great truth that "Yahweh is
good", full of mercy to those who trust in Him; them He "*knows*",
as He did Rahab in Jericho and Hezekiah in Jerusalem, and as the
Psalmist asserts: "The Lord knoweth the way of the righteous"
(1: 6). It is against this profound Old Testament background that
we must read the New Testament declarations: "I know my sheep",
and "The Lord knoweth them that are his" (John 10: 14; 2 Tim.
2: 19), and by contrast, "I never knew you" (Matt. 7: 23).

164   *Nahum 1*

vv: 8–11: Having recited for the encouragement of the faithful the eternal characteristics of the Lord, Nahum now comes more closely to his immediate subject, though Nineveh is still only referred to as "the place". The flood, both of the armies God would send against them, or the swelling rivers which passed through the city (by tradition one of the means whereby the city was taken) would drive the Ninevites into the darkness of death. For was it not Sennacherib who had "reproached" the Lord, "defied the Holy One of Israel" (2 Kings 18: 35; 19: 15–34), by contemptuously enquiring how the Jews could expect Him to deliver them from his power, since none of the gods of the surrounding countries had been able to do so? Thus did he "imagine" against the Lord. But though the Ninevites take refuge behind their defences like tangled thorns, and drench themselves in their drink, yet they shall blaze like dry stubble. The "wicked counsellor", literally "a counsellor of impiety or belial", is usually understood as a reference to Sennacherib, but there is no reason why it could not be an allusion to an Assyrian monarch nearer to Nahum's time and to a particular historical event of which we have no precise information.

vv. 12–15: The address: "Thus saith the Lord", in verse 12 suitably marks the fact that the following words are directed to Israel rather than to Assyria: although the Assyrians are in full strength ("many") and self-confident ("quiet"), yet they shall be mown down as grass and shall pass *away* (not "through"). Israel's Divinely imposed affliction shall come to an end. It is said that the verb "afflict", when used of the action of God, applies only to His chastisement of His people (e.g. Deut. 8: 2; 2 Kings 17: 20), or of individuals (Psa. 88: 7; 90: 15; 22: 24) but *nowhere* of the judgement of His enemies, a point which makes it impossible to apply this verse to Assyria. The breaking of the Assyrian yoke is to be "now", suggesting that the event was not far distant when the tributary relation of Judah to Ashurbanipal (the king who took Manasseh away to Babylon, though he afterwards restored him) would come to an end.

In verse 14 the change of gender of the pronoun (from "thee" feminine in verse 12 applied to Judah, to "thee" masculine here) shows that the "commandment" concerns Nineveh and the Assyrians: their gods are to be cut off, their line is to come to an end, they are to be buried, as Ezekiel declared: "Asshur is there (in Sheol), his graves are about him ... set in the sides of the pit" (32: 22–23); for the Assyrian is of small account, dishonoured ("vile"). We may imagine the tremendous declaration of faith contained in these words, delivered at a time when the Assyrian

Nahum 2 165

empire was the greatest power on earth; and the rejoicing in
Jerusalem as the messenger comes hastening over the mountains, no
doubt of Israel, to bring the glad tidings of peace at last from the
ruthless oppressor (the passage is apparently a quotation from Isa.
52: 7). Upon the basis of this deliverance, recognised as the work of
the Lord who has "made bare his holy arm", the prophet calls upon
Judah to keep the feasts of the law and to perform the vows made
in the time of distress; for the "wicked counsellor" (as v. 11) of the
"villainous one", a term of reproach for the Assyrian officers who
"passed through" the land for the collection of tribute, shall be "cut
off".

No doubt Nahum and his contemporaries hoped that the
destruction of Nineveh would be the signal for the complete
restoration of Israel to harmony with God; yet the thoughtful ones
must have wondered how such blessing could be in view of two
facts: first, the manifest corruption of the nation which was not yet
prepared for the blessing; and secondly, the clear indications in
earlier prophecies that Judah was to be taken captive to *Babylon*, a
power which had not yet risen to international status. Standing at
our vantage point we perceive the great scope of this verse; the
oppressions of Babylon, of Rome, and of the times of the Gentiles
had all to pass before the "peace" published by the messengers of
the Gospel of Christ would bring lasting blessing to "all Israel".

2. Nineveh is "empty and void and waste" (2: 1-13)

2: 1-7: The first seven verses form a vivid picture of the besiegers
and the besieged. "He that dasheth in pieces"—the term means
the disperser, the scatterer or devastator—is the besieger of
Nineveh. Ironically the Ninevites are urged to make all preparations for the defence: "fence thy defences, strengthen thy
might"; for the Lord has a work in hand. He "restoreth", "bringeth
again" (R.V.), the seed of "Jacob", to whom He gave the name
"Israel"; for the vine of Israel had been "emptied" by the
"emptiers", their land had been plundered. As a result the Lord
would send *His* mighty men, the fierce Medians and the Babylonians who would unwittingly be carrying out His will, to bring
about the downfall of Nineveh, just as later He commanded His
"sanctified ones" (the Medes and Persians) to destroy Babylon
(Isa. 13: 3). These "valiant men" have red shields (such as appear
regularly on the Assyrian monuments), their chariots "flash with
steel" (R.V.; the meaning of the phrase translated "with flaming
torches" in the A.V. is uncertain), and they brandish their spears
with shafts of fir.

166   *Nahum 2*

The scene now moves to the inside of the besieged city: the chariots drive madly about the "broad ways". The Assyrian king "remembers his mighty men"; when summoned they come "stumbling" (perhaps from wine, or the expression may just convey fear) to their places on the walls; there they find the attackers have already prepared "the mantelet", the covered shelter used for the protection of the soldiers who were attacking the defences with battering-rams, as the monuments illustrate so graphically. "The gates of the rivers shall be opened"; Nineveh was surrounded and guarded by the rivers Tigris, Khauser and the greater Zab, the second of which actually ran through the city. Although there is no particular historical evidence on this point, it is obvious that the gates must have been a weak point in the defences; indeed tradition asserts that an inundation washed away the foundations of the walls. The "palace" was to be dissolved; since archaeologists have revealed that at least two of Nineveh's palaces were burnt, the sense is probably "dissolved by fire". Huzzab is an unknown word; in view of the allusion to "her maids" it has been suggested that it is the name of the queen, or a cryptic name for Nineveh (like Sheshach for Babylon), but no certainty is possible. In any case the women go forth, almost certainly into captivity, moaning and beating upon their breasts.

vv. 8–13: The inhabitants of Nineveh, multitudinous like a great pool of water, shall flee in panic, despite efforts to make a stand. Her despoilers shall strip her of her silver, gold and pleasant furniture, until she is "empty, and void, and waste", or as the Hebrew is said to sound: "bookah, comebookah, comebullakah", three words with the same basic sense but in ascending order; *Speaker's Commentary* suggests: "sack, sacking, and ransacking". Her people show all the physical signs of distress. The Lord now returns upon Nineveh the words of Sennacherib to Hezekiah: "Where are now the gods of Arpad ... that Yahweh should deliver *you* out of mine hand?", by enquiring: "Where is (now) the dwelling place of lions?", for the lion was conspicuous on the monuments of Assyria as a symbol of proud strength. "Behold I am against thee, saith Yahweh of hosts"; the title occurs in Nahum only here and at 3: 5. Micaiah had seen "Yahweh sitting on his throne and all the host of heaven standing by him" (1 Kings 22: 19), and in Psalms 103: 21 and 148: 2 His hosts are His angels. The use of the title is a rebuke to the idolatrous worship of "the host of heaven". As a result Nineveh's chariots and swords should be burned, and no longer would her emissaries (like Rabshakeh) bear throughout the countries her imperial demands.

Nahum 3   167

3. "Woe to the city of blood!" (3: 1-19)

3: 1-7: The third chapter is a mingled lamentation, indictment, and description of Nineveh's overthrow. Her crimes are lies, rapine and the devouring of the prey like a lion; as Sargon, father of Sennacherib, boasts on the monuments, "I have ground to powder the nations"; but the invading armies shall come with their prancing horses and leaping chariots, their horsemen armed with sword and spear, and the city shall be filled with corpses. The "witchcrafts" and "whoredoms" of which Nineveh is accused are the efforts to force the subject peoples to worship Assyrian gods. (See the words of Rabshakeh before the walls of Hezekiah's Jerusalem, Isa. 36). Rawlinson (see *Speaker's Commentary*) comments upon the "attempts ... to diffuse everywhere a knowledge and recognition of the gods of Assyria. Nothing is more universal than the practice of setting up in the subject countries the 'laws of Asshur' or 'altars to the Great Gods'". A similar charge is brought against Babylon by Isaiah (47: 9). Assyria's "selling" of nations would then be an allusion to the transportation of whole communities to other lands, sometimes to be sold as slaves.

But the Lord of hosts would expose the "graceful harlot" (v. 4) to ignominy. Her skirts should be lifted and thrown over her head, in accordance with the practice with women convicted of unchastity (Ezek. 16: 37; Hosea 2: 3), so that her shame might be witnessed by all nations. She shall be exposed in the pillory as a spectacle and she shall find neither helpers nor comforters in the day of her desolation.

vv. 8-10: The short section cites the case of "populous No", that is the great Egyptian city of Thebes, called No-Amon because of the god Amon worshipped there. Thebes had been the capital of Upper Egypt and famous from antiquity for its splendour and military power. Its Pharaohs, conquerors for six centuries (1700 to 1100 B.C. approx.), had made it the centre of a world empire, like a former Nineveh in fact. Its palaces and temples were immense, as the ruins of Karnak and Luxor bear witness to this day. "Its great temples, ... halls, colonnades, colossal statues, obelisks, sculptures" were "on a scale of imposing magnificence to which there is probably no parallel in the world" *(Century Bible)*. The great hall of Karnak was 170 ft. wide by 329 ft. long, with 134 columns of colossal proportions supporting the roof, some of them 62 ft. high and 35 ft. in circumference. The Pharaohs were gods; their palaces were therefore temples, in which the statues of the monarch were ten times the size of the rest of his soldiers. Thebes was situated "upon the Nile streams" ("among the rivers"); the word is the

168   *Nahum 3*

plural of the usual word for the Nile. The "sea" was the Nile itself
which formed one of the city's defences. In her strength she
received the homage of Kush (Ethiopia), the people of South Egypt,
as well as of Put and the Lubim, the inhabitants of North Africa.
Yet, as Isaiah had prophesied (20: 3–4), this great city had quite
recently been brought to the dust, through two Assyrian invasions
of Egypt, when Ashurbanipal in 663 B.C. had completed its sack.
How should Nineveh think herself worthy to escape a similar fate?

vv. 11–19: Nineveh too was to "become drunken", with the cup of
the Divine wrath that is, as Jeremiah was to prophesy about
Babylon (25: 15–16, 27) and Isaiah had done of Jerusalem (51: 17);
she was to be "hidden", that is obscure, after her centuries of glory,
a prophecy which was accomplished through the sands of the
desert; her strongholds should collapse like figs shaken off the tree
when they are ripe. Her people should be as "women", a not
unfamiliar image for weakness and fear, used of the Egyptians in
Jeremiah 50: 37, and of the Chaldeans in 51: 30. The mountain
passes ("the gates of the land") would be undefended and the
"bars" of their city gates should be burned with fire. During the
two-year siege which they were to endure the Ninevites are
ironically urged to make every effort in their own defence: they
should draw water and make plenty of bricks to repair the damaged
ramparts.

But in the very place where they make these preparations the
Ninevites should be slain with the sword, devoured by the locust
("cankerworm", see Joel 1: 4; 2: 25) and ravaged by fire, despite
the multitude of their merchants and of their "crowned" officers
and captains. On the Assyrian monuments the high officers wear
diadems resembling the lower band of the royal mitre, a fact which
may throw some light on the words: "Are not my princes altogether
kings?" (Isa. 10: 8). The word translated captains is not of Hebrew
origin, and is found elsewhere only in Jeremiah 51: 27, being
probably the Assyrian name for a high-ranking officer. As the
locusts grow dormant in the cold, but disperse rapidly as soon as the
warmth of the sun reaches them, so these mighty men of Assyria
shall vanish.

The king of Assyria is now addressed directly: his nobles and his
governors slumber, while his people are scattered over the mountains like a flock without a shepherd; his "bruise" (a grievous bodily
injury) and his "wound" (often used of plagues inflicted by God, as
in Lev. 26: 21, Deut. 28: 59, 61) are both beyond healing. All who
hear the tidings of his fall break into rejoicing, for upon all the

Nahum 3

nations his "wickedness", his extortion and cruelty, had been a continual burden.

Concluding Reflections

So Nahum's "burden of Nineveh" comes to an end. Not many years later, about 612 B.C. according to the Babylonian Chronicle, the Medes, Babylonians and Scythians besieged the city. Upon its fall the Medes thoroughly sacked it, and the long era of its desolation began. Today the site of Nineveh is formed by uninhabited mounds, the province of the excavators whose spades have revealed the former glory of the ancient capital of Assyria.

Compared with most of the other prophecies, Nahum's work is of limited scope, but a knowledge of the tremendous part played in the affairs of the Middle Eastern nations for more than two centuries by the empire of Assyria, and of the sheer misery and suffering which it inflicted upon its subject peoples, should enable us to imagine the immense sense of relief and joy that the news of its fall would produce. To a prophet of one of the smallest of those nations, Nahum of Israel, was granted the rare privilege of announcing that fall in advance in the name of Yahweh whom the Assyrian had despised. To the ignorant heathen the fall of Nineveh was just one of those political adjustments which are the result of natural causes; Assyria was vanquished because her enemies were now too strong for her; but to the faithful in Israel it was the work of God, for had He not told it in advance through the mouth of a true prophet, as He had promised His people He would do through Moses? The affairs of Judah were desperate; the "knowledge of God" was little found in the land; but evidently the Lord had not abandoned His people and the heathen would not triumph for ever. The time of "peace" would come, when Judah should keep the law of God once more and pay her vows.

As we look back over the centuries we can see the judgement of corrupt Nineveh as the type of God's final controversy with the nations, when their power will be subdued and His Name shall be glorified in all the earth. So came the judgement of God only a few years later upon rebellious Judah by means of the Babylonians; so it came less than a century later upon proud Babylon itself, and six centuries after that upon the city of the Israel that rejected the Lord. So will it come again upon all powers that resist the coming King.

170   *Nahum 3*

Note 14: THE "VENGEANCE OF THE LORD"

There is in the robust language of Nahum a problem for some modern minds, who find unpalatable his blunt statement of the "indignation" of the Lord, the "fierceness of his anger" and His "vengeance on his adversaries", and are quick to charge the Old Testament prophets with "barbarity". There is one important principle to be kept clearly in mind here: the ultimate standard of God's judgements upon men is not human feelings; it is the expression of God's own character. He is merciful and gracious to those who heed His word, but His holiness must in the end require the destruction of the obdurate and unrepentant sinner. No doubt the smaller nations of the Middle East rejoiced in a vengeful spirit at the destruction of their great oppressor. But Nahum, who declares that God is "good" and "slow to anger", knows also that He is "great in power and will by no means clear the guilty" (1: 7, 3). The New Testament message is the same: Jesus will say to some, "I never knew you: depart from me, ye that work iniquity" (Matt. 7: 23); Paul describes "the wrath of God ... revealed from heaven against all ungodliness and unrighteousness of men" (Rom. 1: 18); and the Revelation makes plain not only "the wrath of God" but also "the wrath of the Lamb" (6: 16).

As for us, we must act in all mercy and compassion towards those we meet, and seek to bring before them God's grace in the Lord Jesus. But we do no real service to them if we conceal from them the holiness and righteousness of God, so perverting their understanding of His Name, or fail to make clear that God will reveal His judgements upon sin. The pressure of the spirit of our age is great upon us in this matter; let us see that it is countered by the spirit of the Word of God.

11
ZEPHANIAH
"SEEK YE THE LORD, ALL YE MEEK OF THE EARTH"

Introduction

Very unusually the record of Zephaniah's family is carried back four generations; the point of this must be found in the name Hizkiah, or Hezekiah, which suggests that the prophet was of royal descent. His date is given as the reign of Josiah, but since he describes Jerusalem and Judah as full of corruption and idolatry, he must have written *before* the reforms of that king, that is between 630 and 621 B.C. The state of the people of God is degraded: the land is full of violence, the judges are corrupt, the prophets false, the priests are idolaters who break the law and defile the sanctuary of God. The worship of God is abandoned and many are now indifferent or openly sceptical of God's intervention on behalf of His servants. The account strikingly resembles that of Israel 100 years earlier, or even that of Nineveh given by Nahum. Human corruption ever takes the same notorious paths from age to age, a striking testimony to the power of natural instincts, and a standing warning to all subsequent generations.

Zephaniah has a good deal to say, understandably in these circumstances, about judgement, first of Judah and Jerusalem. Upon them the day of the Lord shall be one of wrath, darkness and distress; the language is very like that of Joel 150 years before. The land and the city are to be desolate and the people taken into captivity. What power could in Zephaniah's day be expected to carry out this work of judgement upon Judah? By 625 B.C. the Assyrians had ceased to be a threat to Palestine, while the Babylonians had not yet appeared, nor indeed did they seem likely to do so. The date falls into the period of the domination of the Scythians, the barbarians who had crossed the Caucasus about 630 and who are said to have reached Egypt by 626. They were known as ruthless marauders and they could well have seemed an imminent threat to Judah, but in the event it was the Chaldeans (whose advent was revealed to Habakkuk) who proved to be the instruments of the Divine wrath. Judgement is next pronounced upon the nations, who are named: Philistia, Ammon, Moab, Egypt

172   *Zephaniah*

and Assyria, the sentence upon the last named being the remarkable one of utter desolation delivered at a time when Nineveh was
still a great name in the Middle East.

The grand design of the Lord is revealed in Zephaniah as
twofold: first the preservation of a remnant and their regathering to
Israel and Zion, where "the Lord thy God" was to be mighty "in
the midst of thee". He would save them with joy and love (the
language is very expressive of the deep feeling of God for His
people). Next, the subduing of the nations with a view to their
conversion to "a pure language, that they may all call upon the
Lord with one consent". This was a final result which Israel had not
at first contemplated but to which their prophets were now
accustoming them. There is however no precise hint as to how this
result is to be achieved and no mention of a personal Messiah, but
the assurance that Yahweh, the God of Israel, shall be known in the
eyes of many nations and that His faithful remnant shall be to Him
for a name and a praise in the earth.

Modern critics generally tend to reject some parts of Zephaniah,
but as usual their reasons are based on their own prejudices: the
prophet is said to switch too abruptly from judgement to
redemption; or the judgement of Assyria could not have been
written before its fall; or the taunts of Ammon and Moab must
refer to the attitude of these nations on the capture of Jerusalem by
Nebuchadnezzar. These verdicts are based upon the critics' own
opinions as to what Zephaniah could or would have written, and
upon the refusal to believe in prophecy; they have no positive
evidence whatever to support them, and the divergencies among the
critics themselves as to what Zephaniah did or did not write, are
wide. In the words of E. J. Young, "There is no sufficient reason for
denying to Zephaniah any portion of his prophecy" (*Introduction to
the Old Testament*, p. 291).

The prophecy falls into four parts: the coming day of the Lord
upon Judah (1: 1–2: 3); the judgement of the heathen nations
(2: 4–15); the sins of Judah (3: 1–7); restoration and redemption
(3: 8–20).

1.   The Coming Day of the Lord upon Judah (1: 1–2: 3)

1: **1–6:** That Hizkiah was really Hezekiah the king is the only
suggestion which explains why the descent of Zephaniah should
be given with such detail. The circumstances revealed by his
prophecy make it practically certain that it must have been uttered
in the earlier years of Josiah, before the reforms. The language of
vv. 2–3 suggests that the judgement is to be a universal one: "I

Zephaniah 1 173

will utterly consume all things from off the face of the *ground*" (R.V.). The phrase recalls the Flood (Gen. 6: 7), as do the particulars: man and beast, fowls and fishes; and the assertion, "I will cut off man from the face of the ground" (R.V.), that is, man generally, the race of men. But as in the Flood it was the race of the wicked which was cut off, here it will be "the stumbling-blocks with the wicked". So in the Parable of the Wheat and the Tares it is declared that "the Son of man shall gather out of his kingdom all things that offend" (all stumbling-blocks) (Matt. 13: 41).

The next three verses are directed specially to Judah, the charge being idolatry and abandonment of their God. The hand of the Lord shall now be "stretched out", as it was over the land of Egypt (Exod. 6: 6), to cut off the Baal worshippers and the Chemarim or black-robed ones, evidently some kind of idolatrous priests (see Hosea 10: 5). The addition of the phrase: "with the priests" suggests that these latter were priests of the Lord, but were faithless to Him. The offering of incense to the host of heaven on altars erected upon the housetops was common, as Jeremiah 19: 13 and 2 Kings 23: 12 show. So was the divided worship of Yahweh and at the same time of the idol called Malcham, "their king". No doubt "the king" was Baal (or lord). (The Hebrews, to show their contempt for this "melech"—Heb. "king"—took away from the word its vowels and replaced them by the vowels of the word "bosheth", shame or abomination, so producing "Molech".) God's hatred of their divided worship is well expressed in Jeremiah: "Will ye ... burn incense unto Baal and walk after other gods, and come and stand before me in this house?" (7: 8–10). There was another class even: those who were just indifferent to the question of religion and had not "diligently sought the Lord", as it is clearly necessary to do (so the verse implies). Three types of sinners are therefore found in this passage: the open idolaters, those of divided allegiance, then the irreligious and atheists.

vv. 7–13: In verse 7 are blended a number of features found in other prophets: Habakkuk has, "Hush before the Lord" (2: 20); Isaiah, Joel, and Obadiah all have, "Nigh is the day of the Lord"; Isaiah (34: 6), Jeremiah (46: 10), and Ezekiel (39: 17) all have the idea of a sacrifice. The day of the Lord spoken of by Joel (at least in its first application) had already come and gone with the invasion and the defeat of Sennacherib, but the expression is used by the prophets of any signal judgement by God either upon the nations or upon His own people, and especially of the *last* such judgement which should usher in the uninterrupted reign of Yahweh. The sacrifice prepared by the Lord is Judah and Jerusalem (as it was

174 *Zephaniah 1*

Bozrah in Isaiah 34: 6), and the "guests" or sanctified ones are the nations "set apart" to carry out this judgement, in this case the Babylonians. The heathen called to punish Babylon were "my sanctified ones" (Isa. 13: 3), and Jeremiah makes use of the same figure: "I have sanctified against thee (Judah) destroyers, a man and his weapons" (Jer. 22: 6–7).

The punishment is to come upon "the princes, the king's children", but with no mention of the king, who would be at the time the young Josiah. In fact the Babylonian judgement came upon his sons. The "foreign dress" (R.V.), which the Israelites were adopting, replaced the band of dark blue upon the fringes of their garments which they were commanded to wear "that ye may *remember* the commandments of the Lord" (Num. 15: 37–41). Since the band was also found on the mitre of the high priest, its intention was to designate the whole nation as "holy" to the Lord. That the Israelites were now imitating the more ostentatious dress of the Gentile nations (that of Babylon was especially luxurious in scarlet and vermilion, Ezek. 23: 14) was a sign of their departure from God in spirit, for dress has always been an indication of the mind; and so it significantly remains to this day. Although the precise allusion in the expression "those that leap on the threshold" is unknown, it must be some idolatrous custom, connected probably with the fate of the god Dagon and the subsequent refusal of his worshippers to step upon the threshold (1 Sam. 5: 1–5). It is remarkable that the superstition that it is unlucky to step upon a threshold is still widely held.

Violence and deceit were the marks even of the servants (how often these two are associated as the prime traits of corruption: "the earth was corrupt and full of violence", Gen. 6; and the Messiah shall "redeem their soul from deceit and violence", Psa. 72). In the day of judgement there should be a great wailing in the city: from the Fish-Gate, thought to have been in the North wall, from the "second" or lower part (the term is wrongly translated "college" in 2 Kings 22: 14); from the "hills", probably Zion and Moriah, there would be the "crashing" of demolition. Maktesh (the word means the "pounding place"), is Jerusalem itself, soon to suffer judgement. The "merchant people" are the people of Canaan, used here of the inhabitants of Jerusalem, because their deeds are like those of Canaan, for with their ill-gotten wealth (silver) they shall be cut off. Jerusalem is to be searched with lamps as devout Jews searched their houses before the Passover to remove every trace of leaven, so no deed will remain concealed by the darkness.

As wine allowed to settle on the lees becomes curdled or thickened, so are those who declare their disbelief that the Lord will

Zephaniah 2   175

ever *do* anything. These men are like the ungodly of all ages, who do their own pleasure and say to themselves: "Thou wilt not require it"; "the Lord shall not see, neither shall the God of Jacob require it" (Psa. 10: 4, 5, 11, 13; 94: 6–7). It was the challenge of the Lord to His own people that their idols "cannot do good, neither can they do evil" (Isa. 41: 23; Jer. 10: 5); these faithless Israelites were in fact treating Him as no better and no worse than an idol. Therefore utter desolation should come upon them with the destruction of their material possessions, their houses and vineyards, in which they delighted.

vv. 14–18: In language like Joel's, Zephaniah now returns to the subject of the day of the Lord, when the warrior shall cry out in despair because he is helpless to deliver himself. Verse 15 contains a number of linguistic features; trouble and distress are words of similar sound; wasteness and desolation are derived from the same root; both pairs of words had been used before (in Job 15: 24; 30: 3; 38: 27); darkness and gloominess occur together in Joel 2: 2, while clouds and thick darkness are used by Moses in describing the giving of the covenant (Deut. 4: 11). Zephaniah was clearly well acquainted with the earlier writings held as holy by Israel. Although the application must be to Judah and Jerusalem here, the language reminds us of the world of Genesis 1: the earth waste and desolate and the heaven dark, before the Lord commenced His work of creation. So for the faithless majority in Judah it is back from the light of the Lord they have rejected to the "power of darkness" they have preferred. Upon the walled cities and in the corner turrets an alarm shall be sounded; the inhabitants shall find no refuge in their wealth in which they have trusted, but shall stumble as the blind and shall be destroyed from off the land ("speedy riddance" is Isaiah's "consumption" and Jeremiah's "full end": Isa. 10: 23; 28: 22; Jer. 4: 27), because "they have sinned against the Lord", in despising His holy Name for the honour of which He is jealous. The violence of this denunciation of Judah is hardly less than Nahum's upon heathen Nineveh.

2: 1–3: The first three verses of chapter 2 contain a last appeal to the people to consider their ways. "Sift yourselves, yea sift" (Pusey) as dry sticks are selected one by one for the fire; the idea is evidently one of self-examination. The nation is "shameless" (R.S.V.); the expression is said to mean "does not grow pale", that is with shame or fear. Before the "decree" of judgement come to pass, in the day of the Lord's anger—for "as chaff a day passeth", that is the days of grace yet remaining are quickly passing—the

176   *Zephaniah 2*

"meek" of the earth are urged to seek the Lord. Their meekness is
rather a humility, not primarily towards man but towards God, a
bowing down before Him (cf. Peter's, "Humble yourselves therefore under the mighty hand of God", 1 Pet. 5). Like "poor" and
"afflicted" the term is of frequent use in the psalms and prophets as
the contrary of the "wicked", "proud", and "evil-doers" (see p. 57).

Their characteristic is that they have "wrought his judgement",
another word of immense significance for the understanding of the
Old Testament. The "judgement" was firstly the statute delivered
by God for the government of His people ("keep his commandments and his statutes and his judgements", Deut. 30; 16):
then the religious ordinance with the moral obligation attached;
hence it comes to be a synonym for the "way of the Lord", as in
Jer. 5: 4–5—"They know not the way of the Lord and the
judgement of their God." This way of the Lord is only found by
those who "seek righteousness", that is who obey the righteous
requirements of God (this implies a recognition of sin, for the
requirements are only necessary because of sin). They accept His
offer of pardon, and "seek meekness", that is they humble
themselves before Him by "trembling at his word" (Isa. 66: 2).
Such faithful ones shall be "hid" in the day of wrath, an expression
which must contain an allusion to Zephaniah's own name, "The
Lord hath hid", and to certain passages in the psalms: "In the time
of trouble he shall hide me ... How great is thy goodness which
thou hast *laid up* (same root) for them that fear thee. Thou shalt
hide them ... Thou shalt *keep them secretly* (same root) ..." (Psa.
27: 5; 31: 19–20). Even amidst the general corruption a remnant of
faithful ones existed, and here was the message of comfort and
encouragement for them. (For more detailed study of the Old
Testament sense of Meekness, Judgement, Righteousness, see the
author's "The Knowledge of God", *The Christadelphian,* 1967.)

2. The Judgement of the Heathen Nations (2: 4–15)

vv. 4-7: The word "For" at the head of this section suggests the
idea of warning to Israel as they consider the fate of the surrounding peoples. The overthrow of Philistia is predicted in Jeremiah 47
and Ezekiel 25, but like Amos, Zephaniah mentions only four cities,
omitting Gath, which may have remained under Judah since the
days of Uzziah and Hezekiah. The names of the cities suggest their
doom: Azzah (Gaza, strong) shall be "azubah", desolated; Ekron
(deep-rooted) shall be "teaker", uprooted; Ashdod (waster) shall be
"driven forth violently"; Chebel, the "band of the sea coast", shall
be "chebel" (another sense) an inheritance for Judah (see v. 7).

Zephaniah 2   177

The appearance of the name Cherethites between the Philistine cites of verse 4 and the "land of the Philistines" of verse 5, shows that they were part of that nation (1 Sam. 30: 14; Ezek. 25: 16). They are thought to have come from Crete (Amos 9: 7), and a detachment of them evidently joined David's army (2 Sam. 8: 18). Their name means "cutters-off". Philistia is to become desolate and the sea coast pasture lands for shepherds. The "cottages" of verse 6 are really "diggings", which may signify wells. The general fulfilment of these Biblical prophecies upon the Philistine cities is well reviewed in books like Urquhart's *Wonders of Prophecy*. The word "coast" is "chebel", a cord or line, hence a portion or inheritance measured by the line; the inheritance of the land of the Philistines is to fall to Judah, a thought found also in other prophets. Ashdod's doom was to come at noon, that is suddenly, when least expected; but the restored remnant of Judah are to lie down like a flock in the evening, the time of rest after the exertions of the day, for Yahweh their God shall accomplish it for them.

vv. 8–11: Moab and Ammon, blood-relations of Israel through their descent from Lot, were long-standing enemies of Israel. They are here charged with "reproach" and "reviling" (or cutting speeches) against "my people". The reproach of these nations was in their contempt for the God of Israel, who allowed His people to be oppressed by foreigners, and was therefore blasphemy, against which Yahweh reacts strongly. "As I live, saith Yahweh of hosts", asserting by these words that *He alone* has life and has the host of heaven at His command, while all the gods of the nations are dumb idols—Moab and Ammon shall be like Sodom and Gomorrah, cities which had become the type of utter destruction. The particular example may here be chosen because Sodom and Gomorrah were close to the border of Moab and Ammon who, themselves descended from Lot, were rescued by the mercy of Yahweh from the fiery destruction of those cities. But they are to become the possession of the "remnant" and the "residue" of God's "nation". Since Israel have never yet fully occupied the territory of Moab and Ammon, this prophecy manifestly still awaits its great fulfilment. These nations shall be judged for their pride, but the time will come when Yahweh will destroy all the gods of the earth by "famishing them" (that is by taking away the offerings upon which they have "fed", the "fat of their sacrifices ... the wine of their drink offerings", Deut. 32: 38), so that all the nations shall worship the God of Israel, "every one from his place", that is each in his own land.

vv. 12–15: The Ethiopians, a section of the old oppressor Egypt, are put here for the whole nation because of the dominant part they

178   *Zephaniah 2*

had played in Egyptian politics. They are to be destroyed by the
Lord's sword, that is by Nebuchadnezzar, three times called the
Lord's "servant" in Jeremiah, and by the Babylonian armies raised
up by Him for the task. After the destruction of Jerusalem,
Nebuchadnezzar invaded Egypt, which remained desolate 40 years.
The desolation of Assyria and Nineveh, however, was to be of a
much more lasting character. Abandoned by men, the site was to be
the haunt of animals (the cormorant is said to be the pelican and
the bittern the hedgehog or porcupine). The palaces and temples
would be desolate, their cedar-panelled walls exposed. The proud
city of Nineveh, who used of herself a phrase ascribed to *Himself*
by the Lord: "I am, and there is none beside me" (Isa. 45: 5, 6, 18,
22)—perhaps thereby indicating that the ruler of Nineveh, like the
Pharaoh of Egypt, considered himself a god—was to become an
utter desolation, a refuge of wild animals, and a subject of
contempt. But if Judah was disposed to rejoice at this judgement,
she should have remembered that Isaiah and Micah (39: 6 and
4: 10) had already declared that her captivity was to be to *Babylon*.

3.   The Sins of Judah (3: 1-7)

3: 1-7: In verse 1 the charge against Jerusalem is rebellion
("filthy" is really rebellious, or defiant), defilement by sin, and
cruelty; the same charges are here levelled against Judah as those
by Hosea and Amos at Israel. Her people had not obeyed "the
voice", of God that is, through the law and the prophets. When
chastisement followed upon disobedience, they were resentful
instead of submissive, and trusted in Egypt or Assyria instead of in
their God. Jerusalem's evil is within herself, for the rulers and
judges are like wild beasts, the prophets are boastful ("light"
suggests water boiling over) and unprincipled, and the priests
pollute the temple and break the law, by offering perverse interpretations of it which in effect violate its spirit. But there is Another
"in the midst" of Jerusalem as well as the unrighteous princes:
righteous Yahweh Himself. Every morning (the traditional time for
doing justice) God gave proof that He was a righteous Ruler in
their midst: He had "cut off the nations" for their iniquity—the
Canaanites for example before Israel—expecting Israel to learn the
lesson of His righteous judgement upon sin and so to "receive
instruction", that is to profit by correction; but the unjust were
unmoved at this evidence of the Lord's righteousness and set
themselves the more determinedly to follow corrupt ways. God's
purpose in chastising them had not been attained; there would now
be no alternative to their utter destruction.

Zephaniah 3 179

4. Restoration and Redemption (3: 8-20)

vv. 8-10: The new section opens with a call to "wait upon" the Lord, evidently addressed to the "meek of the land" (2: 3); for there will come "a day" (the definiteness of the expression is to be noted) when He will pour out his judgements upon all the nations of the earth, a sweeping declaration which has certainly not been fulfilled up to the present day. The prophecy resembles those of the close of Joel, or Zechariah, of Ezekiel 38-9, and of Revelation. But the result of these judgements is to be striking: "For then will I turn to the *peoples* a purified lip". As the world, before the dispersion at Babel, was of "one lip" (Gen. 11: 1, 6, etc.), though rebellious in heart, so now their words will be cleansed (the fruit of the lips is the sacrifice of praise, Heb. 13: 15), and they will all serve the Lord with "one shoulder", that is steadfastly, like oxen pulling against a single yoke. Thus the chastisement of the nations leads to their conversion; at the same time is the restoration of God's people.

The R.V. margin offers a more understandable rendering of verse 10: "From beyond the rivers of Ethiopia they shall bring mine offering, my suppliants, the daughter of my dispersed" (The *Speaker's Commentary* and others agree). In favour is the parallel prediction of Isa. 66: 20. The rivers of Ethiopia are probably chosen as the area farthest south with which the Jews had any dealings, a fit representative therefore of the whole world beyond. The word "offering", by contrast with the word "sacrifice", suggests a bloodless gift.

vv. 11-13: The day of the judgement of the nations is also to be that of Israel's purging, for those who "exult in pride" shall be purged out (as Ezek. 20 describes: "I will purge out from among you the rebels and them that transgress against me ... they shall not enter into the land of Israel", v. 38); "thou shalt be no more haughty *in* my holy mountain". There will be left over, as a remnant, an afflicted and poor people, that is those of submissive and obedient mind, and they shall "take refuge in the name of the Lord", or as Isaiah says, "The Lord hath founded Zion and the poor of his people shall trust in it" (14: 32). The old sins of lying and iniquity shall be removed, and the remnant shall lie down and feed like a flock, and "none shall make them afraid", the very phrase used in Leviticus 26: 6 as a promise, "if ye walk in my statutes".

vv. 14-17: The next four verses are a remarkable expression of the reconciliation which God intends for the regathered remnant of His people, when they are purged. The verbs are in the "prophetic perfect", the past tense which looks upon their actions as already

180   *Zephaniah 3*

accomplished. The remnant are bidden to rejoice utterly, for God
has taken away their "judgements", that is the evils inflicted upon
them by Him in His righteous anger; in the midst of them is now
their King, no less than the Lord Himself. Fear and half-hearted
service shall be banished from Jerusalem, for God is their Saviour,
who will rejoice to do them good. It is a thought found in other
prophetic passages: "As the bridegroom rejoiceth over the bride, so
shall thy God rejoice over thee ... The Lord delighteth in thee"
(Isa. 62: 4–5); and Moses had declared long before: "The Lord thy
God shall rejoice over thee for good", if they sought Him (Deut.
30: 9) —rejoice is a strong term, implying full and exuberant joy.
Very strikingly, God will also "be silent in his love" (R.V.m and
R.S.V. note, for "rest in"), implying that He will no longer
remember the sins of His people. So He promised through
Jeremiah: "I will remember their sin no more" (31: 34), and Micah:
"God ... who pardoneth iniquity ... passeth by the transgressions
of the remnant of his heritage" (7: 18). The verse concludes: "he
will exult over them with singing"; truly a striking declaration of
God's real joy in the accomplishment of redemption among the
remnant of those who respond.

vv. 18–20: Verse 18 is obscure, but literally reads: "Them that
sorrow for the solemn assembly, I gather. Of (or from) thee they
are, a burden upon her is reproach." Jerusalem is addressed and it
is her exiles who "sorrow for the solemn assembly" because they
cannot take part in the feasts of the Lord. Them God will gather,
for they are *of* Zion, her true children. Meanwhile there is a
burden, the reproach of her foes. But at the time of restoration God
will "undo" those who have afflicted Zion, that is, He will deal with
them by way of retribution. Instead of being dispersed like sheep,
His people should be praised and famous in every country where
they had formerly been dishonoured, a fulfilment of the words
spoken to them through Moses: "The Lord hath avouched thee this
day to be his peculiar people ... that thou shouldest keep all his
commandments; and to make thee high above all nations ... in
praise and in name and in honour"; then the verse concludes most
significantly: "that thou mayest be *an holy people* unto the Lord
thy God" (Deut. 26: 18–19). The praise will arise from the fact that
the Lord has acknowledged them as His people visibly, before the
nations; and the cause, that they have become like God and ceased
to be like men.

   Zephaniah's last words emphasise the time: "at that time ...
even in the time that I gather you ... when I turn back your
captivities (plural) before your eyes." This regathering will be the

Zephaniah 3   181

last, the final one before reconciliation with God, and it will be
accomplished openly, even as was the deliverance at the Red Sea,
when Israel were bidden to "stand still and see the salvation of
God"; and as those Israelites who saw that deliverance were called
upon to obey the Lord because "ye have *seen* all that the Lord did
before your eyes in the land of Egypt", so the redeemed remnant of
the future will have before *their* eyes a similar deliverance and will
remain faithful for ever.

Concluding Reflections

As in other prophets the people of God are reminded that if His
judgements were to be poured out upon the nations (as Judah
expected), how much more upon *them* because of their privilege
and their dishonouring of the name of Yahweh. The implication of
chapter 3: 7 is very instructive however for the understanding of
God as Judge: "I said, Surely thou wilt fear me, thou wilt receive
instruction: so their dwelling should not be cut off, howsoever I
punished them: but they rose early, and corrupted all their doings."
The judgements of God were therefore intended as "instruction",
not of course in the mere sense of information, but rather of
correction; God chastised them in measure in order that He might
not have to chastise them *utterly.* It was a correction that Israel
would not receive: in the end their condition permitted of "no
remedy", and their dwelling-place had to be cut off.

The redemption of the residue of Israel will mean the submission
of the nations generally to the God of Israel; but 3: 9 adds: "For
then will I turn to the peoples a purified lip, that they may call
upon the name of the Lord, to serve him with one consent." This is
no longer mere subjection, but reconciliation. The purified lip
speaks of the acceptable nature of their praise of Yahweh; their
"calling upon" Him suggests a conscious and deliberate service,
rendered "with one shoulder", with no desire to depart from Him in
search of other gods. We have met this aspect before—in Micah for
example—and it is noticeable that while the earlier of the prophets
(e.g. Joel, Obadiah) have little trace of it, it occupies a distinct
place in the later ones. Israel, the privileged nation, were being
educated to receive it. How slow and unwilling their reception of it
was is shown by the attitude of the Jews in the days of the apostle
Paul; but it is easy to see why the apostle saw evidence of the call of
the Gentiles in the Old Testament prophets.

Zephaniah too has his conception of the "spiritual worship" God
required: "Seek ye the Lord, all ye meek of the earth, which have
wrought his judgement; seek righteousness, seek meekness: it may

182 *Zephaniah 3*

be ye shall be hid in the day of the Lord's anger" (2: 3): a verse which expresses all the spirit of the prophet. The acceptable of the earth are the humble ones (in contrast with the proud, corrupt, violent, and materialist-minded majority), for they, in seeking to do the will of God, are not ashamed or afraid to "seek meekness", trusting in His mercy that they will be "hid" as treasure in the day of His wrath. Their confidence is based on the conviction that "the Lord thy God in the midst of thee is mighty: he will save, he will rejoice over thee with joy: he will rest in his love, he will joy over thee with singing" (3: 17). We have a note here rather like that of Hosea: God *feels;* He is not just the impassive spectator, or mere manipulator of human puppets. Who can doubt that His "love" for the humble remnant is real and profound? Who can doubt that to be able to "save" them, in harmony with His own righteousness, is for Him a matter of "rejoicing", or even of "exultation"? And who can doubt that the same principles still apply for the benefit of those who "seek meekness" and wait for the God who is their salvation?

12

HABAKKUK

"THE JUST SHALL LIVE BY HIS FAITH"

Introduction

Of Habakkuk himself nothing is known, though he calls himself "a prophet", the only one of the writing prophets to do so. The subscription to his prophecy at the conclusion of chapter 3 (itself a kind of psalm): "my stringed instruments" or "my song accompanied with music", indicates that he was a Levite. The internal indications of date are: (1) the appearance of the Chaldeans as a hostile power; (2) the corrupt state of Judah (despite no mention of Judah or Jerusalem), meriting the judgement of God, a state which must have been that of the period *after* Josiah's reformation and death, that is after 610 B.C.; (3) Jerusalem has not yet fallen to the Chaldeans, which places the date before 598 B.C. We may therefore place the time of Habakkuk's prophecy as during the reign of Jehoiakim, 609 to 598 B.C., with a probability that it was written in the earlier part of that reign. At that time Egypt had temporarily recovered her domination of Palestine, after the collapse of Assyria; but the deeds of the Chaldeans were already known from the events of that collapse. Their ferocious character and military prowess had been sufficiently demonstrated to cause all hearts to quail with fear at the tidings of their approach.

The book itself differs from most of the other prophetic writings in that it is not a series of warnings to Judah, but the discussion of a religious problem (not unlike the book of Job) and a reflection upon principles of God's dealings both with the wicked of His own people and of the Gentiles; and finally with the attitude to be adopted by the faithful in those troubled times. Why does evil triumph in Judah? Why will God punish Judah by means of a nation more evil still, (and perhaps the implication is, at a time when the great traditional oppressor, the Assyrian, has been overthrown: why, in other words raise up *another* oppressor?—though this question is not explicitly put). How can a righteous God act thus? The answer is that the Chaldeans will perish in their turn, that God will come for

184   *Habakkuk*

the salvation of His people, as He did in the past; and that
meanwhile the just must wait in faith.

The book gives the impression of a finished whole; nevertheless,
it has been the target for what E. J. Young calls "negative
criticism". Briefly, some critics cannot believe that Habakkuk could
have written in such terms about the Chaldeans before their
appearance in Palestine; they regard the "archaic" nature of the
language of chapter 3 as proof of a post-exilic date; and they allege
that the character of the book, a religious "discussion", is that of
later literature among the Jews. As an example of arbitrariness of
judgement, we may quote the example of "Duhm, Torrey, and
others", who "have emended the word Kasdim (Chaldeans) of 1: 6
into Kittim (Cypriotes) and maintained that the prophecy was
directed against Alexander the Great and the Macedonians. This
procedure is subjective and without textual support" (Young,
Introduction to the Old Testament, p. 288).

Answering Critical Objections

There are satisfactory answers to these objections: the Chaldeans
were already known to the Israelites through the writings of Micah
and Isaiah, both of whom prophesied the captivity in Babylon.
Hezekiah had actually received an embassy from Babylon in
Jerusalem. There is no reason why the news of their exploits should
not have reached Jerusalem, as elsewhere in the Middle East, and
therefore no objection to regarding Habakkuk 1: 5–11 as an
allusion to an actual historical event. There is no reason why
Habakkuk should not have written chapter 3, *if he knew
Deuteronomy and the Psalms*! The late date of Deuteronomy is the
very point which the critics *assume*, without decisive evidence. If
that point be once abandoned, a large part of the critical case falls
to the ground. There are links between chapter 3 and the earlier
chapters. To quote E. J. Young again: "There is no sufficient
reason for divorcing chapter 3 from chapters 1 and 2. The theme in
both sections is the same ... there are important similarities in the
language: both in 1: 4, 13 and 3: 13 the enemy is designated as
wicked *(rasha)*; 3: 2 seems to have reference to the vision of 2: 3–5;
chapter 3 is *said* to be a prayer of Habakkuk. The fact that it is
introduced and concluded with technical musical terms is no reason
for denying it to Habakkuk, since such terms were evidently used in
pre-exilic times, in connection with the Psalter" (*Introduction to the
Old Testament*, p. 288). The unity of the book is stressed by
Kirkpatrick *(Doctrine of the Prophets)*, who comments upon "the
relation of its parts and the progress of thought in it, which are so

Habakkuk 1   185

striking as entirely to outweigh arguments against the unity of the book derived from some difficulties of detail". Finally, to maintain that Habakkuk could not have written this sort of book about 600 B.C. is baseless assertion. As so often, the critics' case turns out to be much less formidable than it sounds at first sight.

The book divides into three major sections, each coinciding with the chapter divisions, though the sections themselves can also be conveniently subdivided.

1. "Why dost thou show me iniquity?" (1: 1-17)

1: 1-4: Habakkuk, so well known evidently that it was not necessary for him to add any other identifying mark than simply "the prophet", seeing the evils in Judah and Jerusalem, asks how long he will cry to the Lord about them and He apparently not hear. God Himself must behold the vanity and wrong-doing that the prophet sees; for there is violent ill-treatment and injury; "strife hath arisen, contention lifteth itself". Because the wicked "encompass for a hostile end" the righteous, the "law is numbed", or paralysed, and justice does not obtain, for it is perverted or wrested. Justice (*mishpat*, often translated "judgement") is not merely fairness as between man and man, but the observance among God's people of those principles of mercy and truth which were a feature of the law.

The book opens then with the cry of a godly man, distressed at the flourishing of the wicked even in the city of the Lord. The circumstances of the corrupt reign of Jehoiakim, when the alliance of the civil authority with evil-doers made the chance of reformation remote indeed, is sufficient explanation of the prophet's anguished cry. That anguish is increased by the fact that apparently God does not act to prevent it; so the iniquity increases, according to Solomon's principle: "Because sentence against an evil work is not executed speedily, therefore the heart of the sons of men is fully set in them to do evil" (Eccles. 8: 11).

vv. 5-11: To this cry the Lord returns an answer: the people of God were bidden to behold with amazement what was already happening among the nations, for He would perform "in your days", that is *soon*, a work which they would not believe, even though they had been warned about it. The work was to be a judgement upon *them*, the people of the Lord, who had deluded themselves into thinking that because Yahweh was their God, He would never judge them.

The Chaldeans, the instrument of the Divine judgement and a

186   *Habakkuk 1*

new power in Israel's experience, were from Southern Babylonia. They advanced inland, obtained some dominance over the whole of Babylonia, and in 721 B.C. their king, Merodach Baladan, became ruler of the whole country, though Assyria regained control soon after. Under the new dynasty of Nabopolassar and Nebuchadnezzar (from about 625 B.C.) the Chaldeans became the ruling caste. Using the free will of men for His own ends, God has often "stirred up" rulers and powers to do *His* will, as the Medes were later to be employed for the destruction of Babylon itself (Isa. 13: 17).

Here the Chaldeans, "cruel and vehement", are to march through the land of Israel, or perhaps in view of 2: 5 ("gathereth unto him all nations") the *earth* (for the Hebrew word can mean both). They shall seize the territory of others. The soldiers of this dreadful power are a law unto themselves and the embodiment of pride, since they are self-sufficient, like the proud Assyrians before them, whose boast of supremacy over all the gods of the nations, including the "idols of Jerusalem", Isaiah records (Isa. 10: 8–11, 13–14). Like panthers and wolves, notorious for their speed, rapacity and cruelty, their horsemen shall come swarming upon the prey, swift as the eagle: a touch which is a reminder of Moses' prophecy, "The Lord shall bring a nation against thee from far ...as swift as the eagle flieth" (Deut. 28: 49); of Jeremiah's "his horses are swifter than eagles" (4: 13); and of Daniel's vision of a "lion with eagle's wings" (7: 4). The Divine answer to Judah's "violence" is to be the "violence" of these invaders, whose "faces are set eagerly as the East wind" (R.V.; but there is some doubt about the precise meaning). Their contemptuous treatment of conquered princes was notorious; they regard fortified cities with derision, for they "raise a mound" against them (though here it is mere dust) for the siege engines (the technical expression is found in 2 Kings 19: 32; Jeremiah 6: 6).

The literal rendering of verse 11 clearly expresses the sin of the Chaldean: "Then shall he sweep by (having taken the fortress of verse 10) and pass through (the conquered territory) and become guilty, he whose might is his god." The fault of the mighty in the earth is always pride: as Nebuchadnezzar, "Is not this great Babylon that *I* have built ... by the might of *my* power and for the honour of *my* majesty?" (Dan. 4: 30); as Tyre, "I am a god" (Ezek. 28: 2); and as antichrist, "sitting in the temple of God, showing himself that he is a god" (2 Thess. 2): a principle of self-worship explicitly denied by the Lord when He said to His people: "*I* will be to thee God" (Exod. 6: 7). This great fault is to bring about the Chaldean's destruction.

Habakkuk 2   187

vv. 12–17: The reply of the Lord that the sins of Judah are to be judged by means of the Chaldeans, creates for Habakkuk another problem; for how can a righteous God contemplate the execution of this judgement by a nation which is even worse than Judah?

Habakkuk commences with a profession of faith: his God is Yahweh, who is from everlasting and is the Holy One of Israel. For that reason the faithful will not perish, for their God will preserve them, as the Psalmist says: "The Lord hath chastened me ... but he hath not given me over unto death" (118: 18); and God Himself in Malachi 3: 6, "I am the Lord, I change not; therefore ye sons of Jacob are not consumed". Yet it is Yahweh who has ordained the Chaldean for the judgement of Israel and for their correction, He who is a "Rock" ("mighty God"), a very familiar title for God in the Scriptures; it occurs five times in the Song of Moses (Deut. 32) and frequently in the Davidic psalms. Habakkuk had "looked on iniquity" (the same original as "behold grievance" of verse 3) when he contemplated Judah.

How could the righteous God behold the treacherous and rapacious dealings of the "wicked" ("a word used only of the utterly depraved and godless", *Speaker's Commentary*) against those "more righteous than he"? Before these cruel invaders men are as helpless as the beasts of the earth, with no ruler to protect them; for the Chaldeans exultingly scoop them up like fish in a net, and then offer sacrifices unto their gods, to whom they ascribe their success. Ancient nations were accustomed to worship their weapons (cf. the veneration of their eagles by the Romans), and in verse 16 the Chaldeans are depicted as worshipping the "net" and the "drag", evidently symbols for their gods. Habakkuk concludes his plea with the fearful enquiry: Are these marauders to be allowed to enjoy the fruits of their "catch" and then go on to seize fresh prey?

2.   The Lord answers: The proud shall be judged (2: 1–20)

2: 1–4: Habakkuk now imagines himself as a watchman upon a tower who "looks out" (like the prophets who were "watchmen", the verb here being related to the same noun) to see what the Lord will say *in* him or *with* him (that is, would reveal to his understanding) concerning his plea, complaint (R.V., R.S.V.), or even arguing, as the A.V. "when I am reproved" has been variously rendered. In answer the Lord tells him to "write the vision" plainly, thus implying that it will be necessary for others to read it in later times; its fulfilment will not be immediate, but when others read it in later times they will see the truth of the prophecy. It is to be written so plainly that even the hasty reader will gather the message

188   *Habakkuk 2*

(the "running" is in the reading). The vision is for *the* appointed
time; that is, it will require a certain period of time to develop, fixed
of course by God; nevertheless "it breatheth, hasteth to the end" as
though it were yearning towards its fulfilment, and it will not fail to
be accomplished nor will it be behindhand, because it comes from
God who "cannot lie" (Num. 23: 19) and "is not slack concerning
his promise" (2 Pet. 3: 9).

So the prophet is to "wait for it", that religious act of "waiting
upon the Lord", so often referred to in the Old Testament. So
Jacob, "I have waited for thy salvation" (Gen. 49: 18, at the *end* of
his long life); the Psalmist, "Our soul waiteth for the Lord"
(33: 20); and Isaiah, "I will wait upon the Lord", who then adds
most significantly, "that hideth his face from the house of Jacob"
(8: 17); and the apostle who adapts Habakkuk's language, "Yet a
little while ... he shall come ... and will not tarry" (Heb. 10: 37),
while encouraging the Hebrew Christians to "patience". The
expression sums up the very spirit of the prophets, that "patience of
hope" accompanied by "joy in the Lord" which is our great need in
these disturbed days when the "vision" seems to "tarry".

Despite the arrogance and unrighteousness of the proud, the just
shall live; not however by similar deeds, but by his *faith.* The idea is
not however the abstract quality of faith, for which the Hebrew has
no precise word, but rather *faithfulness,* steadfastness, firm belief in
and reliance upon Divine promises. When Israel had witnessed the
deliverance at the Red Sea, they "believed the Lord", but later
when trials came they "rebelled ... believed him not ... nor
hearkened" (Exod. 14: 31; Deut. 9: 23); Abraham "believed in the
Lord and it was counted unto him for righteousness" (Gen. 15: 6);
Jehoshaphat at a time of national peril called upon Judah to
"believe in the Lord your God ... believe his prophets" (2 Chron.
20: 20) (in these passages "faith" and "believe" are from the same
root word). So the remarks of the apostles that "without faith it is
impossible to please God" (Heb. 11), and that the saints are "kept
by the power of God *through faith* unto salvation" (1 Pet. 1: 5),
imply not just some vague emotional experience or spiritual quality,
though in the New Testament the emphasis is upon the attitude of
mind, but in a thorough acceptance by the whole personality of the
fact that God will do as He has said, and a steadfastness of life in
that course.

vv. 5–8: The remainder of chapter 2 is a series of judgements,
largely in the form of "woes", pronounced upon the Chaldeans.
"Yea, how much more since wine is a deceiver" (R.V.); that is, how
much is the Chaldean arrogant, for wine is ever a"mocker" (Prov.

Habakkuk 2   189

20: 1). The Babylonians had the reputation of drunkenness, as
Belshazzar, flushed with wine and desecrating the vessels of the
temple, illustrates. The "proud" Chaldean is restless in his ambition
("neither keepeth at home"), but goes insatiably devouring fresh
victims, conquering fresh peoples, as Sheol endlessly swallows up
the dead.

These peoples are now represented as uttering a taunting song
against the Chaldean: Woe to him that plunders others and to him
"that ladeth himself with pledges" (R.V.). The A.V. "thick clay" is
got by dividing the Hebrew word *ab-tet* into two words. There are
good reasons for thinking, however, that the term here is rather
derived from *abet*, to borrow, and (in a certain form) to lend on a
pledge; hence the R.V. rendering "heavy pledges", a rendering
made more probable by the fact that "he loads himself" (R.V.)
hardly suits the idea of "thick clay"; and also that there would be
three separate allusions within two verses to the subject of *usury*:
the verb "increaseth" of verse 6 is related to one of the words for
interest; and the original of "them that bite thee" (verse 7) is
probably a play upon words, for *nashak* means literally "to bite",
and then "to bite off" from the principal lent, to give interest. So in
these two verses the Chaldean is compared to a merciless usurer,
who compels the nations to give him heavy pledges, but in the day
of retribution the victims will rise up and bite him, exacting
payment for his depredations. (See note in the *Century Bible*.)

These same nations will torment ("vex") him, or shake him to
make him disgorge his plunder. "The remnant of the peoples", all
those left from the aggressions of Nebuchadnezzar, the Medes and
Persians and their confederate tribes, would exact vengeance for the
Chaldeans' violent acts. Thus the forecast of the destruction of
Babylon is clear.

vv. 9-12: The Chaldean, thinking himself safe from calamity behind
his immense walls, set no limits to his covetousness, but he has only
brought shame to his nation and has involved his soul in guilt. The
very stones and beams of the houses, the unfeeling works of men,
shall call for vengeance against him: "Woe to him". Woe to him,
too, because he has founded his empire upon blood and violence,
using forced labour and oppression, a denunciation which reminds
of Daniel's charge to Nebuchadnezzar: "Break off thy sins by
righteousness and thine iniquities by showing mercy to the poor"
(Dan. 4: 27).

vv. 13-14: Turning now momentarily away from the particular case
of Babylon, the prophet considers the case of the nations generally.
Is not all their labour for the fire and do they not weary themselves

190   *Habakkuk 2*

just for nothing, and has not the Lord of hosts ordained it so? (The
verse is quoted by Jeremiah, 51: 58.) But the Lord's ultimate
intention is that the earth shall be full, not of these works of men
destined only for destruction, but of the knowledge of His glory.

This "knowledge of the glory of the Lord" would first be a
recognition of the God of Israel as the God of the whole earth,
supreme among the nations, as in Ezekiel 28: 22, where "I will be
glorified in the midst of thee (Sidon): and they shall know that I am
the Lord, when I shall have executed judgements in her"; and then
a recognition of the holiness, truth and mercy of the Holy One of
Israel, cf. Isaiah 11: 9 where "the knowledge of the Lord" refers to
His ways. The prophecy offers one more example of the way that
the word leaps forward in time to the final fulfilment, for the Lord
was not glorified in the earth at the destruction of Babylon (except
among those who knew the prophecies); yet the time will come for
its full realisation.

vv. 15–17: The fourth woe is pronounced against the Chaldeans
because they have degraded the captive nations by drunkenness,
and "addest thy venom thereto" (R.V.); *henah,* literally heat, being
used first for fury (Nah. 1: 6), and then for poison, venom, as in
Deuteronomy 32: 33, "the poison of serpents". The allusion may be
to actual practices, but may well be figurative for idolatry;
"uncovering nakedness" is exposing to shame. But instead of glory
Babylon herself shall have shame, and having made all the nations
drink the cup of bitterness, she shall see the same cup returned to
her, as in Jeremiah 25: 26: "The king of Sheshach shall drink after
them"; and in Psalm 75: 8: "For in the hand of the Lord there is a
cup ... the dregs thereof, all the wicked of the earth shall wring
them out and drink them." (This figure is applied to the latter-day
Babylon in Revelation 16: 19, "the cup of the wine of the fierceness
of the wrath" of God.) In "the violence of Lebanon", the name may
be used as a figure for the whole of Palestine, or the expression may
be an allusion to the cutting down of vast quantities of cedar for
building, which the inscriptions say that Nebuchadnezzar did; the
destruction of the beasts would be accomplished by the cutting
down of their natural shelter, the cedars of Lebanon. For these
crimes the Chaldean would be afraid, but also for his violence
against men.

vv. 18–20: The last three verses contain a satirical attack upon the
foolishness of idol worship. As Isaiah had used in the same
connection the very words which express the relation of God to
man: "(Shall) the thing *framed* say of its *framer,* He hath no
hands?" (29: 16), so Habakkuk enquires how the idol, that "teacher

Habakkuk 3   191

of lies", was any more valuable because its very *creator* trusted in it? What foolishness to expect the wood or the stone to teach, even if it is covered with silver or gold, seeing there is no breath in it! But, by the great contrast with such useless gods, the Lord is in His holy temple, that is in heaven His "dwelling place" (1 Kings 8: 30), "his holy habitation ... heaven" (Deut. 26: 15); or as the psalmist says: "The Lord is in his holy temple; the Lord's throne is in heaven" (11: 4). With a due sense of reverence, Habakkuk concludes: "Hush! before him all the earth." So the saints of the 20th century, in all their rejoicing and thanksgiving for God's infinite mercy and grace, must never lose their sense of reverence before His majesty and holiness.

3.   "Thou wentest forth for the salvation of the people" (3: 1–19)

3: 1–2: Habukkuk's third chapter is a remarkable composition from more than one point of view. It is a *tephillah,* or prayer; in psalm titles it occurs only in Psalms 17, 86, 90, 102 and 142. The exact meaning of the term Shigionoth is unknown, but it implies a psalm with a musical setting. Students of the Hebrew point out some striking features: verse 6 consists of 15 words in 5 combinations of 3; verses 3 and 10 of 12 words, in 4 groups of 3; verses 4, 9, 19 consist of 9 words in 3 groups of 3; other combinations in which the number three plays a prominent part are found in verses 8, 11, 16 and 17. There was evidently some law of composition here, which is now unknown.

Habakkuk first prays to God: he has heard "the report of thee" (R.V.), for, as the psalm puts it, "our fathers have told us what work (of deliverance) thou didst ... in the times of old" (44: 1). Yet as he considers the years of Israel's affliction, both already past and those which are apparently still to come through the Chaldeans, he is afraid; so he prays earnestly that God will "revive his work", that is perform again a great work of deliverance like the Exodus, alluded to by Isaiah: "Awake, ... O arm of the Lord, ... as in the ancient days ... Art thou not it which hath dried the sea ... that hath made the depths of the sea a way for the ransomed to pass over?" (51: 9–10). So the prophet now prays that in the midst of the wrath of judgement, God will remember His ancient mercies.

vv. 3–7: There follows a picture of the manifestation of the power of the Lord in the terms of the great deliverance of the past. Verses 3–15 contain a number of allusions to "Exodus" psalms (e.g. 18 and 68), to the book of Joshua and the song of Deborah (Judges), so showing how well known these writings were. But while the

192   *Habakkuk 3*

tenses are mostly in the past, it is "the future being vividly imagined as past, a usage frequent in the prophets" *(Century Bible)*. The fact that Yahweh has performed these great deeds for his people is an earnest of the future deliverance which He will equally perform. "God *shall come* ..." (with Pusey and Ellicott), or "cometh" or "came" (with R.V. marg, and *Speaker's Commentary)*; the tense is immaterial, for the first great act was *past*, but the deliverance God will surely bring is yet *future*. It is part of the genius of the Hebrew language that this elasticity in the significance of the tense is possible, and inevitable. "To the Oriental mind, with its disciplined and well-stored memory, the law of association meant far more than it does to us. A word suggested a whole train of thought. A phrase implied an argument. And so it is here. The recollection of the past is the ground of hope for the future. He who once wrought these wonderful works for His people will not fail to work the like again in His own time and His own way" (Kirkpatrick, *Doctrine of the Prophets*, p. 282).

"God came from Teman ... mount Paran"; the language resembles that of Moses in Deuteronomy 33: 2, though an old poetic form of Elohim, Eloah, is used instead of Yahweh. Why is Sinai omitted, when it is included by Moses and in Judges 5: 4–5? For two reasons: Sinai was the symbol of the law, that law which was now "slacked" and virtually rejected, and so Habakkuk was looking forward to the coming of a new law-giver; and then, Sinai was the scene of the laying-down of the law for Israel, but Habakkuk's theme here is the judgement of God upon the nations. The brightness of the Lord is as the sun (the light); the rays (R.V., R.S.V.) coming forth from His hand are the symbols of His power (cf. Deut. 33: 2, "from his right hand was a fiery law for them"). *There*, in the light, was His power concealed. Pestilence and burning heat are the means of His judgements ("I will send the pestilence among you", Lev. 26: 25, for disobedience). He stands and "measures" the earth, or land, as one who has supreme disposal of it, granting it by lot to the tribes of Israel; He causes the nations to tremble, as in the song of Moses: "The people (peoples, R.V.) shall hear and be afraid; terror shall take hold of the inhabitants of Palestina" (Exod. 15: 14); and Rahab's testimony to the spies: "Your terror is fallen upon us" (Josh. 2: 9). Even the age-old mountains and hills are "broken down" and "sink", for Yahweh's "goings are as of old" (as in Psa. 68: 24, "They have seen thy goings, O God", a psalm with many references to the Exodus). Cushan and Midian, neighbours in the Sinai peninsula *(Soncino Bible)*, represent the peoples overwhelmed with terror at the events of the Exodus. The "curtains" are the tent-hangings.

Habakkuk 3   193

vv. 8–15: The thrice repeated question of verse 8: "Was the Lord displeased ... angry ... wrathful ... against the rivers ... the sea?", which must be an allusion to the dividing of the Red Sea and of the Jordan, imply that these acts were especially significant, because they illustrated God's "salvation" of His elect. The verse concludes: "thy chariots *are* salvation", and recalls other allusions to the chariots of God: "The chariots of God are twenty thousand, even thousands of angels; the Lord is among them as in Sinai the holy" (Psa. 68: 17). "And Elijah prayed, Lord, ... open his eyes, that he may see ... And behold the mountain was full of horses and chariots of fire round about Elijah" (2 Kings 6: 17); at Elijah's ascension he was parted from Elisha by "a chariot of fire and horses of fire", which Elisha immediately recognised as "the chariot of Israel" (2 Kings 2: 11–12). The expression is evidently a figure for the power of God put forth on behalf of His anointed.

Verse 9 has proved a mystery for most of the commentators, who cannot understand the relevance of "bow" or "oaths of the tribes". If these words are taken in their natural sense, which the Hebrew usage certainly permits, they are intelligible. The bow, or weapon, of God (like Jacob's bow in Gen. 48: 22) is taken out of its sheath, ready for action, in accordance with His oath sworn to Abraham, Isaac and Jacob, and hence to the *tribes* their descendants. So the "riddle which all the ingenuity of commentators has not been able to solve" (G. A. Smith) is not so obscure, if we are content to remain within the framework of the Divine revelation.

"Thou didst cleave the earth into rivers" is an allusion to the water brought from the rock for the benefit of these same tribes. The trembling of the mountains and the impetuous, sweeping flow of the water are the signs of Yahweh's power; the "lifting up" of the hands by the deep is an allusion to the dividing of the water, when the Lord "rebuked the Red Sea" (Psa. 106: 9), which raised its hands to Him as if in submission. The standing still of the sun and moon is a reference to the intervention of God in the battle with the kings of Canaan, when "the Lord fought for Israel" (Joshua 10: 11–14), upon the prayer of Joshua. The "arrows" of God, shot from the "bow" of verse 9 ("thine arrows also went abroad", in the context of the deliverance of Israel under Moses, Psa. 77: 17–20), and the glittering spear, are symbols of His might for the discomfiture of Israel's enemies.

Verse 12 refers to the subjugation of the Canaanites: "Thou dost march through the land (or the earth, revealing the wider and later application) in indignation"; the same verb is used as in the historical allusions of Judges 5: 4, "When thou marchest out of the field of Edom, the earth trembled, the heavens dropped"; and of

194   Habakkuk 3

Psalm 68: 7, "God, when thou wentest forth before thy people, when thou didst march through the wilderness, the earth shook, the heavens dropped; even Sinai itself was moved".

The verb "thresh" is really to tread or trample, for threshing was often performed by animals, usually oxen, driven round the threshing floor till their hoofs trampled out the grain. Two remarkable passages with this figure are found in Micah 4: 11–13, "Arise and thresh, O daughter of Zion; I will make thine horn iron and thy hoofs brass; thou shalt beat in pieces many people"; and Isaiah 41: 15, "I will make thee (as) a new sharp threshing instrument ... thou shalt thresh the mountains" (where the instrument was a kind of iron-toothed sledge, drawn round over the corn by the oxen). The implication of Habakkuk's allusion is that as God "threshed" the Canaanites, so He will subdue the nations.

The expression "going forth" (v. 13) conveys the demonstration of God's power: Judges 5: 4, "thou wentest out of Seir"; Psalm 68: 7, "thou wentest forth before thy people", both of the manifestation at Sinai; so Isaiah 26: 21, "the Lord cometh out of his place to punish the inhabitants of the earth for their iniquity"; and 42: 13, "The Lord shall go forth as a mighty man ... as a man of war". This positive action of God was "for the salvation *of* thy people, for salvation *with* thine anointed", the change of preposition signifying a difference in the Hebrew. The "anointed" (the word has the idea of choice or election for a particular task) would in the first instance be Moses, and then Joshua, and in the final phase the "son of David", the Messiah, a sense which must be implicit in the prophecy; but the parellelism of the first line of verse 13 suggests that the whole people of the elect is included. The word "anointed" occurs in Psalm 28: 8; 84: 9; 89: 38–51, in all of which passages it is difficult to say whether the allusion is to the whole people or to a chosen *one*; but in Psalm 105: 15, "Touch not my anointed (ones) and do my *prophets* no harm", the allusion is to the fathers. This Old Testament usage is doubtless one of the origins of the New Testament expression "the saints" for the whole body of believers in Christ.

The expression "wound the head" occurs in Psalm 68: 21 and 110: 6 of the judgement of the wicked by God; Habakkuk would have primarily in mind the king of Babylon. "Thou wilt strike through with his own staves the chief of his warriors" (R.V.) suggests the casting of confusion into the camp of the "wicked", as is forecast of Gog in Ezekiel 38: 21 and of the nations gathered against Jerusalem in Zechariah 14: 13; despite their "coming out as a whirlwind" to destroy the "poor"—the innocent and defenceless, the Hebrew *ani* meaning humbled, afflicted, deprived of rights by

Habakkuk 3   195

oppression; so the *godly* poor (see Psalm 10: 8–11; 12: 5; Isaiah
14: 32; 26: 6). Verse 15 is another allusion to the waters of the Red
Sea, divided as "an heap", the horses perhaps being a reminiscence
of Isaiah 63: 13, "God led them through the deep (by the right
hand of Moses, ... dividing the water before them, v. 12) as an
horse in the wilderness", with a general association with "the
chariot of Israel and the horsemen thereof".

vv. 16–19: As Habakkuk contemplates what all this vision will mean
in the way of trouble for his own people, he trembles and feels his
strength utterly fail; he foresees that he must "wait calmly" (rest)
for the "day of trouble" (cf. v. 3–15) which, though it implies
deliverance for Israel, will involve terror for those who experience
it, "when the troop of invaders cometh up against my people". Yet
though human hopes will fail, all the benefits of the fruits of the
ground being destroyed by pestilence and pillage (cf. Jeremiah
5: 17 of the ravages of the Chaldeans), the prophet for his part will
rejoice and exult in the Lord; for He alone is the God of his
salvation, He alone is his strength, who will cause him to walk as
securely as the sure-footed hind (2 Samuel 22: 32–34, "God is my
strength ... He maketh my feet like hinds' feet, and setteth me
upon my high places"); those "high places" of which the apostle
made the "heavenly places" in Christ. Thus does Habakkuk
conclude with a great profession of faith in the midst of present
calamity and approaching trouble, becoming himself an example of
his own message: "the just shall live by his faith".

Concluding Reflections

As we briefly compare the prophecy of Habakkuk, among the
last of the minor prophets to write before the exile, with one of the
earliest, say that of Joel, what major differences do we notice to
have developed in two hundred years?

There is in the later prophets a deep consciousness of the
corruptions of Israel and a realisation of the inevitability of Divine,
final judgement for the majority of the nation; salvation will be for
a few, the remnant. This conviction leads naturally to the question:
what then is to be the fate of God's kingdom, centred in Jerusalem
where He had placed His Name? How is His purpose to be
fulfilled? Why are the pagan nations allowed to triumph, even
admitting the iniquity of Judah, especially such violent and corrupt
idolaters as the Assyrians? And when the Assyrian is destroyed,
why does God permit another, equally corrupt and evil power, the

Habakkuk 3

Chaldean, to arise and continue the oppression? How long, O Lord, how long?

To which questionings the answer of God falls into two parts. The vision is for a long time, but Yahweh will arise as He has done in the past; He will deliver His faithful and vindicate His great Name among the nations. Meanwhile, pride is the destruction of man; but the just shall live through the present troubles by his faithful service and patient waiting, sustained by the thought that the gods of the nations are mere idols, but the Lord is the God of his salvation.

The relevance of these conclusions to ourselves in the 20th century needs no stressing. We too see the violent and corrupt of the earth triumph, and are moved to wonder how long this course can last and what troubles the future may have in store. To us too the lesson is pointed: the Lord who brought Israel out of Egypt is He who raised from the dead the Lord Jesus Christ, the future bearer of His Name in the earth and the ruler of all nations. For his coming we are bidden to wait with the same faithfulness as were the prophets, remembering that the Lord will look with favour and blessing upon "the poor and contrite", that is those who rely not upon their own strength, nor are proud, but are the humble before God, "trembling at his word" (Isa. 66: 2). In these studies of some of the prophets we have been able to sample a little of the quality of that word. It is however a quality which reveals its true depth only to those who read it with reverent devotion, for it is a quality of spirit rather than a mere recital of facts; but the prize is great, for the "spirit" so absorbed becomes a source of strength in this time of probation; it is "the knowledge of God" by which we are able to draw near to Him, who is the Holy One, the Saviour and Preserver of His saints.

13

EPILOGUE

Our survey of the Minor Prophets up to the Exile, from Joel to Zephaniah, has covered a period of more than two centuries when God was constantly sending His faithful messengers to His erring people. Politically the period begins with Israel in conflict with Edom, Ammon, Moab and Philistia, before Assyria began to exert its power over the Northern Kingdom; it extends through the growth of that power, the overthrow of Samaria about 720 B.C., and the beginning of its pressure upon Judah of which the invasion of Sennacherib in the reign of Hezekiah and the carrying away captive of king Manasseh were the high points; and it ends with the threat of Babylonian power which was to engulf Jerusalem. In this very significant period of Israel's occupation of the Land under their kings, the writings of these "minor prophets" throw a great deal of light upon the writings of the "major" prophets, Isaiah, Jeremiah, Ezekiel and Daniel.

The Need

Why was there a need for this "ministry of the prophets"?

The short answer is that the spiritual condition of the nation made it essential. The messages of His prophets were God's own provision to meet the needs of Israel's situation, as they came increasingly under the influence of the neighbouring nations, particularly at first the smaller ones surrounding the "land of Canaan". As Israel began to absorb their ways, there was first a dwindling of their faith in the Lord *their* God; then a worship of the pagan idols, often with corrupt rites; then a growing materialism and sensuality, a pursuit of property and wealth, so that the leaders of the nation built their houses of ivory and cedar, and gave themselves up to self-indulgence in, for example, eating and drinking; and finally a spreading immorality, in which adultery, oppression and violence became common among the powerful; the whole leavened with a "ceremonialism" in which the Israelites outwardly observed the feasts of the Lord and offered their sacrifices, comforting themselves with the thought that since "the

198   *Epilogue*

temple of the Lord" was in their midst, no serious judgement would
come upon them, no matter what the prophets were saying.

The plain fact is then that God provided the prophetic word for
His people because it was what they desperately needed; and the
character of that word, with its clear rebuke for their sins, its
warnings of judgements to come and its recall to obedience and
faith, with frequent passages of encouragement for the faithful and
promises of their eventual redemption, is a priceless indication of
what *God Himself evidently considered was the right remedial
treatment for their spiritual sickness.* It is further significant that
this precious "word of the Lord" came to Israel *not* through the
consensus of Israel's "enlightened opinion", nor through the
leadership of a unanimous "school of prophets", but always through
an individual prophet, called by God Himself and speaking the
message given direct from Him.

In these reflections there is much of value to us today. As a
people of God, "called to be saints", we too live in a world
increasingly influenced by a modern sophisticated idolatry,
materialism, sensuality, immorality, deceit and violence (how
unchanging are the works of human nature throughout the ages!);
and we too must rely for our guidance not upon the prevailing
enlightened opinion, even religious, from whatever source, nor upon
groups who arise from time to time to tell us what our belief and
practice must be, but upon the word that comes direct from God
Himself; and that word we are privileged to have in a permanent
form in the "holy scriptures", alone able to "make us wise unto
salvation".

The Unity of the Message

Careful reading of these prophetic writings inevitably brings out
one striking feature: their tremendous unity and unanimity. From
Joel to Habakkuk, though particular circumstances changed over
two centuries, the basic message remained the same. It was first an
appeal to return to what had already been revealed to Israel
through the writings of Moses and the Psalms. The references to
the Law, especially to Deuteronomy, are frequent; and the
numerous references to psalms—in Jonah's prayer uttered from the
belly of the great fish, for example—are unmistakable. The word
through the prophets recalls God's people to His earlier word for
them and demonstrates its basically unchanging character.

But most significant of all is the spiritual unity of the prophetic
message with its call for a life of uprightness, truth, mercy for the
weak, and humble obedience before the majesty and holiness of

Epilogue 199

God. And how should it be otherwise, for this message was founded upon the spiritual character of the unchanging God Himself, who had first declared His Name and His "goodness" to Israel through Moses ("the Lord, a God full of compassion and gracious, slow to anger and plenteous in mercy and truth, ... forgiving iniquity and transgression and sin; and that will by no means clear the guilty ...", Exod. 34: 6–7, R.V.), and had then demonstrated His spiritual nature by His acts for His people: His mighty deliverance at the Exodus, which caused the hearts of the surrounding nations "to melt" (Josh. 2); His constant provision for their natural needs; His judgements intended to bring about repentance and a return to Him; His reproof of their sin and His forgiveness and provision of a redeemer when they responded; and His constant insistence that His people must be like Him, and thus be prepared for fellowship with the God they professed to serve.

In the literature of the whole world there is nothing approaching this broad and profound manifestation of the Spirit of God at work among men, seeking all the time their redemption. Its presence in all the writings of Scripture, from Genesis to Revelation, so contrary to the natural inclinations of men, is the strongest possible proof of their Divine inspiration. As a 19th-century writer put it, "The Bible is not such as men would have written if they could, nor could have written if they would" (Henry Rogers, *The Superhuman Origin of the Bible deduced from Itself.* If you see it secondhand anywhere, buy it at once.)

Our Foundation

Here too there is a great lesson for us, for this must be *our* firm foundation. In the course of receiving the word of God, we shall rightly accept and uphold its clear doctrines concerning the Gospel of the Kingdom of God and the Name of Jesus Christ, and we shall be warned and encouraged by its prophecy; but we shall find that the secret of steadfast devotion to our God in the midst of a world of clamouring and seducing voices is really to be found in our appreciation of His spiritual nature as declared to Israel, manifested in their history, and revealed most vividly in the person of His Son; and the realisation that this supreme and unique revelation requires a response from ourselves: "for as he which called you is holy, be ye yourselves also holy in all manner of living ..." (1 Pet. 1: 15, R.V.). For our understanding of this unique Spirit of God the writings of the prophets are a priceless treasure. In the wisdom of God they have been preserved "for our

200   Epilogue

learning"; it is our wisdom to take heed. Thus we too may be prepared for fellowship with God through our Lord Jesus Christ.

God's Care for His Saints

Out of all this rich material there emerges one constant and encouraging theme: God is ever mindful of those who acknowledge Him and His word. As Zephaniah wrote: "Seek ye the Lord, all ye meek of the earth, which have wrought his judgement (sought to carry out His revealed will); seek righteousness (acceptance with God through repentance), seek meekness ..." (2: 3). The spirit of the faithful remains the same in all ages. There is no room here for asserting rights to act in our own way, or for demanding our own self-fulfilment; but only for a sincere reception of God's verdict upon our nature and of the riches of His grace in our redemption; and a willingness to accept what He has revealed both for our belief and our conduct. To this end we may well meditate upon the concluding words of Micah:

"But as for me, I will look unto the Lord; I will wait for the God of my salvation: my God will hear me ... Who is a God like unto thee, that pardoneth iniquity ...? He retaineth not his anger for ever, because he delighteth in mercy. He will turn again and have compassion upon us; he will tread our iniquities under foot: and thou wilt cast all their sins into the depths of the sea."

And in the firm conviction that God will "perform the truth to Jacob and the mercy to Abraham" which He has "sworn unto our fathers from the days of old", we may go quietly on our way in faith, earnestly desiring the manifestation of the sons of God.